George A. Hamid

To susie 6-28-10 — I hope you enjoy meeting the Acrobat. Sincerely [signature]

THE ACRO BAT

A Showman's Topsy-Turvy World...
...from Buffalo Bill to the Beatles

George A. Hamid
as told to
George A. Hamid, Jr.

C**M**MTEQ
PUBLISHING
MARGATE, NEW JERSEY

Published by:
    ComteQ Publishing
    A division of ComteQ Communications, LLC
    P.O. Box 3046
    Margate, New Jersey 08402
    609-487-9000 • Fax 609-822-4098
    Email: publisher@ComteQcom.com
    Website: www.ComteQpublishing.com

ISBN 0-9674074-5-1

Book and cover design by Rob Huberman
Hamid group photo on page 272 by Rob Huberman
Cover photo from the Hamid family album.

Second Printing
Printed in the United States of America
10 9 8 7 6 5 4 3 2

Dear Reader:

Did Buffalo Bill and Annie Oakley ever have a son? Maybe they did!

George A. Hamid, Jr.

Contents

Part One
Stories as told to George A. Hamid, Jr. by George A. Hamid.

Part Two

Episodes and incidents from the perspective of George A. Hamid, Jr.

Foreword by Dick Clark

It is hard to imagine one showman's career spanning the first half of the 20th Century from Buffalo Bill's Wild West Circus to the British invasion of the Beatles.

When I first met George Hamid, Sr. most of the bumps in his perilous ride to success were behind him. Our introduction occurred a year or two after my Philadelphia television debut on *American Bandstand* in the mid-fifties.

For the then unheard of sum of $10,000 George hired me to host a two-day show featuring relatively unknown teenage newcomers such as Chubby Checker, Frankie Avalon and Bobby Rydell to perform in the Steel Pier's ten-thousand capacity Marine Ballroom on the Boardwalk in Atlantic City. The concept was so successful that I starred on Steel Pier into the late sixties.

I was actually in Atlantic City playing the Steel Pier on the day George and his son George, Jr. brought the Beatles to the Boardwalk Convention Hall during the band's first U.S. tour, one of the fascinating accounts later in the book told by George, Jr.

The tales of the Hamids' show biz era are remarkable and entertaining and will take readers on a journey through a time we will never see again. I'm proud to have been a part of it.

Dick Clark

Author's Introduction

"George," as my father is alternately referred to by me in this book, experienced only four years of formal education (if one can call a deprived Syrian parochial school a "formal" education) and thereafter did his best to educate himself.

By the time I reached high school age, George was determined to fulfill his dream of an education through me, his only son.

In 1932 he saw to it that I was enrolled in a private high school and in 1936 underwrote my journey through Princeton University. As a result of my minoring in English, and much reading and writing, upon graduation I was awarded Princeton's Manners Prize for creative writing.

During and after WWII I had little opportunity to exploit my writing skills, if they still existed. When it came time to compose George's autobiography, I decided to give it a try.

The result speaks for itself and I invite you to come in and see. I don't think you'll be disappointed.

Chapter 1
ALLEY-OOP

"Alley-oop!"

Where the phrase came from, I don't know. It probably originated in French, then was appropriated by Arab acrobats like me. In my early days, "Arab" and "acrobat" were synonymous.

"Alley-oop" is not an order, it's a battle cry. The tried-and-true acrobat may slumber tranquilly through earsplitting screams of "Help!", "Fire!", and "Save my child!", yet the mere echo of "Alley-oop!" will zip him to his feet before he's awake.

Although I have graduated from earning my livelihood by my own handsprings and pyramids, this command still sends a tingle through my veins, still alerts my muscles. With an "Alley-oop!" I tumbled through a full thousand cities, towns and villages, from Saskatoon to Halifax, Tampico to Nogales, from Brussels to Vienna to Marseilles. My hands and feet thumped the dirt of almost every hamlet in America.

My earliest acrobatic recollections are tumbling through the streets of the little country of Lebanon (then a part of Syria), where, more than anywhere else, the practice of springing and whirling is cherished; virtually a national sport.

The stony streets of Lebanon, the beginning of my story...

"Line up! On your feet! Alley-oop!"

The story of one's life ought to begin with the date of birth. Born in Broumana, Lebanon, of a poor family, my birth date was unrecorded. A family's first son (I was the third of four boys) created a stir; the rest were lucky to get names.

Some old papers of my Uncle Ameen, of whom you will hear

more, confirmed my christening date to be February 4, 1896. Barring the unusual, my birth occurred shortly before. Since nobody knew how long any baby would last, and living in a population one-third Mohammedan, one-third Jewish, and one-third Christian, parents christened their children quickly. If the baby died, they wanted no doubt in the Lord's mind which heaven it should enter.

The practice was apparently justified, since our family's fifth didn't survive the first day. At three and a half, I experienced my first and undoubtedly greatest tragedy when the little boy took my mother with him.

Living without a mother anywhere is tough. Where survival depends on luck and help from someone (like a mother) who loves you, it is worse.

My father and grandmother fed us when they could. My grandmother sometimes skipped eating so the young had food. My father may have done the same thing. We saw so little of him, it is hard to say.

We were ragamuffins. Third in line to get wearables, originating with my big brother, Saleem, by the way of the next oldest, Nahim, my garments barely resembled clothing. If I ruined a shirt or pants before they reached Michel, the baby, I received an easy-to-remember beating. I took more punishment than Nahim, because the clothes were in worse shape when I acquired them. Furthermore, I attracted fights; an added detriment to my wardrobe.

Trouble and I were companions; I created it, horned in on it, or was roped into it.

One day – I was five and half years old and not yet at school – I saw Shaheen, my cousin, slightly older than me, behind my house.

A row of stone huts, (ours included), bordered the road across from the schoolhouse. In order to shed rainwater toward the fields behind, away from the dirt road in front, the roofs slanted sharply and the eaves dropped within six feet of the ground. Shaheen busily tossed stones onto one of the slanted roofs.

"Hello, Puabla," he called. Puabla is an Arabic nickname for George. "I'm throwing stones on the roof. Come help me."

The stones rolled along the sloping roof, but not enough to fall off. Soon he climbed onto the roof, tugging me behind.

"Help me put the stones in little piles," Shaheen said.

I did, after which he revealed his big secret.

"I'm going to *get* someone," he whispered.

The school bell began to ring. We crept to the front edge. Before I could take a good look, Shaheen yelled, jumped up and aimed a stone at a trio of kids. He scored a direct hit. I don't know if he hit the one he wanted, or if he cared. In five seconds, a schoolyard full of children returned his fire, hurling stones, lumps of dirt, anything they could find.

We had the advantage of surprise, the protection of the slanting roof. Shaheen threw rocks as fast as he could pick them up. Naturally, I joined him in the assault; not the best marksman in the world, but with so many kids grouped together, hitting a few.

Soon my "partner" (by this time I couldn't dissolve the partnership if I wanted to) exhausted the stones, leaped from the roof, and without looking, waiting or worrying, disappeared into the bushes. I ran to the edge of the roof and looked down. Six feet – – higher than the side of a mountain. Shaheen, bigger than I, had been practicing that leap. A bare three and a half feet tall, I trembled. The voices in the schoolyard, swelling toward me in a roar of victory, made up my mind.

I landed with a terrific jolt. If the earth hadn't been soft from the rain, I might have broken a bone. I jumped to my feet and beat it to the woods.

A speedy runner, I soon overtook Shaheen. We hid in a thicket, hearing the tumult gradually fade. They'd given up the chase. Even so, I began to cry. I could feel the sting of my father's hand.

Shaheen cried too. Always in trouble, this time he had gone too far and he knew it. His father didn't pay attention to him even when he was bad, which was most of the time. After listening to the priest who ran the school, Shaheen's father, one of the strongest men in Lebanon, would usually explode. Only four-feet-four and toothless, he could dispose of any two normal men in hand combat.

Shaheen's agility usually kept him safe from his muscle-bound father. But once or twice he'd caught him, when he really wanted to, and Shaheen had never forgotten the results.

We didn't dare to go home. When night came, as it soon did, we were so hungry we had no choice. We crept first to Shaheen's house and peered inside. His father lay back in a wooden chair near the only light. He grumbled to himself, then slammed the table with his fist.

"That Shaheen!" he growled. "I'll kill him."

Shaheen seized my arm and dragged me through the night to my own house. I tiptoed to the window and looked in. My grandmother wept.

"Don't hurt him," she pleaded. "He's just a baby." My father sat silent, making me shiver.

Shaheen tugged me toward the woods, but I wouldn't go. I peered through the window again. When I turned, Shaheen had disappeared. (He showed up two days later at his house. His father hit him twice, once with each hand, leaving him against the wall, unconscious. Three days later, he managed to crawl from the house.)

I shivered by the window. After my father went to bed, my grandmother blew out the candle and walked toward her tiny room. I hadn't felt the darkness until she snuffed the light. I didn't care about my father, the priest, or anybody but my grandmother. I ran through the door, not stopping until I bumped into her, nearly knocking her down.

"Puabla!" she cried, pulling me close to her. "Are you all right?"

Momentarily, I was. In seconds, I doubted so, as my father filled the doorway.

"Give me the boy," he said.

My grandmother didn't say a word.

"Give him to me."

"No," she finally whispered.

"My mother," he answered slowly, "you are an old woman and I do not want to hurt you, but I am going to punish my son."

Grandmother should have held her ground. That's one whipping I might have avoided.

"No," she said. "Not until he has eaten."

"Very well. After that, you return to your room and out of sight."

My father spun away. My heart sank and my appetite vanished.

What a compromise! My five year old body for a few scraps of food. I ran for the door. It was locked. With one big arm, he grabbed me, with the other he hit me, inflicting my body with the next-to-the-worst beating I got in the old country.

The worst came two years later, nearly starting a revolution. Again, my father played the heavy. This time, he saved my life.

The Near East, in those days, was dominated by Turkey. With three religious groups in almost every community and each group antagonistic toward the others, the pot always boiled. The few available Turks did little to settle disputes. When they did act, they supported the Mohammedans.

Seven years old, I had begun my brief schooling. Children competed for the privilege of going to the well to fill the priest's *braak,* a long-necked jug, wide at the bottom, with a tiny spout on one side and a little handle on the other. One drank from a *braak* by holding it in the air and aiming the stream of water from the spout into the open mouth. All of us mastered the art at an early age. No one ever drank from glasses.

A fairly good student, on occasion I was chosen by the priest to go to the well to fill his little *braak.* One day, as I came to the well, a Mohammedan girl approached with a big *braak* under one arm and another, almost as big, under the other.

The well was fed through one small stream. I raced her. She won, forcing me to wait. I picked up a few pebbles and tossed them aimlessly.

"Hurry up!" I called. "Besides, you're on our side of the well." Not that it mattered, with only one spigot.

"Be quiet," she said, poking her tongue at me.

When she had filled the big jug, I pushed in to fill my little one.

"Wait till I'm through," she snapped, giving me a shove. Being about nine, she sent me flying. The priest's *braak* popped out of my hands and crashed to the ground.

Horrified, I stared at the broken pieces. The priest's face flashed into my mind. I could feel my humiliation, his wrath, the snap of his sharp switch. I looked at the Mohammedan girl, lowered my head and charged. A second later, she sprawled on the ground, groaning and holding her stomach. I jumped on her. I grabbed nearby stones by the handful and piled them on top of her. I covered everything but her face. Throwing weeds over her face, I picked up her full *braak* and sped away.

I crept into the schoolroom, placed the *braak* on the priest's table, and walked to my bench. The priest stopped talking, picked up the jug, drinking deeply.

"Puabla," he said, "I see my *braak* doubled its size."

I nodded, looking proudly at the other kids.

"Does this happen every time you go for water?" he asked, in a sharper tone.

I nodded yes then shook my head no. The other kids snickered.

"Quiet!" the priest commanded. "Puabla, come here."

I went. "Tell me what you did," he said.

"I..." – zing! His switch stung my legs. That was for nothing. Wait till he heard the story.

I stammered that a Mohammedan girl at the well had broken his *braak* and I made her give me one of hers. The switch snapped at my legs again.

"Is this true?"

"Yes," I insisted. It was, as far as it went. He smiled at me, then sent me to my bench.

Not for long. A strange noise grew in the distance. Soon, a shouting mob of Mohammedans, led by fifteen men with clubs, stormed to the schoolhouse door.

"Where is George, the son of Joseph?" shouted the leader.

The priest barred the way. "Why do you want George?" he asked.

"Keep out of this, Christian priest!"

"Why do you want him?" the priest insisted.

"Ha!" the Mohammedan spat, a wicked gleam in his eyes. "We are going to kill him."

Kill me! I tried to swallow, then to disappear into the wall behind me.

"If you don't turn him over," the leader added, "we'll kill every child in this schoolhouse!"

As killing was common practice, wholesale massacre no rarity, these Mohammedans meant business. The priest would gladly hand me over if he believed it would end the matter.

He started to speak, perhaps to seek such assurances, when my father burst through the back door, leaping on the table.

Casting his arms in the air, he shouted, "Hold, I am Joseph, father of George. What has my son done?"

The leader's dark face curled into an evil smile, happy to report what George, son of Joseph, had done. He described how I entombed his daughter in a rock pile, how she might now be dead if someone had not unpiled her, heaping indignity on his family, on the Mohammedans in general, and on the Great Prophet himself. He ended by announcing that they were going to kill me – and maybe my father, too. They might wipe out all the Christians in the village!

As the men moved forward, my father raised his hand. They hesitated enough for him to look straight at me.

"My son, is this true?" he demanded.

I stood up, slowly. "Father, I…" I began.

"Silence!" he roared.

No one heard or cared about my futile words, "She was on our side of the well."

He turned to the Mohammedans. "Neighbors," he said. My father actually called them *neighbors!* (If Joseph, father of George, had possessed plaguing powers, there would be no Mohammedans left in the world!) "Good neighbors," he continued, "I can plainly see that my cur of a son has done you an unforgivable injustice. I, his father, demand the privilege of killing him."

I jumped. First *they* were going to kill me. Now him! I often feared he might slaughter me with one of his whippings, never deliberately. I glanced at the back door to make a fast run for my life. To my dismay, my father, my newest enemy, luckily blocked my escape, or the Mohammedans would have finished the matter.

My father seized me, carried me in front of the table, and lifted me high above his head. For a moment, I had the best view in the room. I saw terrified school kids, happily angry Mohammedans, and the priest, who had retired to as neutral a corner as he could find.

Crash! – I hit the floor. Pain lashed through me as I absorbed two heavy kicks. My last conscious sounds were the eager jeers of the Mohammedans, satisfied with my apparent death. My grandmother burst into the room, screaming. She ran out of the back door, carrying my corpse home. The Mohammedans, certain that justice had been served, returned to their third of the town.

My father did not want to kill me, if he could avoid it, but make it look convincing. He performed an extraordinary job, for it took a month to repair me.

Chapter 2
The Baker's Three

A desperate, ignored little country, Lebanon lacked food, shelter, education, opportunity. Relatives schemed, plotted and connived to get their children to Europe or, better yet, the United States.

One day, my grandmother called me to her small room and lifted me to her bed. "Little George," she said, "I see you tumble in the streets. Do you like to tumble?"

I had been doing cartwheels and somersaults for fun. On Saturday nights, I sometimes tumbled with Shaheen and another cousin, George Simon, in the village center, enticing the villagers to toss pennies. If the pennies were as valuable as the American pennies, the villagers would not have parted with one for the greatest acrobats in the world.

"Yes, I like to tumble," I told my grandmother.

"Are you a good tumbler?"

I looked into her fine, gray eyes. "Shaheen and George Simon and I are the best in town," I told her. As I learned later, we were awkward beginners.

"Fine," said my grandmother. "You must practice hard and become the best of all."

I asked why.

"Your Uncle Ameen," she went on, "you know of him?"

"Yes, Grandmother."

"Your Uncle Ameen is in America," she said, emphasizing *America*. "He owns troupes of tumblers, with circuses, with bazaars, and the men are happy in America. He will need more tumblers. If you are good, he may send for you."

"America" was just a word. I had no particular grudge against

Lebanon. Yet, if my grandmother wanted me to be the best tumbler, I'd manage to be just that!

Shaheen, George Simon and I tumbled regularly. Naturally, we improved. The next summer brought our first job, at a fair before the annual merchants' bazaar. After school, the three of us were twisting and turning in front of our house. A baker from the village watched us. The longer he watched, the more daring we became. Finally, the baker called out, "Shaheen, come over here!"

We stopped. Shaheen looked suspiciously at the man without moving. "What do you want?" Shaheen had better sense than to advance within reach of a grownup.

"I want you three boys to work at my tent when the bazaar opens."

I decided to take over. "What will you pay us?"

"You're hasty, little fellow, for someone who never had a job." He smiled and continued. "At the end of the day, I will give you the bread and pastry that I have not sold.

Bread and pastry! Our heads swam at the thought, comparing it to our diets of lentils, rice, and stale bread. Shaheen and George Simon jumped up and down. "Yes, yes, yes!" they cried.

I pulled them to one side. "What if you sell all you bake?" I asked aloud.

The baker shrugged. "Then you have nothing to take home, but..." he added after a pause, "that does not often happen."

Shaheen and George Simon cooled to the idea as quickly as they had embraced it. They shook their heads and started to walk away. "Don't pay attention to them," I told the baker. "We'll do it."

I sat my two cousins down and explained, "The baker hopes to sell a lot. He'll make more than he can sell. Most of the time, we'll get ours."

Two days later, the little fair started. My reasoning had been sound, except for the drawing power of the three acrobats. The baker hired us to attract crowds to his booth. I did not foresee the hit we'd make. The crowds we attracted exceeded his (and our) wildest dreams. As he sold out the first day, we left empty handed.

The baker was smart enough to know he had a hot property, and didn't want to lose us. He gave us each a small piece of bread, which we gobbled in seconds. "Tomorrow," he promised, "I shall bake extra loaves and extra pastry, so there will be some for you."

Our fame spread, business better than the day before. For four hours, with a few short rest periods, we tumbled our hearts out. We wolfed our slices of bread. When we spread out our handkerchiefs for our real earnings, there were none. Tired, dirty and miserable, we dragged ourselves home. Before my grandmother could comfort me, I was asleep in her arms. Quitting was the smart thing to do. When the weather broke hot and threatening the next day, I was convinced it was our only sensible option. I wouldn't tumble in the rain – baker or no baker.

My grandmother sat me in a chair. "Do *not* give up, Puabla," she said. After a long pause, she added, "Today it may be better."

I coaxed my reluctant partners into giving the job another try. At the fair, the thunder rumbled. The worried baker put us to work before we could say hello. A small crowd gathered. Then the rain fell. On we tumbled, though the crowd thinned from few to none. Cold and miserable, we crawled into the cubicle and huddled in a corner, teeth chattering. The baker looked out at the steady rain, cursing with his most descriptive Arabic oaths. He refused to notice us, except when he tripped over Shaheen. He gave us a tongue lashing, favoring Shaheen with a short kick in the ribs.

We would have sneaked away, except for the relentless rain. Finally, the baker slammed his shutters closed. "Get out, you dirty ragamuffins," he spat.

We scurried from under the counter.

"Where are you going?" he screamed.

"Home," I answered.

"Well, then," he shouted, "take your baskets with you!"

I stopped in my tracks. George Simon and Shaheen bumped me hard. Back we scrambled. Sure enough, three baskets stood on the counter.

"If you stupid little pigs don't remember what you're working for, perhaps I shouldn't pay you," he grumbled as we snatched our baskets. In a twinkling we were gone.

My grandmother laughed, seeing me rush into the house with my basket. "Aren't you glad you went back?"

"Of course! Hurry up and open it!"

My eyes bulged. Our baker was either the best in Lebanon or fresh bread and sweet pastries were such rarities that the angels might have baked them.

Chapter 3
Circus a la Buffalo Bill

We had little trouble eating for the next three weeks because the fair season coincided with the rainy season. Bazaars followed each other in nearby hamlets, our baker having cubicles in all of them.

Summer ended the fair season and I returned to school. One day, I found my grandmother sitting in her chair, sadly reading a piece of paper. She called me to her, pulled me on her lap, saying something very special had happened. My grandmother's eyes were wet.

"What's the matter?" I asked.

"My Puabla," she said quietly, "you are going on a trip."

In fear and alarm, I whispered, "Not if you don't go with me."

She continued as if she hadn't heard. "You are going to America to join your Uncle Ameen. Your father has not seen this letter yet. Your uncle needs four tumblers. Your father will let you go. If he doesn't I will make him." Her voice cracked.

This was not easy for her. "Puabla," she went on, "I have told you stories about Bible lands flowing with milk and honey, about the Garden of Eden. There are no such places on this earth. Where you are going, Puabla, is close to it. You can make for yourself a little garden of your own design. You are smart enough, my child, and sensitive enough."

She stopped. I put my arms around her, telling her not to worry. I wouldn't go.

My father came home after I was in bed. I heard muffled voices, but you could not catch their words. In the morning, he left the house, never mentioning my leaving. Grandmother had decided for her, as well as her grandson.

On departure day, we headed for the Beirut waterfront – my

grandmother, Father and I, Shaheen and his father, and George Simon alone. (Uncle Ameen was to get delivery of only three tumblers because no one else fitted his age requirements.)

We were scared and we showed it. Our few belongings wrapped in our handkerchiefs, we were dressed in our pathetic best – gathered from brothers and cousins.

Reluctantly approaching the gangplank, we looked suspiciously about, my grandmother holding my hand, my father walking beside me. Suddenly, he reached down, lifted me and carried me the last few feet. He kissed me furiously all over my face, almost smothering me. Just as suddenly, he put me down, kissed Shaheen, then George Simon, and turned away.

Grandmother kissed Shaheen and George Simon first. Then, sobbing, she picked me up and held me close. When she put me down, all three kids burst out crying. We had to be pushed up the gangplank.

At the ship's rail, we waved to those on the dock. Slowly, almost imperceptibly, the boat began to move. Our families stood like statues looking at us. Occasionally, one of them waved. My grandmother crossed herself and made a cross toward us. As I stared at her, she grew smaller and smaller, until distance and tears blotted her out forever.

Before the mountains of Lebanon faded below the horizon, we were homesick for Broumana, soon to be considered heaven compared to the ship. We knew that we were not headed directly to America and Uncle Ameen. We were to join a circus on tour somewhere. Life aboard ship made the details insignificant.

Somebody showed us our room. We traveled steerage, of course, in quarters cramped beyond imagination. The odor, heavy and relentless, sickened us until we got use to it.

Traveling in steerage on a small Mediterranean freighter, already old in 1906, is impossible to conceive; the food, the world's worst, the filth knee-deep. No one once attempted to clean anything. We had no windows or ventilation, roasting all the time. We roomed with one other person and an unimaginable variety of animal life. In two nights, Shaheen, in the bottom bunk, lost his fingernails, and toenails to the rats.

Shaheen decided to correct the food situation. "Puabla," he said, "come with me and we'll steal some bread and lentils." The despised bread and lentils.

I answered, "I won't steal bread, or even lentils. They'll kill you if they catch you."

"You won't tell if I do it?" he asked.

"No, I won't tell," I promised. Shaheen left. George Simon and I followed without his knowing it. We wound through passages completely new to us. Our pathfinder seemed familiar with this dim part of the ship.

I made a note of the turns, leading George Simon by the hand. A light flashed and we stopped. Shaheen flattened himself against the wall of the passageway, inching forward almost imperceptibly, as we held our breaths with him. A door widened, his arms darted through and quickly withdrew, loaded with food.

He teetered from the light, unaware of us in the dark. The maneuver had been managed perfectly until the door flew wide open, framing an enormous hulk of a man. Having better sea legs and carrying no load except a club, he gained on Shaheen. By the time he reached our corner, Shaheen was surely doomed.

George Simon and I had the same idea. After Shaheen passed, we dove together for his pursuer's legs, pulling him to the deck. I bit the leg I had hold of; George Simon jumped on the man's head. In seconds, we darted down the dark passageway. Two turns later, we reached the safety of complete darkness. I led George back to our room. Shaheen sat on his bunk, the picture of innocence.

"Where's our food?" I asked

"What food?"

"The food you just stole from the kitchen."

"I – well – you see," he began.

"Listen," I said, "did you hear somebody fall down when your were running away?"

"Yes," he admitted, "I guess that's what it was."

"Well," I said, "George and I tripped the giant chasing you – *with a club.* Give us our share of the food or we'll push you in the ocean."

Shaheen uncovered the hidden food. We stuffed ourselves, and promptly forgave him.

At Marseilles, we couldn't quit the ship fast enough. A Frenchman from a cheap hotel met us, having been paid in advance to take charge till we were called for. He found us huddled on the dock. After a look and smell of three filthy brats, he emitted a string of strange noises, like cracking branches on dead trees.

He spat on us, then motioned to follow him.

Wide-eyed, we walked, an odor-reducing distance behind. For the first time since Broumana, the world looked fit to live in. The streets narrowed as we reached lodging.

We fearfully climbed four flights of winding stairs to a small room containing three miserable beds, nothing else. A window and a cover on each bed lifted our spirits.

In self-defense, the proprietor forced a bath on our bodies, as well as our clothes. We were confined to our rooms until our clothes dried. By evening, we were familiarly starved. The Frenchman eventually delivered a meal he obviously considered inedible. Not having traveled steerage on the Mediterranean, he miscalculated. We gobbled every scrap, impressing him to the extent that he treated us with a touch of respect.

While we couldn't speak French and he couldn't speak Arabic, our landlord soon discovered our meager acrobatics, putting us to work in his beer (or wine) garden. He stopped trying to poison us, either to repay us or to preserve his entertainment.

We survived on this basis for two weeks until one day, hearing a clamor outside, we saw people lining the street. Our innkeeper handed us our belongings, led us to the door, and shoved us into the crowd.

We held each other's hands for dear life. Finally, when an opening appeared in the human wall, we crept through the legs to the curbstone, sat and waited – for what we did not know.

A noise up the street grew louder and closer. To an earsplitting crowd roar, a circus parade drove into view. *Our* circus! We knew it! What else could it be?

Shaheen trembled, as George Simon's mouth hung open. I felt as foolishly happy as they. On prancing horses rode strange creatures in costumes – Indians and cowboys! Then, on the most beautiful horse in the world, rode a straight, square, white-haired, white-bearded man who looked like a prophet out of Grandmother's Bible. Next came a strange, wild-looking woman carrying two rifles. She pointed one in the air and fired.

Now came the thrill we could barely stand, the Arab tumblers; one in front, eight across, costumes sparkling blue, red, green and gold. One or another of them repeatedly sprung into a cartwheel or flip-flap.

"The acrobats!" I gasped, pulling Shaheen and George Simon to follow alongside the troupe.

We tried to trail them into the big tent, bigger and brighter than I could imagine.

An ugly-looking man in a black suit loomed ahead. "Where do you little punks think you're going?" he boomed. We couldn't recognize the words; the meaning we understood.

We spoke in Arabic, he spoke in English, and everybody else spoke French. Now what?

"Shaheen," I said, "show him we can tumble and maybe he'll let us in." Shaheen's cartwheels made no impression.

"You and George Simon wait right here," I ordered, "no matter what I do." I cartwheeled in a circle, straightening out toward the gate tender. With a burst of speed, I shot past him through the opening. I was inside a circus tent!

The attendant let out a yell, chasing me as I fled toward two men in Arab costumes at the far end of the tent. I raced to the nearest one, gasping my troubles. A puzzled look told me, to my horror, that he didn't understand a word. Sprinkled among the Arabian Arabs were two Irish Arabs and a Jewish Arab. I had chosen one of the Irish Arabs.

There was no time for explanations in any language. My pursuer, now joined by a gendarme, yelled something that might have been, "Bastille!"

I headed for the other Arab. As I grabbed him, they grabbed me.

"Ameen!" I pleaded, my only chance. "Uncle Ameen, save me!"

The Arab looked at me, startled, "Who are you?" he asked in Arabic, waving the men back. I was so grateful to hear him speaking Arabic that I seized his hands and kissed them. The two representatives of law and order tried to drag me away. My new protector shouted something at them in English. They released me, but did not leave.

"I am your nephew," I said. "George, son of Joseph. Call me Puabla."

"You are Ameen's nephew?"

"Yes, and there are two more outside, Uncle."

The Arab frowned at me. Could I be engineering a three-way sneak? He quickly sensed that no little French kid would learn Arabic to crash a circus.

He turned to the gate man. "Were there two others with this boy?"

The man nodded. The Arab stated, "These are the three nephews whom Ameen Buhamid expected. Let the others in at once." In a trudge of defeat, the gate man collected my two frightened cousins.

My new Arab friend, not Uncle Ameen, who had remained in America, was Haj Shiraff, a young man in charge of Ameen's troupe. Haj put us to work as soon as we were in the tent.

"Who's the best one?" he asked.

"Me," I declared.

Haj called to the other acrobat in Arab costume, "Alley-oop!" In a flash, the man leaped to Haj's shoulders.

"Get up there," Haj commanded me.

"Where?" I asked.

"On his shoulders."

Shaheen and George Simon giggled. Gritting my teeth, I started climbing. I consumed a full minute, but made it to my first *three-high*. I didn't dare look.

"Now down!" Haj yelled.

I later learned the universal method of completing an acrobatic formation; leaning forward, falling to the stage, rolling to a standing position. Not knowing it then, I landed on my stomach. If the surface had not been soft dirt, it would have knocked me unconscious. As I groaned in agony, George Simon, Shaheen, the Arabs and a few onlookers roared.

I raged. George Simon stood closest to me. I socked him on the jaw as hard as I could. Down he went. He shot to his feet almost as quickly. We tangled to the dirt.

Haj separated us. "Sunday," he said, pointing his finger at us. "Sunday you settle this."

I didn't care about Sunday. I wanted it settled now. Haj commanded, "In this circus, we fight all fights on Sunday. Start tumbling."

I aimed a cartwheel at George Simon, but Haj spun me in another direction. The grudge was forgotten in trying to outdo each other around the arena. Quite a sight, as I think of it now; three street urchins in rags, springing furiously through cartwheels and handsprings, unnamed acrobatic twists thrown in for good measure.

Haj found three outfits that resembled his own, gave a few simple instructions including, "Be ready for the act this afternoon."

An acrobatic act, such as ours, consists of two parts. The first, built-up formations, in which the *understander* supports from five to ten men on his shoulders, in what are called pyramids. An act of nine men executes a dozen various pyramid structures.

The second, tumbling, requires individual act members to run forth into handsprings, (forward somersaults, hands touching the ground), forwards (full forward somersaults in tuck position, without touching), flip-flaps (backward somersaults, touching), backs (backward somersaults, not touching) tinsicas (oblique, four-beat, foot-to-foot, cartwheels), pirouettes (acrobatic spins) – or a combination of these.

Haj's sense of timing demanded the others to stop and us to start after the pyramids and adult tumbling. We posed, like Haj said. We watched. We waited. It seemed like forever.

Formation followed formation, tinsicas followed flip-flaps. Seeing the others tumble, our feet and hands itched. Haj sensed this, glaring at us appearing to doubt his judgment.

On cue, the others stopped. As they drew to one side, he motioned. We tore into our routine; cartwheels, handsprings, a variety of flip-flaps, with such speed and energy it took everyone's breath away – including ours. As we kept the furious pace, using every twist and turn we knew, the applause mounted. We loved it; a hit of the show in our first performance. Like every ingenue, I wanted to be the hit of the show thereafter.

Chapter 4
Annie Oakley, Benefactress

The glamour of stealing the show faded upon discovery of the system of distributing (or not distributing) food. That first night, when the dinner bell rang and nobody bothered to tell us what it meant, we didn't eat. Next morning, we took our places at the barrier half an hour ahead of time. At the bell, we were trampled by the bigger performers. We barely managed a few pieces of stale bread.

The performers were fed in a catch-as-catch-can manner at two long tables. The grub boys spread their attention in accordance with the importance, the physical strength or the secret tipping habits of the eaters. Thus, landing a palatable meal of any size became an art. Three new kids were swamped by the experienced food snatchers.

Nightfall of the second day found us heartsick – and weak. We complained to an unsympathetic Haj. He had himself to provide for.

After the night show, George Simon and I curled ourselves into a corner, shamelessly sobbing. Even Shaheen, the clever one, couldn't sneak a plate of food.

As we sat crying a shadow fell on us. I looked and saw the first smile of friendliness since leaving home. The smiler was a woman who spoke in foreign words. I stood up, shook my head and pointed to my mouth and stomach.

Her eyes were pleasant, sharp. She knew what I meant, for she knew the circus. She called for a passing attendant and ordered him to bring food to her tent. She beckoned, smiled and we followed.

Our benefactress was Annie Oakley. People have written of her hard-bitten manner, her callousness. That is only a small part of the truth. Her surface obscured her honest compassion.

The first night, and a hundred times after, she fed me bits from her own meal. She cared when no one else paid the least attention. Our routine won applause and had attracted Annie Oakley to us, the young show-stealers. She found us merely three hungry little kids.

After she first fed us in her tent, she took our hands and led us across the lot. The crisp black night, the overpowering smell of the circus, and what we were about to see are still indelibly in my mind. We approached a special ten, yellow lamplight seeping through its slits. We entered quietly, Annie speaking to a man in a chair, his back to us. Her turned and I recognized the awesome man on the beautiful horse, the man who had stepped out of Grandmother's Bible. I looked for the first time into the face of Buffalo Bill.

Unfamiliar with legends, I openly felt his power, his stature, his poise and the depth of his bluish-gray eyes.

Annie told him our story. Such innocent babes, she advised, should get some regular meals – that is, if he wanted to keep his three stars in working condition. Though I couldn't understand, I knew what she meant.

Buffalo Bill called an attendant who appeared, nodded and disappeared. The great man looked at us, smiling his truly wonderful smile. When he spoke, Annie explained that we could not understand. We left his tent, having acquired a grub boy of our very own.

Annie Oakley's ideas of our innocence suffered a rude shock two days later.

It was Sunday morning. After those who cared finished church, the performers, top men, riggers and greasers (kitchen help) and everyone else connected with the circus trickled into the arena. An impromptu boxing ring was pieced together, more to keep watchers out than fighters in. Its often-unaccomplished purpose was to settle grudges, as well as to entertain the spectators.

The rules of battle were few and flexible, satisfying fighters and audience alike. Some appeared more often than others in the Sunday ring. The regulars had their supporters.

Haj led George Simon and me to a spot not far from ringside. We wondered why he was so kind, while we appreciated the good view. Colonel Cody occupied the seat of honor, Annie Oakley sitting near him. I caught her eye and grinned, thinking of her generosity. She smiled back and my heart skipped a beat.

Shouts greeted two men who entered the ring. I didn't know them, but enjoyed their bitter struggle. One of them gave up, bloody and battered, the "referee" bringing forth the next pair. We watched, commented on fighting techniques, argued over our favorites, enjoying the spectacle.

After four fights, the referee yelled, "Puabla against George Simon!"

This we understood! Our names had been called. We looked around in alarm. Haj pushed the two of us forward to the ring, explaining that we were next. George Simon grabbed me and started to cry. "I love Puabla, " he sobbed. " I don't want to fight him."

I didn't feel belligerent myself. George Simon and I were having so much fun together. In front of Miss Oakley, I was ashamed to be labeled a quarreler and brawler.

George Simon didn't care what Annie thought. He did not want to fight his cousin except when he was angry. He loved me (right then), and probably would have refused to fight if Shaheen hadn't pinched him and laughed in his face, calling him a coward. As he turned to Shaheen, Haj picked him up, seized his arms, and hustled us into the ring.

Muffled laughter ran through the crowd. Despite Annie, I didn't like the snickers. I'd show them a good fight.

George Simon let his love for me last two seconds too long. I jumped on him. He got up and ran.

I caught him in the face with a wild swing. Down he went. We wrestled until my stranglehold brought the fight to an end.

On our way out of the ring, George Simon, now in a rage, leaped at me. We were separated. To our subsequent horror, we found ourselves number one on next week's card.

Whether to our credit or discredit, George Simon and I were thereafter the most popular and frequent ring entrants on the show. After the second week, we were never in opposition to each other.

I was angry at Haj. Because I had an argument with George Simon on Thursday was no reason for him to make us fight on Sunday. Especially in front of my only friend, Annie Oakley. I told him what I thought of him. He was pleasantly indifferent until my prattle annoyed him and he pinched my ear.

"Come with me," he cried, calling Shaheen and George Simon to follow. "You have had your fun. I would have started the *real* work tomorrow. Since you are ungrateful, we begin today."

Fun? I couldn't believe my ears! We worked like dogs in the act; we slept on wooden bunks in the dressing tent; we ate only the meals Annie Oakley provided; we had been forced to fight each other!

Introducing us to the "real work," Haj declared, "Your Uncle Ameen would writhe in agony if he saw you tumble. It's your good luck that we won't see him for another six months. If you don't practice hard, he may beat you to death the first day he sees you."

Shaheen and I looked at each other in astonishment. He was speaking to the three greatest tumblers in the world with total disrespect.

"The people like us better than they like you!" I flung at him.

"How much would they like you," he snapped, "if you were *good!*"

I started to ask why *he* didn't make his act good. A crack on the neck stopped me.

Practice began. We didn't stop till the Sunday dinner bell rang. Though Haj's teaching lacked compassion, it was long on persistence. He showed no awareness of the limits of the human body. We dragged ourselves to our food. Our grub boy laughed when he saw us. Too hungry and too exhausted to eat, we trudged to our bunks. In no time, Shaheen and George Simon fell asleep.

Tired as I was, I crept across the clearing to Annie Oakley's tent. I called her name, which by now I knew better than my own.

Her voice came back, warm and friendly. Encouraged, I tiptoed inside, stood in front of her as she smiled inquiringly at me. Something compelled me to speak. I couldn't help myself. Although I knew she couldn't understand, I burst out in Arabic, the only tongue I knew, pouring forth my adulation and my shame, telling her how sorry I was to disgrace her by being a public brawler. I hoped she would forgive me, and promised never again to humiliate her.

How true it is that the language of love is universal! How lucky I was for Annie's rarely seen tenderness.

She could easily dismiss me with a few indignant or indifferent phrases. Instead, she took my hand and lifted my chin. I hadn't dared to look into her eyes. She spoke to me, softly and slowly. The strange sounds meant reassurance, confidence. She spoke until, as she could see, joy and happiness filled me.

I have often wondered about that meeting. If she had turned me away, would I have ever learned to read or write?

It was Annie Oakley who first taught me English. Poorly educated herself, she persisted in ABC's, patiently teaching me the strange new letters. She bought primers and helped me understand the first easy words, told me how to pronounce them. Many hours of her free time were spent helping this little Arab ragamuffin – because she knew I was desperate to learn. While others played, gambled or loafed, I worked. I might have learned anyway, maybe not. Had it not been for Annie Oakley, this book might not have been written. How much else in the life it describes might never have happened, had I, like so many others in my day, stayed illiterate.

Chapter 5
The Sunday Ring

My first circus trip remains the greatest I ever made. Buffalo Bill and his show played every worthwhile theater and amphitheater in Europe, to applauding masses. We performed before Kaiser Wilhelm I; in the palace of Versailles; Europe's royalty toasted Colonel Cody, their American idol.

We felt the reflected glory, although we received little direct benefit. My memory recalls the endless hours of practice, the fight with cleverer hands for the decent meal, the mystery of a new language, strange people and a new life.

After two weeks of steady eating, Buffalo Bill called us in and explained to us that he couldn't allow any more favoritism. We must take care of ourselves at mealtime, on our own, Miss Oakley or anyone else to the contrary, notwithstanding.

Despite the prospect of imminent starvation, we realized the Colonel's word was law.

As we turned to leave, Buffalo Bill put his strong hand on my shoulder and beckoned to Haj. "Can this boy ride a horse?" he asked.

Haj translated. I vigorously shook my head "No!"

"Well," Bill ordered, "see that he is taught. I want him in the maze."

In most circuses, a parade of performers preceded the performance. The Buffalo Bill Show, not content with the *usual,* opened with the "maze"; riders racing in opposite directions, in concentric circles. The formations were so tight that the required precision was tricky and dangerous; so dangerous, in fact, that it was privately called the "Ride of Death." This is what Buffalo Bill wanted me to join!

I received the news with mixed feelings. Being an optimist, I didn't doubt my ability to ride. Would Haj reduce my acrobatic lessons to improve my horsemanship? Never.

Having no choice, I reported as scheduled to the equestrian director, who gave me a cowboy suit and a barely broken horse. My steed bucked, jumped, ran away and threw me a dozen times, to the merriment of the assorted cowboys.

One laugh rang above all the others – that of a Japanese cowboy named Sinko. He taunted me; rode up to my horse when it settled down momentarily and snapped its nose with his whip. As the horse bucked again, he cackled, continuing long after the others had stopped. I vowed revenge.

Before the show, Sinko normally sat outside one of the tents. Finding him there, alone, I walked to him.

With my few English words, I warned him to leave me alone. He cackled. I lifted him from his chair, scolding him in Arabic. His eyes widened in fright, as I dropped him into the chair.

I turned to walk away. After two steps, I found myself on the ground, with the Jap clawing and biting me. We rolled in a scramble, me getting the worst of it.

A voice boomed, a heavy hand seized my shoulder and we were both jerked to our feet.

Buffalo Bill!

My eyes were gouged, my legs scratched, my arm bitten. Blood poured from the gashes made by Sinko's sharp teeth. Buffalo Bill looked me up and down, then lowered his eyes on the Jap. He roared at him in English, shook him and staggered him with an open-handed slap on the face. He called someone to him, ordering a renewal for Sunday.

The circus buzzed as Sunday arrived. My scraps with George Simon were kid affairs. This battle was for real. Sinko, a vicious, hateful devil, had pulled more than a few nasty tricks. Being twelve years old and small, he avoided direct encounter, due to the shortage of people smaller than himself.

I was ten, not very big, and a decided underdog. It made no difference. Circus rules dictated that the fight be fought regardless of a mere discrepancy in age or size.

A grim Buffalo Bill sat in his usual spot, Annie beside him. I walked to the ring, amid a silent circle of faces. Except for the dozen biased Japs opposite me, every face showed me sympathy, some pity. The referee explained a few rules. Haj interpreted them, staying close to me, encouraging me in a quiet voice. I didn't need it, because of my increasing hatred of the Jap.

The battle began. Sinko sprang at me – and I went down. His arm tightened around my neck, as unyielding as iron. With his other hand, he tried to gouge my eyes – which the referee stopped. He bit me – the referee stopping him again. It was, however, permissible to choke me to death.

I gasped, I wriggled and twisted to break his hold. It would not break. The arm drew tighter. By desperate design, or accident, I looped into a somersault. When the arm loosened for a bare second, I grabbed it, yanked it from my neck, and leaped to my feet. For the first time in my life, I heard people cheering *me*.

Sinko sprang again – an animal. I dodged and swung my fist with all my might. He was a basic infighter, relying on teeth and claws. A hard fist at long range was not his game. I caught him in the face. His eyes widened, then glazed, as his knees buckled. I leaped on him and smashed my fists into the face that had laughed at me, into the mouth that had bitten me.

When they finally pulled me away, the Jap rolled over bloody, sobbing and half conscious. People roared their approval. I hardly heard. "Hooray for Puabla!" they cried, as Haj led me from the ring.

I passed Buffalo Bill. "Good boy, Puabla," he said. I heard *that*.

To complete my glory, Annie favored me with her very best smile – and a wink.

Haj was so proud, you'd have thought he won the fight himself. He cut my tumbling practice to an hour. At dinner, the grub boys presented me with a plateful of food, without my fighting for it. Winning had its rewards.

Chapter 6
America and Ameen

When the tour of the Buffalo Bill Circus ended in Germany, we sailed for America.

On the ship, it was steerage again. Would we be forced to steal to eat? Our fourth roommate was a boy our own age. He had received a terrific send-off, with fruit and food baskets, which he carefully guarded. Within twenty-four hours, he became so seasick he couldn't lift his head from his bunk. Shaheen, in his own deft manner, took gradual possession of the delicacies. We stood no chance in the mess hall wars. Thanks to Shaheen, we survived.

Our roommate disembarked on a stretcher when we reached Ellis Island.

Ellis Island was no more pleasant for us than anyone else. Three days passed before we were transported to the mainland, arriving at night in Hoboken – early in the year 1907. The dampness penetrated our skins. The dock, with its four or five yellow electric lights, resembled a tomb.

Huddled at the foot of the gangplank, we clutched our handkerchief's belongings, waiting for Haj. I looked into the gloom. America. A shiver ran down my body. Now what?

Now what turned into a miserable train ride, through what Haj told us was New Jersey, to a fairground where we would await orders from Uncle Ameen.

Our lodging, which we somehow found in the dark was a horse barn. Three cots in a stable defied rest. We rolled into the relative comfort of the straw.

Shaheen and George Simon still slept when the morning sun woke me. I crept toward the barn door and peered outside – at America.

The trees were bare, the sparse grass still brown. Nearby stood another small red barn, in the distance a grandstand like some of the arenas we had played in Europe. I walked out the barn door and inhaled the crisp air.

In America, anything would have thrilled me – (except a dismal dock in Hoboken.) A country fairground on a frosty morning in early spring accomplished as much as skyscrapers might have.

We practiced daily, getting acquainted with the other performers quartered there. Finally, we were summoned to New York to meet Uncle Ameen; a huge event, as we could tell from the awe in Haj's voice. Another big event came first.

Haj, instructed to give us each a dime a week in Europe, saved the money instead. Before we left Paris, he had used it to buy us (without fittings) three suits of clothes, hidden until we were to meet Uncle Ameen. Now, with impressive ceremony, he opened the boxes. Our eyes popped. Black velvet with lace collars!

Shaheen took one look and ran. I jumped him and pulled him back. George Simon could hardly wait to don the outfits; Shaheen, so disgusted, he wanted to fight both of us.

Dressed as we had never dreamed of being dressed, we departed with Haj, via train and ferry, to New York. To explain what the sight of the city meant to me is impossible. Huge and noisy, it frightened me. We walked the streets lined with tall buildings until we came to a red brick house with a huge brown stoop. Haj's attitude changed. The man who disciplined us and ordered us about now seemed as spellbound and frightened as we. Why? Of course, I had not yet met Uncle Ameen. Despite the cool weather, perspiration wet Haj's forehead. Was he sick?

Haj tapped the door. It opened and we entered a hallway. A woman, who turned out to be my aunt, bent and kissed us, leading us to the living room. By later standards, the house would be judged barely habitable. Our eyes, unaccustomed to the shabbiest of splendors, were dazzled.

A gigantic figure loomed over us. Haj scurried to a shadowy corner.

"What are these?" the giant thundered. I glanced at the source of the thunder into the squarest, fiercest face I had ever seen. Black eyes, black hair, and two unbelievable handlebars of mustache – that was Uncle Ameen.

"Well?" he shouted impatiently, as his jaws propelled the ends of his mustaches up and down. "Answer me – somebody!"

"These are your new nephews, Uncle," Haj whimpered. He, too, was apparently one of Ameen's nephews.

"Hmph!" Ameen grunted. "They look like little *girls* to me."

George Simon started to say something nasty. Half frightened, half angry, I grabbed him. "Uncle," I said quickly, "I am George Joseph, this is George Simon, and here is Shaheen."

Ameen ignored me. He jerked at Shaheen's lace collar. "Never have I seen such clothes as these," he grumbled. Haj crawled deeper into his corner. The clothes were his "wonderful" idea. He prayed no one would mention it.

Shaheen, without intending to, saved him. "Uncle," he blurted out, "I'm hungry. Will you feed us soon?"

Crack! Shaheen reeled from a wicked slap on the cheek. "Don't tell me when to feed you," Uncle Ameen growled. "I am the one to decide that – or whether you are worth feeding." He turned away, losing interest in us.

Haj pulled us outside. Shaheen trembled. George Simon and I shook. Haj's mouth twitched. Haj said, "Stay here," and walked down the steps, the sidewalk, around the corner. He did not return. We sat, silent and depressed. Not for long.

A gang of roughneck kids strode the sidewalk, saw us, laughed at our clothes, and started making fun of us. Shaheen and I tried to ignore them. Not George Simon. He hurled Arabic insults at our tormentors. They jeered. He spat at them. They understood that language! Two of them lunged up the steps, grabbed him and pulled him to the sidewalk, where they pounded. I tried to help, but we were outnumbered, both taking our licks. Shaheen ran after Haj for help, but they caught him, too.

On even terms, these little pugs would have given us a merciless shellacking. At two-to-one, we were doomed.

Suddenly, Uncle Ameen appeared on the stoop. He threw his big cane into the tangle of fighters, voice bellowing. The kids scattered like leaves on a windy day.

In the gutter lay Ameen's three battered Lord Fauntleroys. He speared us with a glance. "Into the house!"

We, inside, lined against the wall facing Uncle Ameen. "Ha! This is more like it," he grunted. "Maybe you are *boys* after all. You are not *men* or you wouldn't have been beaten."

We wanted to point out we were outnumbered, that the toughs who had attacked us were vicious fighters. One did not protest to Uncle Ameen – without risking damage. We had enough damage for that day.

"You did not *run* from the fight, anyway, which is a good sign." He looked sternly at us. "But you have foolishly ruined your fine new clothes." We looked at each other. A half-hour before, he had almost disowned us for wearing them. "They cost at least three dollars a suit. Since you will be paid twenty-five cents a week when we work, this means that for the first twelve weeks you will get nothing."

"But, Uncle..." I interrupted, despite the peril of a cracked head, "We have already paid for the suits out of our European pay of ten cents a week. Uncle, we..."

"Silence!" Ameen roared, and lifted his hand from his knee.

I looked at the big, hairy hand, silently bidding goodbye to twelve weeks' pay.

Chapter 7
Flip-Flaps and Tinsicas

Uncle Ameen was a slave-driver whose brutality was open and undisguised. When we pleased him, he rewarded us little, if at all. When we crossed him, or he thought we did, punishment was swift, sure and strong. Yet, in his own bitter, twisted fashion, Ameen respected us, maybe loved us.

I collected most of his respect, most of his wrath. He chided me when he found me sitting in a corner with one of Annie's primers. The chiding didn't bother me because he knew that whether for practice or on stage, I'd be the first to arrive and the last to leave.

We remained at Uncle Ameen's house until he got us some bookings. Not a period of rest, as we virtually lived in the gym, practicing for long hours on our stunts, learning new ones. Under Ameen's pitiless instruction – far more demanding than Haj's – we became fast, expert acrobats, possibly the best he had ever produced.

Uncle Ameen designated me the topmounter. Although number one in altitude, topmounting is the lowliest status in the troupe.

We practiced through the winter, in the spring rejoining the Buffalo Bill Circus. I sought Annie, not finding the lady. Then Colonel Cody greeted me warmly. Thanks to her, I now understood the Colonel's words. "She has married, Puabla. Work harder for her sake."

Renewing old acquaintants, I exchanged guarded greetings with Sinko. We clashed once without being caught, but we never again met in the Sunday ring.

I soon acquired an enemy more potent than Sinko – Minnie, the elephant. Minnie led an act consisting of a dog, a pony and an elephant. Minnie was a mean old hellion whom nobody ever knowingly antagonized.

My extracurricular money-making activities caused my trouble with Minnie. Although Uncle Ameen had grudgingly raised my pay from twenty-five to forty cents a week, I earned a few pennies more by shining boots and making lemonade.

Ten cowboys paid me two cents a week to shine their boots, fifteen others paying three cents a week to belong to my lemonade club. At noon, I filled a large bucket with lemonade, my members dipping into it until six o'clock.

One early afternoon, a thirsty club member demanded to know why the lemonade had run out. Morally obligated to keep up the supply until dinnertime, I made another bucketful – cost: a nickel.

For the next three days, the same thing happened. I found myself near bankruptcy.

Shaheen, a non-paying member of the club, volunteered his advice. "I don't like to see you go out of business." (Naturally, that would end his free drinks.) "Put some Epsom salts in the lemonade. Keep your eyes open. Whoever runs in and out is the guy who's stealing your lemonade."

I informed my regular customers to keep away for one day, loading my bucket of lemonade with salts. I couldn't watch the bucket, so I kept an eye on the man who left practice too often. There was no more than the regular traffic. The culprit had been warned off, I thought, as I returned to the dressing tent. An empty bucket again stared at me.

That night, I sought Shaheen. "I'll have to go out of business," I told him, "unless one last idea works. I can only try it if Uncle Ameen lets me out of the rehearsal tomorrow."

Shaheen shook his head at such a proposal. "I'll talk to him anyway," I said. Uncle Ameen was my biggest lemonade customer; complimentary of course. "Where is Uncle?" I asked Shaheen.

"He's talking to Buffalo Bill."

"What's the matter?"

"He's trying to get our spot in the show changed." Shaheen said. "He can't stand following the elephant anymore. It's making him sick."

Uncle Ameen returned and I explained the plan. He immediately rebelled at the thought of letting me out of work from twelve to two o'clock. When I reminded him of "his" lemonade, he reconsidered.

Alone in the tent the next day, I loaded the bucket with water, a few lemons, and the cheapest, nastiest alum I could buy. I hid, watching the bucket, as everyone else rehearsed. Twelve-thirty, nothing. One o'clock, one-fifteen. A tent flap raised. Something slithered into the bucket. I dove and grabbed, coming up with Minnie's trunk. She sucked the bucket dry. With an angry blast, she blew the alum lemonade from her puckered mouth.

I rolled out of the tent, almost under her feet. She saw and smelled me. She lifted one foot. I scrambled as the big hoof thumped into the earth. The elephant snorted, charging me.

"Minnie!" her owner yelled, stopping her in her tracks to crouch by the tent. I eyed her; she eyed me. She no longer rumbled. Her glare never left me until I crawled to safety. After that, my very presence evoked Minnie's snorts.

When the circus season ended, we lived with Uncle Ameen in the 17th Street house, after which we moved to a shabby red brick flat on the corner of 103rd Street and Park Avenue. One bedroom faced the street and the other faced the railroad tracks. We drew the tracks. At thirteen years of age, it took more than bellowing steam engines to disturb our sleep. After all, for three-quarters of the year, we lived on a train.

Our wooden circus car was more my home than any of the many immovable dwellings we occupied. Although it housed no family, it carried whatever friends I could claim in the world; a few enemies, too. Even a familiar enemy is more reassuring than a stranger. Despite the bedbugs, lice and other assorted creatures that inhabited the crowded, smelly circus car, I always felt a pleasant tingle when the time came to throw my pack in my bunk and start traveling.

By 1909, my salary had risen to two dollars-and-a-half a week. Even more important, I had gained Colonel Cody's special attention when the Colonel recognized me publicly as one of his top horseback riders. The Maze in the Buffalo Bill Circus now consisted of Wild West Riders, Indians, and Far East Riders. Complicated and furious, it was to all circusdom, "The Ride of Death." Falling off while riding in the tight, opposing circles, could result in a rider being trampled, even killed.

When the leader of the Far East group quit the circus, Buffalo Bill, without prior hint, announced that the new director of the Far East Riders was Puabla Hamid.

He not only selected me for this important post, but even dignified me by using my last name. I was a man at last – though not yet fourteen.

That year, the chief circuses of the country decided to hold a tumbling contest for the world's championship. Buffalo Bill and Uncle Ameen determined, after much deliberation, that I was to be their entrant. The prestige of our circus would tumble with me.

Old Madison Square Garden was packed to the rafters with circus enthusiasts, half of them performers. The biggest circus owners in the world sat in flag-draped boxes. Buffalo Bill, the center of attention, even among the top celebrities, occupied a center box, Uncle Ameen beside him.

At the end of the arena, the contestants practiced cartwheels and backs. I eyed the others to see how good they were, just as they looked at me. Shaheen became my "second". Since George Simon also wanted to get into the action, he became my "third."

A cannon-voiced announcer boomed the details of the contest. We were to be judged in five competitions – cartwheels, tinsicas, pirouettes, handsprings and forwards. From the first set, eight competitors would be eliminated by the judges. The remainder would move on to stationary flip-flaps, moving flip-flaps, and flip-flaps with backs, during the course of which four more tumblers would be ruled out. The final test, to determine the prize winner, would be long distance tumbling – twenty handsprings, twenty tinsicas, then flip-flaps as far as the tumbler could go.

My "third" did not boost my morale as we waited for the contest to begin, calling my attention to an outstanding forward here, a fancy tinsica there, with such remarks as "Gee, look at that guy!" and "Wow, he's good, Puabla – you'll have a tough time beating him!"

He finally got to me, and I warned Shaheen, "If you want an

assistant, you'd better shut up George Simon. Otherwise, I'll get along without a "third."

Shaheen's simple and direct method was to kick George Simon on the shins with a message-bearing growl. Before George Simon could reform or get fired, the contest began.

His unintentional needling served a useful purpose. He had focused my attention on the one contestant who stood out above the others. He represented, naturally enough, Barnum & Bailey. Since Barnum & Bailey preceded Buffalo Bill alphabetically, he preceded me in each test. I noted every move he made, determined to do a little bit better.

He and I survived the first elimination into the second series. He tumbled beautifully. The crowd adopted him, applauding loudly every time his turn came up. Too busy trying to out-do him, the obvious one to beat, I didn't hear how they applauded me.

He and I and another acrobat repeated the entire second group of stunts before the judges could select the final two contestants. After five long minutes of deliberation, the announcer walked to the center of the arena, held up his hands and roared, "Ladies and gentlemen. The judges have decided on the two finalists. From the Barnum & Bailey Circus, we have…" Cheering drowned out the name. "And from the…" – my heart stood still – "… Buffalo Bill Circus, Puabla Hamid."

For the first time, I realized I had a following, because the cheering sounded as loud for me as for my opponent.

The announcer bellowed the final rules; long distance tumbling, to be judged on endurance as well as form. Circling the Old Madison Square Garden consumed at least five hundred feet. Our assigned course ran counter-clockwise from the center boxes, six feet off the outer wall.

In the trials, I had loosened myself, chasing the butterflies out of my stomach. Shaheen, now more nervous than me, asked if he should station George Simon at one of the turns to trip the other tumbler. I told him to sit down before he collapsed.

A drum-roll launched my opponent. He did the handsprings, the tinsicas. Away he flew into the flip-flaps.

"Oh, oh," Shaheen moaned, "He's good on form."

I didn't need Shaheen to tell me that. Up one side of the arena he rolled, around the end and down the other side. As he passed the starting point, a roar swelled form the crowd. On he went, Shaheen moaning louder. He rounded the bend and returned down the far side. The roar subsided as the thousands in the audience watched tensely, silently. The only sound in the arena was the steady thump-thump of his hands and feet as they hit the sawdust.

George Simon, standing beside me, began to sob. "Oh, look at him – just look at him!" I shoved him away. My heart grew fainter the longer I looked. The tumbler became a red and gold blur, like the wheel of a moving circus wagon. He approached the finish line a second time, the roar of applause starting again, mounting and bursting like thunder as he crossed the line. Ten more feet and he crumpled into a red and gold heap on the ground.

The people shouted themselves hoarse. His second, who had run alongside, tried to lift him to his feet. He could not stand, waving weakly from his knees.

I limbered my arms and legs, looking at Shaheen, who had paled.

"Come on," I whispered. "You're my second. You've got to go along with me."

"Do you really think you can go around this place twice?" he asked. I shrugged my shoulders. "If he can, I ought to be able to," my bravado speaking for me. A swarm of butterflies returned. I'd never tried a distance like that – or near it.

I took my place at the starting line. For a moment, the drum rolled. I steadied my feet, grinding my slippers through the sawdust to the solid earth. "Go!"

Shaheen counted for me – twenty handsprings, twenty tinsicas, then a full twister through the air into the flip-flaps.

The wind sang in my ears. I felt strong. Around the turn and down the other side, my wrists beginning to grow numb. Shaheen's voice pounded in my ears. Through the lower bend, then to the finish line I whirled, barely hearing the roar of the crowd as I crossed it.

Over and over I went. Feet – then hands. Feet – hands,

thumping into the sawdust, my ears ringing. The building looped crazily. My eyes saw the ceiling, the ground, my wrists now so numb that I had to concentrate to keep them holding me as I landed on them. I no longer heard the crowd, nor could I figure out where I was on the track. I couldn't even try.

Only Shaheen's voice urged me, guided me. "Good boy, Puabla! Keep going, Puabla. Keep it up. Don't stop now, Puabla. Good going, Puabla."

Breathing grew difficult. My lungs ached, then pained. I wasn't dizzy anymore, because I lost sight of the tumbling world around me.

Finally, my wrist gave out. With a crash, I fell to the ground like a broken toy. The building spun too fast for me to sit up. Shaheen bent over. "Are you hurt, Puabla?"

I shook my head. The building settled. Shaheen lifted me to my feet. I wobbled and leaned against him, but I stood up. In the tradition of all acrobats, I waved to the crowd. I focused my eyes to get my bearings. I had ended at the far turn, at what amounted to about the three-quarter mark. Only one and three-quarter turns, I thought to myself. It seemed as if I had gone miles. I was too exhausted to care. Shaheen led me toward the finish line, where I fell onto a canvas cot. He wiped me with a towel. Several minutes passed, during which I breathed more normally, settled my insides to their proper location, my mind regaining its whereabouts.

"What do you think, Shaheen?" I asked. "My form – how was my form?"

"Relax, Cousin," he cautioned me. "You look terrible – relax."

The announcer strode to the center of the arena, raising his hands. The buzzing of the audience subsided.

"The judges have decided as follows," he boomed. "On form, the two contestants are equal." He paused. "Since the Barnum & Bailey entrant circled the arena twice, plus ten feet, and the Buffalo Bill entrant circled the arena two and three-quarter times..."(I gulped) "the Champion Tumbler of the United States and the World is none other than"...with a flourish, he pointed at me, as I tried to sit straight and smile... "Puabla Hamid."

Chapter 8
Stanley's Sparring Partner

Everybody enthused about my victory – except Uncle Ameen. Being Ameen, he found it difficult to show his approval.

Before dinner that night, the rest of us talked happily. I possessed a bright medal, plus five dollars that Buffalo Bill had given me as a reward. Ameen sat stonily silent in his armchair, until he spoke.

"Puabla," he said, "you have had a great day, have you not?"

"Yes, Uncle," I replied, rubbing my sore wrist.

"I know," he said. Then he roared, "I should send you to bed without your supper!"

"What have I done wrong?" I sputtered.

"You now think," Ameen growled, "that you are the Champion of the World, so there is nobody like you." I grew a little frightened. "You think that the act and I, probably the whole circus, would be lost without you. This thought will poison you and you will become rotten."

Though he was the strongest man I've ever known, I wanted to hit him, hard. Not looking at me, he gazed into the distance, his eyes sad. My anger fled, replaced by the all too familiar fright. I walked over, sinking into the floor in front of him.

"Uncle Ameen," I said, "I won't turn rotten. Maybe I'm not the best in the world. If I was, I wouldn't leave you or the act or Buffalo Bill. Honest." I almost sobbed, "You ought to know that."

He didn't answer. For all I was able to eat, he might as well have sent me to bed without supper.

Uncle Ameen probably feared I would launch my own career as

the World's Champion Tumbler. The only danger of my leaving the act would come from a completely different profession.

We usually practiced in a gymnasium, where I liked to work out on the punching bad for fifteen minutes before leaving – for the fun of it. One day, someone approached me as I punched the bag. "Wanna spar?" he asked.

I shook my head no. We fought enough in the circus without looking for outside battles.

"Only take you ten minutes," the man persisted. "You can make a quarter, maybe half a buck."

I stopped punching the bag. "Where?" I asked.

"Over there," he said pointing to a ring where a fighter sat, two men rubbing him.

I was fourteen years old. Weighing a hundred and thirty pounds and measuring no more than five feet, two inches in height. Size never bothered me. I was strong and I knew how to fight.

I stripped off my shirt, ducking through the ropes into the ring. I smiled at my opponent, who smiled back. One of his seconds ordered us to start. As I strolled to the corner of the ring, fists hammered at my head from all directions. I jumped back, stumbling to the canvas. The other fighter grinned down at me.

Hopping to my feet, I surprised him with a right to the jaw, darting back to pull my wits together. Returning to the fight, I ducked and weaved to dodge the blows. I didn't dodge many.

I wobbled to my corner. One of the seconds crossed the ring to me. "Stanley says you're not bad, I should help you," he said.

"Who's Stanley?" I asked.

"The guy you're fighting, stupid – Stanley Ketchel."

I bolted upright on my stool. For fifty cents, I had volunteered to spar with the Middleweight Champion of the World! No wonder I couldn't dodge those fists.

"Holy smokes!" I muttered, trying to duck away from my handler. "He'll kill me."

"No, he won't. He could, but he won't. Besides, he says you're a good sparring partner. You're hard to hit."

To me, on the receiving end, I wondered what would be "easy to hit." The man gave me basic pointers on jabbing and shoved me toward Ketchel again. By the end of the third round, our last, I began to recognize the science of boxing – so different from mere fighting.

Ketchel took off his gloves and sauntered over to me. "How about tomorrow night?" he asked. I shook my head no. "Listen," he said, "you're not bad. I'll give you a half a buck a day the rest of the week if you'll go three rounds with me, same time."

"Will you take it easy with me until I get the hang of it?" I asked. Five days at fifty cents totaled two-fifty, a full week's salary.

"Seventy-five cents."

Ketchel nodded in agreement.

"Give me a handler to tell me what to do?" I asked. He nodded again.

When Shaheen and George Simon learned that I was sparring with the great Stanley Ketchel, I acquired two seconds. They rounded up a bucket, a sponge and some towels for the next night. Between rounds, they worked me over, all the time offering such useful advice as "Kill him! Try a couple below the belt."

My chief goal was to avoid Ketchel's fists. By the end of the week, I started to catch on. Although Ketchel lived up to his agreements, I still took a great deal more than I gave. Gradually, I became a more difficult target. Occasionally, I caught him off-guard with a jab or a lucky right cross. When I did, I could see he felt it.

On the last night that week, after the others had left, Ketchel and his manager walked with me into a rubbing room, sitting me down.

"Puabla," Ketchel said to me, "how would you like to become a fighter?" I frowned.

"Lots of dough in it," he went on. Turning to his manager, he added, "Sparring's okay, but I think we're missing the boat. We can make a pile of money with this kid."

The manager scrutinized me. "Awful short on reach," he commented.

"Doesn't matter," Ketchel said. "He's fast. He can hit."

The manager shrugged, "You ought to know. If you think he's good, I'll try him."

Ketchel looked at me. "How about it, kid? We'll put you up, feed you and take care of you. In three years, you'll be rich."

I couldn't answer him. I needed time to think. I was going to spar on Monday, anyway.

For two days I worried. I couldn't sleep. Conflicting desires split my mind. First, the money, the excitement of the boxing world – and Ketchel, whom I liked immensely. Then Buffalo Bill, Annie Oakley, Uncle Ameen, Shaheen, George Simon – and being Champion Tumbler of the World. I remembered a kid named Gunther, who hung around the gym. He tried boxing for a while. Now "punchy," nobody at the gym gave him the time of day. On the other hand, there was Ketchel, bright, alert, at the top. If you were smart...

On Monday, I tumbled badly and sparred worse. Ketchel came to me at the end of our session. "You look tired, kid. Rough weekend?"

I half nodded. "I didn't get much sleep."

"We'll show you how to take a good time in stride," Ketchel said.

"I've been thinking instead of sleeping." I blurted out, "Mr. Ketchel, I can't come with you. I'm an acrobat, not a boxer. I've got to keep on being an acrobat."

Ketchel looked annoyed, then softened. He patted me, pretty hard, on the chin. "Well," he said, "don't worry about it. I'll be around here another couple of weeks. Any time you want to pick up six bits, you know where it is. If you change your mind...."

I had one more sparring session with Ketchel. For two rounds, I boxed better than ever and wondered if maybe I should be a boxer after all. In the third, Ketchel opened up. He bombarded me with everything. I saw stars, suns and planets unknown to man. He didn't knock me out. If the session had lasted another round, I'd have left on a stretcher.

Whether or not he intended to, Ketchel convinced me I made the right decision. He was my ring hero and I followed his turbulent career with fascination. Never did I see a greater boxer. A year later, I learned he was shot to death.

When I couldn't eat dinner, Uncle Ameen wanted to know why. "You always eat. You sick?"

Only in my heart, I thought. "Don't worry Uncle. Maybe not tonight. I'll be alright."

Chapter 9
Folding Circus

When something goes wrong with a circus, a lot of other things begin to go wrong.

The trouble started when the animal train wrecked. One faulty switch-box and the whole caravan flew down an embankment. The wooden cars splintered. Parts of animals scattered in all directions. When we arrived, Minnie's owner was pounding on the door of his, the only, steel car.

A lantern revealed the car to be upside down, as was the elephant, the weight on her head and shoulders, her hind legs thrust against an opposite wall. If she relaxed those hind legs, her weight would fall against the roof of the car, now the bottom. Under her lay her friend, the performing pony, which would then be crushed to death.

I don't know how she held herself in the contortionist position. Her owner talked to her softly until a derrick pulled alongside. Its crew extricated the pony. Only then did Minnie let her weight settle against the roof of the car.

A cheer greeted her as her head, then her body, appeared through the twisted door. I made the mistake of being too close to her. Despite everything she had been through, she remembered the lemonade with the bitter alum when she saw and smelled me. She snorted. I ran.

The train wreck caused the circus to pass up valuable dates. It took time to accumulate and break in new stock, so it was many weeks before the circus was whole again.

Serious wrangling broke out among the roustabouts, filtering to the performers. For a while, we even had trouble keeping up with our "Paper" (advertised schedules.) We'd play a town two, or sometimes three days late, then skip a couple of spots to catch up with the advertising, the commitments. Falling behind its dated posters is the worst thing that can happen to the traveling show.

It took a full season to restore the circus. The adjustment nearly exhausted Colonel Cody's resources.

At the same time, Buffalo Bill himself faded as a drawing card. Now in his late years, he had played every town in America. When he combined his circus with that of his long-time (likewise aging) competitor, most of us thought that the end had come. Although Buffalo Bill and Pawnee Bill skillfully blended the two shows, the merger only postponed the inevitable.

We arrived in a Nebraska town one day and set up the circus in a lot on the outskirts. One of the boys in the act brought me a message – Colonel Cody wanted to see me. Though I'd been with the circus several years, I still got a thrill when a call came from Buffalo Bill. I hurried to his railroad car.

He motioned me to a seat, his age showing, even to me. "Puabla," he said, "I am an old man. Like other old men, I am tired. Before something happens to prevent me, I want to talk to you."

I listened with all my attention.

"Do you remember the day I told Haj to make a rider out of you?" I nodded. "Since then, I have been watching you. You have brains, you have energy – the right kind of energy. If you were ten years older…" He paused, then sadly shook his head. "There's no use talking about that, because you're *not* ten years older. If you were, I'd turn this circus over to you. And I wouldn't be surprised, Puabla, if you could return it to its old glories."

"Speaking of old glories, I remember this town," talking more to himself than to me. "It was an out-post forty-five years ago. Over there," he pointed, "was a stable where I could freshen up the horses or exchange them. It wasn't far from here I shot all those buffalo for the Kansas and Pacific. Puabla, you would have made a good hunter. I read in a book lately that I shot 4,280 of them in eighteen months." He chuckled, "Sounds like a lot of bison meat, though I wouldn't be surprised if it's the truth." He looked at me out of the corner of his eye. "I had to shoot 'em, you know. I didn't do it because I wanted to kill the beasts. It was a contract with the railroad. A man made strange deals in those days."

I listened quietly, hoping he would go on, fascinated to be hearing these tales from the great man whose deeds had become legends. He continued.

"Puabla, my son, this town grew because it had the strength to grow. My Wild West Show grew because I had the knowledge and the determination to build it." He looked away. "And now, it is failing because I no longer have the power to keep it from failing. Puabla, there is only one will in the world; that is the will inside you."

He talked on, speaking of his confidence in me, urging me to always have confidence in myself. I felt comfortable, somehow at home. The car was elegant, the chair deep and soft, his words warm. Soon, I began to talk. I told him of my grandmother, my father, of my life as a little boy in Lebanon. I talked about Uncle Ameen. I even told him about my great chance with Stanley Ketchel.

"Do you think I should have gone with him?" I asked Buffalo Bill. "I know I could have been a good boxer. Tell me, what do you think?"

He smiled his wonderful smile. "I think Puabla, that you should continue on the road you are traveling. You know the road. Others may look smoother at times, this is yours."

I soon had occasion to appreciate the fighting technique I had learned from Ketchel.

Uncle Ameen's physical strength, his acrobatic supremacy, were almost as much a part of the tradition of the circus as Buffalo Bill's showmanship and his flowing white hair. As understander in our act, he supported nine men on his shoulders. I had moved from topmounter, through several grades, to middleman, the acrobat immediately above the understander. Although I experienced a part of this great weight, I never dreamed of attempting Uncle Ameen's feats.

No one doubted, opposed or challenged Uncle Ameen's strength.

His universal acknowledgement fed his insatiable pride. We, his nephews, basked in the reflected glory.

An ugly threat appeared in the person of one Sharkey, an ex-fighter, now a member of the mess gang. Once a champion of some kind, he was a huge man who knew the techniques of boxing, as he demonstrated by pulverizing three of the best Sunday fighters in the circus.

Could Sharkey beat Ameen Buhamid in a fight? That was the whispered question. If Ameen heard it, he ignored it. I thought, "Just as well." The Ketchel in me warned that Sharkey, with real ring skills, would punch Ameen dizzy before Uncle could lay a hand on him.

One day, a commotion erupted by our railroad car. I hurried to the small crowd and saw George Simon arguing with Sharkey. George Simon said something about the great strength of his Uncle Ameen, disparaging the prowess of Sharkey. A few oaths followed, Sharkey stomping away muttering, "I'll find this Ameen and settle him once and for all."

I felt a chill. For the first time I realized that Uncle Ameen was not invincible. He still thought so; that thought his most precious possession. Without it, Ameen's world, his ego, would collapse. I couldn't stand the thought.

Jumping in front of Sharkey, grabbing his arm, I said, "My God, Sharkey! You're not going to hit Uncle Ameen! He's twenty-five years older than you."

He brushed me aside, walked along the track, the whole circus in curious pursuit.

Sharkey and I were friends. Otherwise, I wouldn't have dared get in his way again. I darted in front of him. "What's the idea?" I demanded. "Uncle Ameen hasn't done anything to you."

Sharkey stopped, glaring at me. "Do I have to beat up Ameen's whole family?" he growled. "Get out of my way." I refused to move. The crowd circled round. I started to speak again. Sharkey whipped his open hand at my face. I pulled back as I felt the wind from the intended slap whistle in my eyes.

My fist closed as he lunged off balance. I threw a vicious right hook, landing flush on his jaw. His mouth hung open as he fell. He crashed, his head clanking against the rail.

He didn't move. For a moment, I could not move either. Somebody said, almost in a whisper, "Puabla's killed him." I tried to disappear.

From behind a tent I watched as three men carried the limp Sharkey.

Shaheen met me. He shook his head. He told me that Sharkey was not dead. "You're in for it," he told me. "You *almost* killed him. His jaw is broken. His head is split open where it hit the railroad track. They took him to the hospital. The grub boys say that as soon as you come down to eat they'll gang up on you. Sharkey was their hero."

"They'll murder me." I moaned.

When Uncle Ameen heard the story, he misunderstood it, as I knew he would. He wanted to punish George Simon and me for getting into a fight with Sharkey. I tried to explain.

"Uncle, Sharkey was on his way over here to fight you. I tried to stop him. Before I knew it, I had to sock him on the jaw."

Crack! Uncle Ameen's cane slashed my shins. Did I think that he, Ameen, couldn't handle the likes of Sharkey?

I tried to describe Sharkey's boxing prowess. With every word, I sank deeper. Ameen stormed out of the tent, not allowing us to think that he needed protections from Sharkey – or anyone. I could expect no help from Uncle. At dinnertime, Shaheen and George Simon left. I stayed alone in the tent, too frightened to move. How long could I get along without food? Two days, maybe. Miserable and hungry, I waited.

Johnny Baker, Buffalo Bill's right-hand man, stuck his head in the tent. "Hello, Puabla," he called. "They tell me you're breaking up the circus." A big, good-natured fellow, his word (next to Colonel Cody's) was circus law.

"You look worried." He commented.

"Of course I'm worried. The grub gang's after me. They'll give me a worse going-over than Sharkey would."

He laughed, "I don't think so, boy.   Sharkey asked for it. Come with me."

I followed him, hearing the clatter of plates, the hum of voices, as we approached the long tables. The grub gang waited ominously in the corner.

Baker beckoned them. Magically, the noises at the table ceased, all faces turning towards us. Baker spoke.

"I want everyone's attention," he roared. "Sharkey's in the hospital. Puabla, here, with help from a railroad track, put him there. I'm not going to say what he did was right. We have enough fights in this circus already. I do say this – Sharkey got what he asked for. If anyone in this show lays a hand on Puabla over what happened today, he'll be accountable to me. Worse than that, he'll be accountable to Colonel Cody."

Baker sat down beside me – a singular honor – and ordered two plates of grub.

The next day I visited Sharkey in the hospital. Surprisingly, he offered me his hand. I cringed at the sight of him – broken jaw, four teeth out, stitches in his head. He tried to smile, mumbling, "I'm not mad at you. Next time, I'll have more sense than to pick a fight along a railroad track."

One of the grub boys sat near his bed. Sharkey turned to him. "You tell the fellows to lay off Puabla," Sharkey said. "He's a good guy."

The show moved on, while Sharkey stayed. He was to catch up in Nebraska, but never did. Nobody I knew ever saw him again.

Sharkey, as merely a threat, had erased the invincibility of Uncle Ameen. His armor showed visible chinks, the realization frightening me.

The end of the circus – for us anyway – came in Denver in early 1913. Uncle Ameen had already taken a cut. Unfortunately for him, his minions received so little that he could not share his reduction.

The circus, now a shadow of its former magnificence, set up on the west side of town, under the overhanging peaks of the Rocky Mountains.

Uncle Ameen and the troupe sat outside the dressing tent before the show opened. We talked aimlessly when, out of the twilight, strode Buffalo Bill himself, a shadow of what he once was. As I stood up, he motioned us to be at ease and sat down next to Uncle Ameen. The chattering stopped.

"Ameen, I want to talk to you."

Uncle told us to leave. "No, Ameen," he said. "Let them stay. They should hear, too." He paused, finding it hard to speak. "Ameen, you have been working for only part of your salary. For many years, you have performed well. Now I must tell you, my good friend, and it breaks my heart to do it, that I can no longer afford to pay you even this small part of your salary."

He turned, looking sorrowfully at the mountains, his head silhouetted against the evening sky. Tears filled my eyes, blurring the sight of him.

"It means that you are no longer with my circus," Colonel Cody said. "The truth is I have no circus. If you offered to work for nothing, it couldn't be done. The show may move on after tomorrow. I doubt if it will move often, or for long. When it moves tomorrow, I am leaving you behind."

He stood up, looking at us, one after the other. He smiled, calling us each by name. "I wish you the greatest good luck this life can provide." He stood for a few minutes. We couldn't speak. He turned and disappeared in the shadows of the tents.

The next day, I left him there, beneath the towering crags of his Rocky Mountains. I say "his" Rocky Mountains. I guess if they are anybody's they are his.

Chapter 10
Innocents Afoot

We trudged downtown to a cheap hotel. Denver wasn't new to us. We had played it before with the circus, but now we paid attention to it.

Though Uncle Ameen received a reduced salary for some weeks, the act had earned good money for years. What Uncle did with the money, I never knew, except that funds were usually low; especially so when the circus departed. I didn't realized *how* low.

Uncle Ameen brought us to his hotel room. "This is how much money we have," he grunted, tossing one dollar bills on the table. "It will take all of us two hundred miles, or it will take one of us to Chicago. Since we can get work only from Chicago agents, the wise thing is for one of us to go all the way. I will take the train to Chicago."

An obvious problem loomed. "Suppose you do get work in Chicago," I asked. "How do you plan to get us there?"

"I have thought of that," Ameen shot back. "You will all walk to Chicago."

We gasped. Walk to Chicago? While none of us knew its location, we did know Chicago wasn't anywhere near Denver. One of Ameen's non-relative acrobats objected. My uncle shrugged his shoulders. "Stay in Denver. It's up to you."

Ameen, leaving, threw the pilgrimage into my charge. Whatever sympathy I had for my aging uncle perished then and there.

Calling a meeting, I said, "We're in a pickle. I nearly got put away asking somebody downstairs the best route for walking to Chicago." I looked at the glum faces. "There's no choice. We have to get there. Any ideas?"

Not even a grumble.

"Here's what I think," I said. "There's lots of towns between here and Chicago. We'll start walking. Whenever we can ride on an interurban for a nickel apiece, we'll take it. We should average twenty miles a day. I found out Chicago is a thousand fifty miles east. We can make it in about fifty-two days."

I expected a few groans. None came. For encouragement, I added, "At least there's no mountains to cross." Nobody cheered.

"We can stay here if somebody can figure out how to make a living."

"What about food?" Shaheen asked. I was afraid of that.

"I know I have the most money," I said. "If all of you want to pool our dough and divide it up, I'm willing."

Each reluctantly walked to the bed, emptying his pockets. George Simon was low man with thirty cents. "Search George," I ordered Shaheen, who uncovered forty cents in a shoe, plus a dollar in a shirt pocket. I banished George Simon to a chair in the corner.

"We're either in this thing together," I growled, "or everyone goes on his own." I handed George Simon his dollar seventy. "Get to Chicago any way you can."

"You're not going to leave me. I don't even know the way."

Ignoring him, I divided the money among the others – six dollars and forty-five cents apiece.

Next morning, I rallied my troops in the lobby. Each of us parted with two of our precious dollars for the hotel bill, which included two days' food. Four dollars and forty-five cents remained.

Each of us carried one small grip. In it were costumes, a few spare pieces of clothing, our meager personal belongings; scarcely wealthier than the day we left Lebanon.

On a bright, sunny, spring morning, we walked out of the hotel, along the streets of Denver to the edge of town, then onto the open road. George Simon followed us, as I knew he would. I had ordered the members in good standing not to mingle with him. I warned Shaheen not to let him out of our sight. The presence of our outcast did the others some good. They pitied him. Until then, they had felt sorry only for themselves – now they could look at someone worse off.

For a week, the weather stayed balmy. At Brush, Colorado, we ate a big dinner. Proceeding outside town, we found a comfortable-looking tree, pulling up for the night. As on the previous nights, we slept in the open, George Simon at an ever diminishing distance.

Night fell and the travelers slept. I walked to a little tree, sat down beside George Simon. He jumped out of his sleep.

"I guess you can come back," I said. He rubbed his eyes. "You shouldn't have cheated back in Denver. That was a lowdown trick when we're all in trouble together."

George Simon sat in silence.

"Do you have any money left?" He shook his head no, and I believed him. "You ate tonight. I saw you. What are you going to do in the morning?"

He didn't know. His isolation was ending barely in time.

"Get your pack," I told him, "and follow me to the big tree." We lay down, side by side.

"Cousin," I whispered, "I'm sorry for what I did."

His arm stretched over me as we fell asleep.

On the ninth day it rained, soaking us. Tom Morocco forced a barn door. We huddled inside, the rain leaking through the roof. We bundled hay around ourselves, shivering till morning, fearing, but not catching pneumonia.

Before reaching North Platte, Nebraska, we entered a little village where a freight train took on water. A boxcar's open door yawned an invitation. We glanced around, tip-toeing our acceptance. We rode a hundred miles – equal to five days on foot.

We walked on again, a bit rested. We spent one morning pitching hay for a farmer; our total pay amounting to two dollars, plus a good meal. We netted food and twenty-two cents apiece.

Bright weather had launched the trip from Denver. Rain, now coupled with impending financial exhaustion, turned our cheer into gloom.

A fifteen cent lunch broke us. We trudged through the afternoon in silence. At evening, we approached the outskirts of Grand Island, Nebraska.

Sitting on the curb, we eyed each other sadly. Shaheen took off a shoe, poking his finger through the sole. We smelled something, having made the serious mistake of sitting in front of the Elite Restaurant.

"Oh God, that food smells good," Tom Morocco groaned.

Sid Amelia's look suggested larceny or murder, if it would produce a meal.

"Take it easy," I warned. "We'll think of something."

The townspeople stared at us – nine rough-looking strangers sitting menacingly on their curbstone. To our dismay, the first person who spoke to us was the constable.

I started to explain to him that we were walking to Chicago. I stopped. That was the surest way to go to jail. Who would believe us? I simplified, "We're acrobats. Our circus went broke and we're trying to get work."

The constable scratched his head. "I ain't heard of no circuses goin' on the rocks around here. Where'd it happen?"

"In Denver," I said.

"Denver? How'd you get here?"

"Walked,"

He pulled me to my feet. "Son, that sounds like a lie to me." He wheezed. "If you're acrobats, let's see you do some acrobatting – or off to jail you go.

I pulled the constable to one side. "How about if we do our act?"

He okayed the idea, taking us down a deserted alley so we could change into our costumes. To the amazement of the townspeople, we emerged onto the main street in full regalia. We lined in front of the restaurant and walked forward.

"Ladies and gentlemen," I announced, "believe it or not, this is a group of circus acrobats." The crowd had quickly grown. "The constable here thinks we're thieves. He wants us to prove we're not. As long as that's the case, you might as well be entertained. We were with a circus. Things got tough and they had to leave us." I started to mention the name of the circus, but couldn't bring myself to do it. "We walked here from Denver."

I heard a few disbelieving snickers. That made me decide to tell the whole truth. "And, we're walking to Chicago."

Someone laughed. Somebody else yelled, "Hooray!" Then the whole crowd, to our surprise, cheered.

I promoted Morocco to my uncle's former position of understander, and Sid Amelia to middleman. The others knew their positions. With a wave of the hand, we alley-ooped into our routines. After six or seven better-than-average pyramids, I stopped the act. Taking the constable's arms, I tugged him to the center of the crowd.

"The best part of the show is yet to come, folks. But I want you to know that when we're finished, the officer here is going to pass the hat. Aren't you, officer?" He nodded blankly, trying to figure out if he had been duped.

"And don't worry, most of what we get will be spent right here in Grand Island."

I yelled, "Tumble!" One after the other, the troupe whirled across the sidewalk. We finished in a flourish of pirouettes. As the others bowed, I grabbed the constable. Some fancy encores held the crowd.

The hat was fuller than I'd dared hope. We counted twenty dollars, gave the sheriff two, keeping two apiece. At that, the townspeople had received their money's worth. We had given them one of the best performances of their lives.

The next day, a farmer drove us ten miles in a wagon for two cents apiece. Two days later, when we arrived in Columbus, a street-corner performance netted eleven dollars, without benefit of a constable; in Fremont, Nebraska, another eight dollars.

We splurged on the interurban. Since the line ended sixty miles east of Council Bluffs, we found ourselves afoot once more. In Des Moines, we could have had our best "free" show, except the police ran us out of town. In Newton, Iowa, our shoes received their second overhaul. (The first had been in Grand Island.) While the shoes were undergoing treatment, I noticed a large group of people gathered in a grove. Walking to one of the kids, I asked, "What's going on?"

"Annual family outing," he answered.

I whistled. Some family! There were hundreds of people there.

"Who's the boss?" The boy pointed to a man called Mr. Pease. I approached, saying, "Hello, Mr. Pease." Four Peases turned to answer me.

I told the family leader I had a circus act. For ten dollars we'd put on a show the Peases would never forget. He frowned, then offered eight dollars, to be paid *after* the performance. I agreed on nine, payment in the *middle*.

Already in our acrobatic shoes, we quickly donned our red and blue costumes behind a clump of bushes, leaping into the act. In fifteen minutes, we became nine dollars richer. To top it off, the appreciative Peases adopted us, one for each branch of the family. We joined their festivities and demolished their food.

By the time we reached Cedar Rapids, we were again penniless. Luckily, a small circus hired us for two performances, at seven dollars per show; less than two dollars apiece. Once again we skirted starvation.

Hunger had ceased to be our chief worry. Our corner shows bought us two or three dollars for meals. Concerned with aching, numbed legs, endless dusty roads, sleeping on the ground on clear nights, in barns when it rained, we rarely spoke.

I tried to keep track of mileage or distances. Unfortunately, in anticipating the Mississippi, I miscalculated, promising it three days too early. Over every hill, around each turn, our eyes sought the river. We ended the second such fruitless day in DeWitt, Iowa. When a farmer informed us that the Mississippi still lay twenty-three eastward miles, Tom Morocco wept. George Simon would have punched me if he hadn't been heartsick. What could be done to restore morale? I found a tiny hotel. The proprietor, a kind old gentleman, heard my story and agreed to bunk us in three back rooms. It was a month since a roof covered our heads, other than a barn. We bathed in water that wasn't a river or a brook.

Refreshed, we sighted the Mississippi the next afternoon. Crossing from Clinton, Iowa to Fulton, Illinois, we at last found ourselves in the right state.

The following day, as we walked along a dirt road in the vicinity of

Sterling, Tom Morocco sided up to me. "Puabla," he whispered, "you'd better take a look at Sid's leg."

I had noticed Amelia limping. I called out, "Let's relax for a while, fellows," dropping under the shade of a tree. I felt Sid's knee. "What's the matter?" I asked. "Where does it hurt?"

"I don't know," he said. "It doesn't hurt any special place. I think it's just given out."

I patted his back. "Don't be silly. We have only a hundred and twenty miles left. You can't stop now. Besides, from Aurora, we can go the last forty miles on a trolley."

After resting, the calf of Sid's leg swelled like a balloon. When I touched it, he paled. I looked at Tom, "I guess we carry him to the nearest town."

We divided into four two-man teams, carrying Sid Amelia for two hundred steps at a time, in rotation. Exhausted, we reached Sterling. Amelia called me to him.

"Leave me here, Puabla.," he pleaded. "Nothing bad will happen. Honest. Look, I'm a cripple. The people, or the cops or somebody will take care of me."

"Go on," he urged. "If you leave me on this corner, they'll be looking after me in an hour."

I spoke to Tom. "We've got to do a benefit," I said. "We have to raise enough dough to buy Sid a train ticket to Chicago, plus a hotel room for a night."

"About four dollars," Tom suggested.

"Four or five."

This had to be a production. Over his protests, we dressed Sid in costume, donning our own. I told three of the others to hoist him in the air. A crowd quickly grew.

"Ladies and gentleman," I yelled, "here you see a crippled acrobat. Notice his left leg. Perfectly normal. Now look at his right leg. Swollen like a poisoned pig." I selected two bystanders to feel for themselves. Amelia winced so genuinely, no one could doubt his pain. "We are all members of his troupe, on our way to Chicago. We're broke and walking. Our partner can't walk. He needs a doctor, plus train fare. We don't ask charity for him. All we want is a chance to do our act. Somebody will pass the hat. You pay us what you think it's worth.

We staged a whale of a performance. Even Sid Amelia applauded. During the encores, Shaheen collected while I thanked. We returned to the place where we changed our costumes, carrying Sid. We counted the money, jumping for joy; our biggest haul yet.

We carried Sid to a doctor, who treated his leg. Buying his ticket, we bid him goodbye at the depot. I bargained for a hotel room and we slept under cover again.

Reduced by one, my caravan rolled on. No more beautiful a June morning ever dawned than on the day we left Sterling. The sun, the breeze, the clouds, the warm moving air renewed our spirits. Shaheen sang a song in Arabic. Tom Morocco told us stories about his childhood in Algeria.

A farmer directed us to a stream in the woods that afternoon. We splashed in the cool water for an hour. The same farmer drove us six miles in his wagon, without charge. In return, we did a five minute show for him.

Two days later, near Aurora, we hopped the interurban. Twenty-five miles to the east we found a comfortable-looking grove, camping for the night. Tom Morocco, Shaheen and I talked long after the others had fallen asleep.

"Well, over there's Chicago," I said, looking into the night.

"About time," Tom mumbled.

"Tomorrow night, we'll be there," I said. "I guess we'll be able to catch a streetcar in a few more miles." I hesitated. "Listen, Tom, you and Shaheen take the others on the streetcar. I'm going to walk it."

Tom grabbed my arm. "If you think I'm going to ride the last few miles, you're crazy."

Shaheen agreed. "Who cares if we get there in the morning or the night. I don't."

I half laughed. "By God, we'll finish as we started – on our feet. The hell with Denver, the hell with Chicago, and for all I care, Uncle Ameen can go there, too." I couldn't get myself to say, "the hell with Uncle Ameen."

The next afternoon, eight ragged acrobats approached Chicago. Spotting the "City Limits" sign, we let out a whoop. A couple of kids playing in the street blinked at us and ran away. George Simon walked to the sign, banged it with his fist, and spat on it. Shaheen sang his Arabic song as the five (out of eight) Arabic-speaking Arabs joined him. Bystanders thought we were crazy. We *were* crazy; crazy happy.

We found Sid Amelia in the hotel we had directed him to. Though he still couldn't walk, the leg looked better.

"I spoke to Ameen," Sid told us. "He got us booked with Eva Tanguay's Burlesque Show – starting in a week."

I phoned Uncle Ameen an hour after we arrived. He seemed almost glad to hear my voice. "How do you boys feel?" he asked.

I told him that, aside from Sid's leg, we were weary. Otherwise, pretty good.

"Fine!" he answered. "There's a gym on Dearborn Street. Have them meet me there at eight o'clock tomorrow morning."

I didn't answer.

"Do you hear me, Puabla? Do you hear me?"

"Uncle, we're in Chicago, not Denver," I answered slowly. "If I tell them you say to practice tomorrow morning, you won't have an act."

"Very well," he growled. "See that they report at eight o'clock sharp the *next* morning." He hung up.

Ameen lost two of the acrobats to another act and had to search for replacements.

I penciled the time we crossed the city limits. Back in Sid's room, I added and subtracted. Thirty-four days, Denver to Chicago; a record that undoubtedly still stands.

Chapter 11
Life with Uncle

In 1913, burlesque shows were amongst the most desirable kinds of employment for stage acts. A popular burlesque could last as long as twenty consecutive weeks. They rated with minstrels in performer preference.

Vaudeville circuits such as the "Pan Times," twelve weeks in a large group of western theaters owned by Alexander Pantages, and "Sun Times," a circuit of small houses in and around Ohio, booked by the Guns Sun Agency, provided most of the remaining indoor work. We had played the "Pan Times" while the circus was in winter quarters.

Eva Tanguay, the peppery, vivacious "hot mama" of her day, operated one of the better known burlesque units. As an attraction, she starred. As a producer, she ranked the best. The result: long routes, good income for her, worthwhile salaries for the acts.

Uncle Ameen, as well as his hired hands, thrilled to find themselves in Eva's Burlesque Show. Steady work would pull Ameen to his financial feet.

Things passed serene and happy for the first five weeks. Eva, fiery and smiling, wowed the audiences. She liked our act, even liked Ameen; improving Ameen's disposition.

A magician named Rudolph-the-Great played pinochle with Ameen and Rudolph's pretty wife. Why anyone would play cards with a magician I couldn't understand, unless Ameen fancied Mrs. Rudolph. We appreciated associating with an amiable Ameen, whatever the reason. His mustache hadn't done its angry dance in weeks, although, when Mrs. Rudolph walked by, it undulated.

As we left the Midwest for the East, Eva's mood soured. Though we never knew why, we suspected either a financial or romantic problem with her manager, maybe both. The farther east we traveled, the more temperamental, less vivacious she became.

Ameen could not afford a layoff. Barely in the clear, he wanted to stay that way. Eva, however, could hand us our week's notice any time, without warning. Uncle Ameen, therefore, headed to New York, naming Habash, a new man, to be understander. I suspected that Ameen, besides looking for future work, sneaked a rest for his forty-five year old back. He was to be gone only three days, during which we would play the Opera House in Clifton Forge, Virginia. With assorted instructions and warnings, Ameen appointed me boss in his absence – my first such authority ever (other than supervising long walks.)

The Opera House copied many other theaters we had played and would play again. To me, it stands out on two counts. One, because for the first day in my life I had charge of an act. Two, because before that first day ended, I almost didn't have an act.

A new game called Chinese wrestling captivated our troupe. Each of two contestants, sitting, placed his elbow on a table. Each grasped his opponent's upright right hand. At a signal, each tried to push the other's forearm flat against the table.

As I entered the theater, Shaheen and George Simon's elbows were planted on a trunk. Shaheen, now a strong teenager, could down the arm of anybody in the troupe. George Simon challenged the champ.

I paid scant attention, picking up a book and finding a chair in the corner. George Simon yelled, "Ouch!"

Shaheen laughed.

"You guys better watch out," I warned. "If Uncle Ameen catches you doing that, he'll wallop you."

"Ouch!" George Simon yelled again.

"I'm telling you, Shaheen, if you put George out of commission, Uncle will do you in. Anyway, I'm in charge. Do what I say. Cut it out."

George Simon glared at me. "If you'd stop reading your silly old books, maybe you could wrestle against Shaheen. Then you wouldn't stand around trying to make other people stop."

"I wouldn't say that."

"No, you wouldn't say that. You wouldn't try it either." George Simon taunted. He looked admiringly at Shaheen. "My cousin is one of the strongest men in the show. He'd break your arm."

His cousin! Shaheen was as much my cousin. "Listen, George Simon," I snapped, "not Shaheen, or anybody else, is going to break my arm. If it will make you feel better, come over and I'll put your arm down in two seconds."

"Just what I thought," George Simon sneered. "Why don't you be a man and try Shaheen? I gave you a good battle, didn't I Shaheen?"

I could stand no more, moving opposite to Shaheen. "After this, I don't want anybody in the troupe Chinese wrestling while I'm in charge." Shaheen and I clasped hands.

"Go!" cried George Simon. Our arms scarcely moved. We strained every muscle, pouring all the power we possessed into our two right arms. The arms inched first in one direction, then the other. Perspiration wet our cheeks. My arm began to give.

Shaheen groaned. I groaned. I drew a deep breath, summoned all my strength, and heaved forward. With a sickening crack, Shaheen's arm gave way, slamming against the trunk. To my horror, the lower arm lay at an angle to the upper arm. Shaheen turned green.

George Simon raged, "You broke my cousin's arm!" My stomach rolled as I thought of Ameen. What would *he* do when he discovered I crippled Shaheen? In his fury, George Simon picked up a knife. I leaped through the door, George Simon in hot pursuit. I raced backstage, around a wing. Behind me, George Simon fell.

"Yeow!" he screamed, in obvious pain. "Help! Somebody help me!"

I turned. He was sprawled over a sandbag, his head against a post, a knife wound in his leg where he had stabbed himself.

He writhed. "You, Puabla," he muttered, "wait until I get you! It's all your fault. If you hadn't broken Shaheen's arm, this wouldn't have happened to me."

I staggered to a chair. Our ten-man act had now been reduced to seven. Thinking of Ameen, I shuddered, wondering if I should leave town and make it a six-man act.

Shaheen and George Simon moaned as the doctor treated their injuries. "A week lay-off for you," he told George Simon. "At least ten days for your dislocated arm," he said to Shaheen.

I held my head in my hands, thinking of my "supervision" of the act. Uncle would beat me to a pulp.

Seven of us did what we could that afternoon and night.

Eva, fortunately, mounted such a terrible mood that she wouldn't have noticed if we had reduced to a double.

The next day as I awaited my uncle's arrival on the afternoon train, I pondered a possible salvation – Mrs. Rudolph. In her dressing room she smiled, asking me to sit down, listening to my story.

When I finished, her eyes twinkled. "Your wave of destruction is not exactly a secret," she said. "Everybody in the show sympathizes with you, Puabla, though no one holds much hope. Tell me, is your uncle really that bad?"

She knew very well he was that bad. I nodded anyway.

"I'll tell you what," she said. "As soon as he arrives, you run over here. I'll try my luck."

I didn't get a chance to leave. Outside, thunder could be heard. "Puabla!" It riveted me. My hands shook. My teeth chattered. Even Mrs. Rudolph paled.

There was a rattling on the door. It opened, Uncle's eyes cutting through me. Up and down jumped the mustache.

"You, Puabla," he bellowed, moving toward me.

He halted as Mrs. Rudolph's voice caressed the air.

"Ameen, friend, what are you doing in my dressing room?" She stepped in front of him. Ameen struggled to work a smile onto his face. Though the mustache stopped hopping, his fierce jaws throbbed.

"Madam," Ameen replied, "I have only come to remove my nephew from your presence."

"Ameen, you are not telling me all," she purred. "You have come to punish this boy because his cousins teased him. He couldn't help it if they got hurt, but..." and she lowered her eyes. "I don't think you are big enough to understand, Ameen." She turned away.

He forgot me for a moment. "Ah, Madam, do not believe this of me," he begged. "I am the boy's uncle. If you say he is blameless, then I forgive him." Out of the corner of his eye he sizzled me.

"Do you mean it?" she asked.

"By my beloved grandmother," he swore, "it is true." Ameen didn't know if he ever *had* a grandmother.

Mrs. Rudolph was not fooled. "Send someone with his costume," she suggested. "He can dress with us. Dear Ameen, I know I won't hear of you being unfair to him later, will I?"

Shaking his head, Uncle wandered from the room. I thanked Mrs. Rudolph, swearing everlasting allegiance. She had put an end to the visible part of the matter.

On stage, Ameen kicked me every chance he got, twisted my arm, and finally, with me on his shoulders, bit my ankle. I yelped, letting go of the men. Seven of us fell in a heap on top of him. One last cuff on the back of my neck completed his hidden assault.

Two weeks later, at the Globe Theater in Atlantic City, Ameen turned the act over to me again. This time he had no choice. After the third night of engagement, Eva Tanguay blew up, knocked her manager cold with a handbag, packed her trunk and left, stranding the entire company in Atlantic City.

Everybody, including Ameen, trekked to New York in search of work. Only the acrobats remained behind.

"Here's some money," Ameen told me. "Feed the boys the best you can. Check with Western Union every day. I can get work in a week."

I looked at the money. Twelve dollars. How could anyone feed nine hungry Arabs for seven days on twelve dollars. I suppose we were to handle our own hotel rooms. On what? After Ameen departed, I led the brood to Childs Restaurant, where each one devoured a fifteen-cent lunch. We passed a summery afternoon on the beach, then ate a twenty-cent supper.

Only Shaheen's good humor held up; Shaheen, possessor of the biggest appetite of the bunch.

We mapped strategy on the beach. Six of the boys had paid their hotel in advance. They were to try to check out and get their money back. The hotel clerk laughed. Shaheen, George Simon and I had already checked out.

I eyed the boardwalk. "George Simon," I said, "that's where we sleep – under the boardwalk." Shaheen laughed. His happiness bothered me. I called one of the other acrobats aside. "What's he so cheerful about?" I asked.

A shrug of the shoulders answered me. "He's usually hungrier than anyone else." I insisted.

"Him?" was the reply. "Didn't you see the meal he put away tonight?"

"What meal? His check was twenty cents, like the rest of us."

"All I know is he gooed and cooed the waitress. She brought him a plateload of something that smelled awful good."

A light dawned, "Shaheen," I called, "come here."

"What is it, Cousin?"

Cousin! Something fishy for sure. "Are you hungry, Cousin?" I asked.

"Why no," he answered sweetly. "I feel all right."

"What did you have for dinner?"

"Well," Shaheen said, "soup, chicken fricassee, dessert, and coffee, I think.

"For twenty cents? This isn't 1900!"

"You paid my check," Shaheen said, "you ought to know."

"What do you suppose I ate for twenty cents?" I demanded. "Some of that danged soup, two eggs, toast, no dessert. I'm still hungry. So is everybody else. What's the idea?"

"Well, it's sort of like this," he apologized. "I don't want to get you mad, but that's my girl."

Three days in Atlantic City and *that* was his *girl!* "Keep talking," I said.

"You won't tell, will you?"

"I'll tell anything I please. If you don't hurry up, I'll break your arm on purpose."

"Well," he blurted, "she gives me whatever I want and punches the check for twenty cents."

I collected my acrobats. "Shaheen, here, has fallen in love," I announced. "Who's he in love with? The waitress at Childs. She's so much in love with him that she gives him a full course dinner and punches the check for only twenty cents." Shaheen blushed.

"Cousin" I said to him, "do you think she loves you enough to feed the rest of us that way and punch our checks for only twenty cents?"

He shrugged. "I don't know. I can ask her."

"Well, boys," I said, "Shaheen is going to find out. If she won't do it, starting tomorrow we'll all eat, Shaheen included, on Atlantic Avenue."

"Yeah," agreed the gang.

Shaheen rushed off. "I think she'll do it," he called. An hour later he returned, arrangements made. The six hotel dwellers departed for their rooms. George Simon, Shaheen and I remained on the sand.

Shaheen peered into the dark chasm under the boardwalk. "What happens if it rains?"

"We get wet," George Simon said.

"Not as wet as if we weren't under the boardwalk," I consoled.

"I ought to quit the act, anyhow," Shaheen grumbled.

"And do what?" George Simon asked.

"I could make more money as a lover."

George Simon and I led him by the hand. Under the boardwalk, we slept.

Next day and the following day, we ate at Childs, sleeping under the boardwalk, during the day sunning ourselves on the beach. When a crowd gathered or when pretty girls appeared, we tumbled. Since we had to practice, that was as good a way as any.

After a spirited session, a large, well-dressed man approached. "Who's in charge here?" he asked.

He looked like a detective.

"Is this an act?" the man asked.

I nodded.

"I've been watching you fellows. How would you like to play a week on the Steel Pier?"

The Steel Pier! Uncle Ameen tried desperately to book us there before he deserted to New York. They wouldn't let him in the office!

I tried not to appear overwhelmed. "I don't know," I told the man. "I'll have to ask my uncle."

"You can ask anybody you like," he said. "I have to know in half an hour. I'm John E. Murphy. I'm in charge of the Steel Pier Minstrel Show." He paused. "Come along with me. We've got phones as good as anybody else's."

I gave the operator Uncle Ameen's number in New York. No answer.

"He isn't there," I said

He looked me over and smiled. "You're big enough to make up your own mind. What do you want a week?"

I did some quick figuring. Having no idea what Uncle Ameen sold the act for, or what kind of prices the Steel Pier paid, any figure I chose would be a gamble. Nine acrobats, nobody earning over fifteen dollars, equaled a hundred and thirty-five. Expenses were certainly low. I could say two-fifty. On the other hand, the office had a rich flavor.

"Five hundred dollars," I said, the words choking their way out.

Murphy whistled. "You're ambitious. Four-fifty is my limit. Sign here."

With a shaking hand, I signed. For the rest of the afternoon, I phoned Uncle Ameen. At six o'clock, we connected.

"Uncle, don't get mad," I said, "I signed the act to play at the Steel Pier next week."

"You what?" he bellowed.

"I signed the act for next week at the Steel Pier."

"How much?" he sputtered. "How much is the price?"

"Four hundred and fifty," I confessed.

"Four-fifty! Take it! Do you hear? Take it!"

"Uncle, calm down," I said, breathing easier. "I already took it."

"Good boy, Puabla. You're a *fine* boy. Go to a restaurant. Buy everybody a special meal."

"Uncle, we have no money yet."

"You heard what I said," he commanded. "I'll see you on Sunday. Goodbye."

His command put no money in my pocket. The special meal waited.

The lucky booking almost backfired. Freak attractions being the current rage, we had one on our bill – Mrs. Bob Fitzsimmons, wife of the ex-Heavyweight Champion of the World. It seems that Fitz, after losing the championship, traded wives with his manager. Legally, of course. The handy switch created lots of gossip with its newspaper publicity. As ultra as the Steel Pier tried to be in 1913, it couldn't resist an act like the new Mrs. Fitzsimmons.

Although she had never appeared professionally, Mrs. Fitz was featured, going on next to closing. We were the finale.

Standing in the wings, we awaited our turn, as anxious as anyone else to see the lady. She walked on stage – an ample, attractive woman with a pleasant smile – obviously nervous.

When the crowd, sprinkled with fight fans, spied her, a peculiar murmuring turned into snickers. I shifted my gaze to Mrs. Fitzsimmons, who still had not started her opening song. Instead, blushing furiously, she tugged at her bodice. Something had come undone. Laughter rolled across the house.

"My God, she's falling apart," Ameen gasped.

Murphy squirmed. More undoing would expose Mrs. Fitzsimmons' entire bosom. Murphy knew it, as did the audience.

The lady burst out crying. "You beasts!" she screamed. "If that's all you came here for, then there!" She tore the top of her dress and ran off the stage.

"Down with the curtain!" Murphy yelled.

"Oh, no!" Ameen groaned. "Our big chance is ruined."

"Hold the curtain," I shouted to the stage manager, striding to the front of the stage, raising my arm.

"Mr. Murphy," I called. "Ladies and gentlemen, *please!*"

The hubbub subsided.

"That lady never appeared on stage before. She's back there now, crying her heart out."

"Let her cry," somebody catcalled.

Another cried, "Be quiet – let him talk."

"She could be a member of your family. She didn't come here to take off her clothes. In panic, goaded by your laughter, she tore her dress. Why don't you forget it? Be good sports." I paused. People returned to their seats. "I'm in this costume because I belong to the closing act, Ameen Hamid's Sons of the Desert. We came a long way, (here I lied; we'd come two blocks) to put on our act for you and for Mr. Murphy, the manager. Do you want to see it?"

The crowd's reaction persuaded the undecided to stay. I looked at Murphy. He wiped his brow as I gave the leader our downbeat. We swept into our act. The crowd applauded every pirouette, cheered our pyramids, and left the theater happy.

Ameen increased my salary a dollar and a half.

Chapter 12
Plaguing The Palace

Ameen's act had gradually become known. Though he played the Sun circuit, plus more Pan Time, like everybody else in the business, he longed to book the Keith circuit. He repeatedly visited the office of Paul Durand, Keith's chief booker. Success convinced Uncle we were ripe for Keith. He had never before been able to get an interview with Durand himself, although Durand certainly knew of Ameen's quality troupes.

One evening, Ameen was particularly silent, as only he could be. Our troupe being out of work, the members were at their own homes. Shaheen, George Simon and I made ourselves as unobtrusive as possible within Ameen's glowering silence. I had bought the ugliest bulldog in the world, Jeff, who made life bearable by being my one true friend.

Ameen did not bellow because the second troupe was earning money in a burlesque show at the Columbia Theatre for at least another five weeks.

The phone rang. I answer it. "IS Ameen Hamid there?" a powerful voice asked.

"Who is this?"

"Is Ameen Hamid there? This is Paul Durand."

"Uncle Ameen, it's..."

"Don't bother me."

"But, it's..."

"Quiet" he roared.

"Uncle, it's Paul Durand!"

He sprang to his feet, ripped the phone from my hand. I bent close to hear the conversation.

"Listen, Ameen, I know who you are," Durand said. "I know you have been trying to play my theaters for years. I might as well tell you I don't think much of you or your kind of act, but I need a closing act at the Palace this week. If you can put on a good one, you can have the spot."

Ameen could not answer. The Palace was the prize! "Well, what do you say?" Durand shouted impatiently.

"Yes, yes, of course." Ameen sputtered. "I'll give you the best act you ever saw."

"Well, this is your chance to show me."

Ameen's mustache quivered as he yelled, "Puabla! Get me Haj."

"Haj is with the other troupe," I reminded him. Ameen caught me in the shins with his cane.

"Get me Haj!" he bellowed.

I trudged across New York on aching legs to the Columbia Theatre. Haj's troupe was just finishing.

"I think you'd better come tonight," I said to a reluctant, tired Haj, "unless you want him to find you tomorrow and let you have it."

Together we walked to Ameen's. Uncle smiled. "My boys, we have the chance of a lifetime," he said. He started to pat Haj with one hand, me with the other. Instinctively, I ducked.

"Haj, you close just before intermission, do you not?" Ameen asked. Haj nodded.

"That would be three-thirty in the afternoon, and about nine-thirty at night, yes?" Haj kept nodding.

"The Columbia is across the street from the Palace. I am the closing act at the Palace. As soon as you are through at the Columbia, I want you to bring yourself and your three best tumblers to the Palace to work with us."

Haj nodded, like it or not.

"Tomorrow and Thursday, practice in the gym with me. This must be the greatest act Paul Durand ever saw."

Since arguing would be futile, Haj agreed and left.

"Uncle, this sounds like a great idea," I admitted, although my shins still hurt. "I'll bet Durand will be impressed." I was excited about the talented combination.

Our rehearsals were beautiful to watch, each member of the troupe an acrobatic artist. When Ameen called for a formation – Tres-flutes, Tukul, Burge – it took seconds to execute. The pyramids were perfect, the tumbling crisp.

Wanting everything to be exact, Ameen himself went to the theater to rehearse the music.

An ill-tempered Ameen grew nervous in the wings. On the stage, he became as poised as I ever saw him. "Tres-flutes" was his first call. Eight nimble wraiths slithered up his back into precise position. "Down," he grunted. As one man, we spun to the stage and into a bow. A pleasant burst of applause hit our ears. This was nothing compared to what would follow; the hard figures, then the tumbling.

We executed four quick pyramids, each fine as the one before, graceful, smooth. Somehow, the applause didn't grow.

I sidled to Ameen. "I don't think we're going over so hot," I whispered. "Maybe we'd better start tumbling."

Although he acted as though he hadn't heard me, the next order was "Tumble."

Haj went first. He circled the stage doing handsprings and finishing with two beautiful forwards. Nice applause. I followed with flip-flaps and backs. I knew I had never tumbled better in my life, but finished to only a mild hand. My heart sank as realization dawned – we were too good! It looked easy.

The others burst into their specialties. By the time the last acrobat crossed the stage, the applause died to a ripple. People walked out.

We sped into our final routine. Everyone pirouetted for ten seconds, followed by handsprings, into a bow. It drew a polite smattering.

We ran off the stage as fast as we could.

In the dressing room, only silence. Ameen looked so baffled I had to say something. "We were too good, Uncle. After the first trick, there was nothing to look forward to. And our tumbling! We were all so terrific, none of us looked very good at all. Only another acrobat could appreciate us."

Ameen could not understand what I meant. You couldn't be *too* good.

Ameen was called to the phone. He hesitated, knowing it was Paul Durand.

"Ameen, how could you do this to me?" Durand demanded. Ameen couldn't answer.

"You were supposed to bring me the best Arab troupe in the world. It was the worst. I saw it with my own eyes."

"Yes," Ameen growled feebly, "but..."

"Don't 'but' me. You finish out the week, because I have to finish out the week with you. If you ever come to my office again, I'll have you thrown out." He hung up.

Ameen rumbled to the dressing room. Between shows, he bought the evening paper. The write-up disposed of us in two lines.

A defeated Ameen's back became so sore that he made Shaheen walk on it, the only relief coming when the bare heels dug into his backbone.

We finished out the seven days. Afterward, Uncle Ameen went to bed for a week. He wouldn't even pay the small gymnasium fee for us to practice. Shaheen and I subwayed to the Brooklyn dumps where we'd worked out before. We didn't particularly mind it in nice weather.

I thought up a trick. Starting backstage center, each of us circled handsprings in opposite directions, then, simultaneously, forwards as we passed each other front center. When we found our timing, we executed the figure well.

Ameen, on his feet again, looked for work, without his old spirit. He found nothing. Two weeks later, as we sat glumly at home, the phone rang – Paul Durand. Ameen refused to talk to him.

"My uncle is taking a bath," I said. It sounded fishy. Uncle Ameen took baths only on Saturdays, and not every Saturday.

"Well, you tell your uncle for me," Durand said, "that he's the worst acrobat in the world. I wouldn't use one of his troupes if I never bought an act..."

"Mr. Durard," I interrupted, my "Arabian" ire rising, "you didn't have to call here to tell my uncle that. He knows how you feel."

"Yes," Ameen growled. "Tell him I don't think he's so good either."

"All right, all right," said Durand impatiently. "You tell him this. I'm stuck. You can bet your life I'm stuck or I wouldn't be calling him. I need an opening act, starting Monday at the Flatbush Theater in Brooklyn. You tell him this is his last chance."

I relayed the message to Ameen. "Oh, my God, no!" Ameen groaned. "The other troupe's in Ohio. You three are all I have left of this troupe. No, I can't do it."

"Uncle, I can get four tumblers." I said hurriedly. "We'll get Freddie Spears for middleman. That will give us a full troupe."

"No," Ameen insisted. "We're in enough trouble with the Keith office without making it worse."

"We're in so bad, what have we got to lose? Anyway, it's a week's work." When we worked, I got paid. When we didn't, my only pay was food, not very good food.

Ameen did not answer. I took my hand off the mouthpiece. "All right, Mr. Durand," I shouted. "We'll take it!" I hung up before Ameen could change the decision.

If his back had been sound, I wouldn't have dared. Even so, he swore, flinging his cane at me.

"Look what you've done!" he roared. "Where can you get four Arabs and break in an act in two days?"

"They may not be Arabs, but I can get four good tumblers down at the Brooklyn dumps."

"Oh, no!" Ameen groaned. "The Brooklyn dumps! Well, call Freddie Spears."

I knew Freddie was available because I had tumbled with him that morning at the dumps. This relieved Ameen, for he knew a good middleman could spare his back. The pyramids might get by. Freddie tumbled, too.

"Be at the gym, two o'clock tomorrow for rehearsal," Ameen instructed.

The next morning, I realized our desperation. Aside from Freddie, there wasn't a professional acrobat in town. To the dumps I went. I had seen five or six men tumbling, paying little attention to them. Now, I watched their every move.

By noon, five men sprang hither and yon. Four of them might

pass, although one was a gawky fellow, too skinny, far too tall to make an acrobat.

No others showed. I collected the four possibilities, offering them all a job for a week. They accepted.

"What's your name?" I asked the tall one.

"John," he drawled. "You might as well call me Long John. Everybody else does."

"Long John, what made you take up tumbling?"

"I like it."

"You know what a forward is, don't you?" I asked. "That's a front flip, without touching the ground." Long John nodded. "Whatever else, don't try a forward. When you land on your feet, you look like a scarecrow. Half the time, you don't land on your feet."

Long John shrugged. Breaking into a smile, he agreed.

"You," I said to the doubtful one, "do a few flip-flaps for my uncle. Act dumb."

"You picked the right guy for that." Long John whispered. "He says nothing and looks sad. His name is Gloomy Gus."

I ordered the other two to avoid their worst figures as we boarded the subway for New York.

At the gym, Freddie Spears stared at Long John and burst out laughing.

"He will look adorable in an Arab suit!"

Ameen spotted us, brushing Freddie out of the way with one arm. His mustache jumped.

"What's this, Puabla?" he asked, waving his cane at my hirelings. He noticed Long John. "Oh my God!"

"These are the acrobats for our act," I said, trying to smile.

"Acrobats? *Acrobats?*" he screamed. "They look like Bowery tramps to me." Maybe they were. I didn't know.

"Get me a telephone," Ameen demanded. "Get me a telephone. I want to call Durand right now and cancel the whole thing."

"Wait a minute, Uncle," I pleaded. "These men can tumble, I've watched them."

"*He* can tumble?" Ameen stormed, whacking Long John across the stomach with his cane. "You insult me by telling me *he* can tumble."

"Show him, Long John. Do some handsprings. Gloomy Gus, do some flip-flaps."

Ameen shook his head. "Long John!" he moaned. "Gloomy Gus! Oh! Oh! Oh!"

Long John, now insulted, leaped into a fair line of handsprings. Gloomy Gus did a string of flip-flaps. Quickly, I shoved the other two into pirouettes and tinsicas.

Ameen stood groaning. "I should live to…."

"Uncle," I interrupted, "with the rest of us, they will look okay. Anyway, this is the Flatbush, not the Palace."

"You fool," Ameen growled. "Even if they could tumble, how do we build pyramids with a freak like him?" Ameen swung his cane at Long John again. John, proving his agility, jumped out of the way.

"I've thought of that, Uncle," I said. "We have eight without him. We can make decent pyramids with eight. He'll stand alongside and point."

Accepted practice, though not custom, omitted one member of an acrobatic troupe from the formations. The extra man stood to the side until a structure was formed, then pointed towards the top, with a sweeping flourish. I could picture Long John's flourish.

We rehearsed Wednesday afternoon and all day Thursday. Freddie Spears turned out to be a fine middleman. The two Brooklyn boys learned fast. Gloomy Gus was a little shaky, nevertheless, our formations developed better than I had hoped. We left the gym, dog-tired with instructions to be at the theater by one the next day.

Ameen was not unhappy enough to be dangerous. His back still pained him. A few good poundings relieved him. He was probably as afraid of his back as of his reputation. In an unbalanced pyramid, the weight of the seven up-men, pulling to one side or the other, can torture a good back. A skillful middleman can partially eliminate such imbalance. Freddie proved to be very good.

At eleven the next morning I checked the music. As I walked down the side of the empty theater, an elegant girl appeared from the wings. She stamped her feet, calling to the orchestra leader.

"Where's Mr. Hamid? I've got to find Mr. Hamid."

"I am Mr. Hamid," I called, smiling my best. She surely didn't mean me. Yet, after all, I was *a* Mr. Hamid, though I was rarely so identified.

"I want *the* Mr. Hamid," she retorted.

"My dear lady," I said, "I can do anything for you that the other Mr. Hamid can." I chuckled, quite pleased with myself.

"Well, I'm Freddie Spears' sister," she said. "You're pretty fresh, but I guess you'll do. I came to tell you that Freddie has the flu. He can't work. Maybe if you or the other Mr. Hamid had let him come home to get some rest, he might not have it."

Something socked me in the pit of my stomach.

"No, oh no! You must get him down here!" I cried. "Get an ambulance, get something, bring him here."

"Impossible," she snapped. "He's running a fever. The doctor won't let him move. If you were decent, you'd pay the doctor bill." She stomped off.

Doctor bills! Who was going to pay my doctor bill when I told Uncle Ameen? At one o'clock our acrobats started to arrive. A little after one, Ameen paraded in.

"Sit down, Uncle," I said. He was going to sit down anyway. "Freddie Spears is sick. He can't work."

"That's a lie," Ameen grunted. "Don't lie to me." He swung his cane at the air.

"There's no use saying that, Uncle Ameen. It's the truth; nothing we can do about it."

"Call Paul Durand," Ameen said. "Call the manager. I won't go on."

I was heartsick. "I'm sorry, Uncle. We have to go on. It's too late for them to get an opening act. Your other troupe closes in a couple of weeks. You have no work for them, no work for us. The Keith office is the biggest in the business. If you walk out now, you're through. They'll blackball you all over the country. We'll be out of show business forever."

"You, Puabla," he grumbled, "you got me into this mess. When I get you home tonight, I will kill you!"

"I know, Uncle, I deserve it. Meanwhile, we have to get by the best we can. Freddie may be better tomorrow. Anyway, Paul

Durand expects us to be bad, so if we're terrible, he won't be surprised. Besides, he won't pay attention to what we do over here in Flatbush."

Ameen lowered his eyes. "Since you seem to be running my act, maybe you will tell me who will be middleman in the pyramids."

"I'm trying to make the best out of a tough situation," I said. "As far as middleman goes, Uncle, we all have our positions already. We can't change the whole act around now, so there's only one person who can be middle man."

I looked at Ameen as he looked at me. We both looked at Long John. "Him" Ameen roared.

"You're on in fifteen minutes," came a familiar cry.

"Let's get into costumes," I said, walking to Long John. Ameen dressed, dazed.

"You remember the formations, don't you, Long John?" I whispered. He nodded. "Can you do them?"

"I guess so," he answered blankly. "I never tried them, but I don't see why I can't."

"Take it easy on Uncle's back," I said. "He's going to kill me as it is. If you make his back worse, he'll build a cross and crucify me."

"Five minutes!" came the call. "Ameen, you're on in five minutes."

We avoided Ameen in the wings. He cursed to himself, almost frothing at the mouth. The handlebars did a jig.

We were on. "Alley-oop! Hip! Tres-flutes," commanded a fearful Ameen. The simplest pyramid in the book. Long John lurched at Ameen's shoulders, as if he were climbing a picket fence.

Ameen winced. I felt every dig of John's huge feet. Quickly, the rest of us scrambled up to our positions. We teetered left, then right. The pyramid collapsed.

"*Harrak deek il mukk,*" cursed Ameen.

"Alley-oop! Hip, Burge!" Up we went again. Crash! Down we came again. The audience snickered.

On the third attempt, Long John's foot slipped, his knee digging into Ameen's neck with the weight of five men. The five flew in five directions.

"Dibh!" cursed Ameen. He stalked off the stage.

I nearly panicked. Here was Ameen's act, with no Ameen. I yelled, "Tumble!"

Gloomy Gus started a clumsy roll of flip-flaps. I followed with handsprings and tinsicas. They were very good, except that I misjudged, finishing the last one into the curtain.

I picked myself up and, to my horror, noticed Long John. In a fit of remorse, he tried to compensate for his wretched pyramids with spectacular tumbling. Full-tilt, he turned the most awkward set of handsprings I have ever seen. Across the stage he clumped. I held my breath. No one in the world, least of all Long John, could halt that string without at least one forward, maybe two. Sure enough, he bounced to the edge of the stage, took a full forward, landing smack in the orchestra pit, spun and finished face-forward, ten feet up the middle aisle.

"Keep tumbling," I yelled. With that, my two Brooklyn Arabs appeared from opposite wings in flip-flaps. Wham! They tripped each other and tangled.

When George Simon nervously missed a trick and duplicated Long Johns leap into the pit, I decided we should call a halt to the mayhem. We'd give them one good trick, if we could, then get off the stage to face the music.

I caught Shaheen's eye, calling "Drum roll!" The music stopped, the drum began to roll. "Handsprings," I called to Shaheen. We started tumbling in opposite circles – our newest trick, the one in which we executed simultaneous forwards, as we passed in center stage. By now we were so upset we lost our timing. We circled too close to the front of the stage. When we took off for the forwards – bang! A mid-air collision.

Shaheen sprawled on the stage. I hit feet first on the footlight guards, burned my feet and yelled and leaped into the kettledrum.

I scrambled to the stage. "Finish!" I yelled as we turned to ten frenzied seconds of pirouettes, fell into our bows, and fled.

We ran into the dressing room, the audience in an uproar. Performers who had come to the wings to investigate the rumpus laughed at us. Ameen glowered in the dressing room.

"You have disgraced me!" He snarled. "I shouldn't wait till tonight. I should kill you now."

I avoided his gaze, took off my blouse, sat down. Suddenly a voice was yelling at the door, the manager!

"Ameen!" he yelled. "Get back out there and do something."

"No," groaned Ameen. "we have done all we can."

"Then take another bow!"

"Another bow?" I cried. "Are you crazy? We never want to see that audience again."

"Listen to me!" the manager was frantic. "You stopped the show. The next act can't go on. For the love of God, at least go out there and take another bow."

I listened. The crowd still roared. "We're half undressed," I called to the manager.

"I don't care how you are – get the devil on stage."

We threw things around us. I peeked out from the wing. A new cheer erupted. I led my startled troupe, nodding to the crowd.

I looked at the drummer. "Drum roll," I commanded

"Go to hell," he growled, looking at his busted kettledrum.

By now, the flush of triumph surged through me. "Leader," I said, "does that drummer do as I say or do I have to punch him in the nose?" the audience cheered.

As the drum rolled, Shaheen and I looked at each other. "Handsprings!" I barked. Off we shot, spinning in a circle at top speed, charging toward center stage. There, we sprang upward into perfect full forwards. We landed with the grace of experts, spun toward the audience, then into a bow.

The house nearly exploded!

Chapter 13
Amen!

Back in the dressing room, Ameen couldn't believe his ears. He kept shaking his head. "A month ago," he mumbled, "I came to the Palace with the greatest acrobats in the world and they threw me out. Today, with a bunch of peddlers, my act makes a hit."

The inevitable phone call came from Durand. "You take it, Puabla," Ameen said. "Durand is a smart showman. We didn't fool him."

"Don't kid yourself, Uncle," I encouraged. "We lucked into a very good act. Come to the phone."

He took the call.

"Ameen, my boy," boomed Durand. "You are my friend for life. They tell me you have the greatest acrobatic act in history. You fox, why didn't you show it to me the last time?"

Ameen was stunned. "Well, I…"

"It really doesn't matter, my boy." I had to chuckle. Neither of them had been boys for years. "Wait where you are. My agent will be down to sign you for the circuit. The Palace, next week."

I had to support Ameen as he hung up. Not for long. He became his old self.

"My boys," he said. Now he was calling everybody boys. "My act is better than I thought. We'll all have dinner, come back and do a big show tonight."

A disturbing thought entered my mind. He saw my face. The same thought struck him. "My God, how can we repeat *that* act?"

"I don't know," I said. "The drummer will murder me if I bust his kettledrum again."

I didn't worry for long. At a nearby music store, I bought a cheap kettledrum with twenty skins and routined our new act.

As long as we used Long John and Gloomy Gus, we couldn't miss. I suggested to Ameen that they tumble more. I framed it with Long John to do full forwards up the aisle. The pyramids, with Long John in the middle, took care of themselves.

George Simon did his flip-flap into the pit, of course. Shaheen and I figured out how to hit in mid-air without killing ourselves. I certainly had no trouble falling into a drum. Keeping it fresh and spontaneous, so that it wouldn't look planned was surprisingly easy. We had enough bad tumblers to insure something ridiculous every show.

The new act wowed them throughout the circuit. After we played every Keith house in the East, Lew Dockstader took us with his minstrel show for fifteen weeks; the first acrobatic act he ever used. He never had an act he liked better – that is, *after* opening night.

We couldn't be blamed for the opening. We just didn't know. A stagehand threw us four cans of 'black face', with instructions to "Put this on." Nothing else. We applied the make-up to our cheeks and foreheads, taking seats in the rear row.

When the curtain lifted, the audience began to laugh. The interlocutor turned, seeing our white eyes, white mouths, and white ears; closed the curtain, good-naturedly explaining to the audience that we were the new Arab troupe. Would they please excuse our ignorance of the customs of black face? He rushed us off-stage. The show started. After a quick repair job, we filed back in, acceptable to Dockstader, as well as the audience.

After the minstrel tour, Ameen booked us with a top burlesque for six months.

While the act triumphed, none of the actors except Ameen enjoyed the success. Our salaries hadn't been raised in the year we were out, Ameen refusing to discuss them. Even so, Uncle's dictatorial control would have held us for a further time, except for his back. The pain tied Ameen in knots that even Shaheen's bare heels could not relieve. Someone suggested treatments at Excelsior Spring, Missouri. Now able to afford it, Ameen went.

I ran the act in his absence; collecting the money, making the payroll, paying the men. The first time I figured the pay, I stared in disbelief. I was top man at $17.50 a week. The other salaries ranged from $8.50 to $15.00 a week. The outlay for nine men totaled a hundred and ten dollars. The act's selling price averaged five hundred. I counted and figured.

For three weeks, I obeyed Ameen's instructions to the letter. Those were his salaries, that was what I'd pay. Each day I confronted more mathematics. We paid fifty cents a night for rooms. At fifteen cents for breakfast, twenty cents for lunch, thirty cents for dinner, twenty-five cents for the after-the-show supper, food came to ninety cents. That added up to $6.30 for food, $3.50 for hotel – $9.80 total expense per man.

Our meager salaries bought clothes, an occasional low cost date. Living in 1914 took considerably more money than in 1909, despite Ameen's refusal to admit it. His performers struggled on pennies while Ameen pocketed four hundred dollars a week.

I did the wrong thing. I pondered, worried and grew angry. On the fourth payday, of my own accord, I raised everybody's salary – except my own – five dollars a week. I wouldn't dare raise my own. This reduced Ameen's remittance by thirty-five dollars. I sent it off, explaining nothing.

The anticipated wire came. "Forward balance at once. Ameen Hamid."

After two more wires, I wrote an answer. "Raised salaries, therefore no balance. George Hamid."

That generated a wire of a different sort. "Depart for Excelsior Springs immediately. Disregard act. A. Hamid."

I boarded the train to Excelsior Springs. My eyes popped when I scanned the spacious lobby of the hotel. The grandeur fueled my courage.

Ameen appeared wan and withered in a corner of the lovely suite. "Puabla, what have you done to me?" he asked. "How dare you raise salaries without so much as consulting me?"

"The men can't live on what you are paying them, Uncle."

The mustache jumped. "You are not the judge of that."

"Uncle, I sent you double all the salaries put together."

Ameen grew angrier. "Who supports them between dates?" he roared. "Do you?" I shook my head. We hadn't been idle more than five weeks in two years.

"Who walks from one office to the next to get work? Do you?"

I didn't move.

"You go back" he ordered. "Restore the old salaries. Send me the proper remittance and never defy me again."

"You are starving the men, Uncle," I said. "If you want them cut back, you'll have to do it yourself or get someone else to handle the act."

If he could have moved, Ameen would have choked me with his bare hands. No one else could handle the act. He knew it. I knew it.

"Do as I say. Leave my sight at once," he shouted. I left.

The acrobats awaited my return apprehensively. "Everything's fine," I told the boys. "Uncle Ameen wanted to put things back the way they were. He changed his mind." I didn't go into details.

My next money order drew real fireworks. By the night show, his wire lay on the dressing table. It was addressed to the act itself, Hamid's Sons of the Desert, not me. It said, "George Hamid no longer in charge of act. My son takes over. Ameen Buhamid."

Ameen had acquired a young stepson, Lucien, through his American marriage. We saw him twice. Being no acrobat, he never ventured into show business.

Long John and Sweeney Sirgany, a wiry little Syrian boy, the current topmounter, were the first to see the wire.

"I don't like this," Long John said.

"Me either, me either," Sweeney shrilled. (His voice rasped so fast, sometimes we couldn't understand him.)

"Puabla, you didn't tell the truth," Long John concluded. "Ameen laid you out, didn't he?"

"No, Long John," I said. "He objected to my raising everybody. He did not lay me out."

"He told you not to pay us high any more. Don't tell me he didn't."

I shrugged my shoulders. "I had no right to do it in the first place."

"I don't know about that," Long John drawled. "He couldn't keep the act much longer if somebody hadn't done something. Anyway, this punk of his better not get funny. I'd hate to have to lay him on my knee and break his bottom."

"Me, too," Sweeny chattered, laughing. "If he tries anything on me, I'll jump from a tres-flutes and land on him."

"He's going to be in charge," I said. "Whatever he says, goes, until Ameen gets back."

Nobody else in the act accepted the young "upstart's" authority. A variety of threats, most of them empty, were uttered for two days. On the third, Lucien arrived.

To everyone's surprise, he acted friendly, almost apologetic. His eyes jiggled nervously from one of us to the other. I pitied the kid. He was only eighteen. I was eighteen, too; not his kind of eighteen.

No difficulty arose until payday. After the matinee, we filed in for our money, which had been sealed in envelopes, each envelope bearing a name. Ameen's son handed them out nervously. Mine, of course, contained my regular salary, which had never changed. I watched Long John count his money. He looked thoughtfully at the bills, then at Gloomy Gus.

Long John spoke. "You underpaid us, son."

"No, no, that is your regular salary," Lucien protested.

"You're wrong," Long John insisted. "That is not the salary we work for." John ostentatiously counted his money again. "Pay us in full, boy," he said firmly. "Or, Seven Sons of the Desert don't go on tonight."

"You can't do that to the kid," I protested. "He's following orders."

No one spoke. The men began to remove their costumes.

Lucien panicked. "I can't pay you any more. I already sent the money to my father."

He lied. He hadn't been able to leave the theater since pay time, let alone send a telegram.

"If you want a show tonight," Long John warned, "you'd better get it back."

That night, Lucien was not at the theater. Seven envelopes were.

I found the miserable kid at the hotel after the show. "He would have killed me if the act walked out," he said. "Now he'll kill me because I sent him short."

"No, he won't," I said putting my arm around his shoulder. "Ameen isn't dumb. He knows what you are up against. You'd be smart to go home to your mother."

"I can't," he moaned. "I sent all the money to my stepfather."

There was no wire this time. Instead, two days later, Ameen strode into town. Excelsior Springs had apparently restored him. He stood straight, walking normally.

He confronted us in the dressing room. "So these are Ameen Hamid's Sons of the Desert," he snarled. "Desert rats would be more like it. George Simon, come here."

"Who brought you to this country, my fine nephew?" he asked.

"You did, Uncle," came the whispered reply.

"Who bought you your clothes? Who gives you the money to feed your stomach?"

George Simon managed an uncertain nod. Our costumes, our trip to America had been paid off many times over.

"Yet, you refused to work when my son paid you your full wages," Ameen thundered.

A thick silence settled over the room. Crack! He sent George Simon reeling with his open hand.

The men looked at George Simon, half sobbing in a corner, back to Ameen, who shifted his black glance from one to another of us.

"Long John," he said. "My son tells me you led the men against him. Men, ha! What kind of men…"

Long John said nothing.

"I would like you to tell me," Ameen persisted. "Where were you living when I picked you up?"

Still silence.

"Then I will tell you," Ameen said loudly. "The Brooklyn dumps."

"Puabla found me, not you," Long John responded.

Ameen's fist crashed against the table. "Puabla couldn't have moved you ten feet from the Brooklyn dumps without me. You make more money with my act than in your whole life."

"I spend more, too," growled Long John.

"Sweeney!" Ameen bellowed, having finished with Long John.

"*Ec-ec-ec-ec-ec,*" screeched Sweeney, scrambling to his feet.

"You – a topmounter, have the nerve to disobey orders from the understander, the owner of this act?"

He turned to Pete Cazzazza.

"Cazzazza, how far can you go defying the orders of the man who employs you?"

Each man received his individual tongue-lashing – except me.

He then addressed the entire group. "Temptations can be understood," he said. "Your desire to keep the extra money is natural. Your defiance, however, is not!"

His eyes wandered from one to the other.

"Bygones will be bygones. The proper wages will be restored." He tried to smile. "If the act continues to improve, sensible raises will be given as they are deserved."

Long John broke the ensuing silence. "The only one you didn't say anything about is Puabla. What about him?"

Ferocity drove the smile from Ameen's mouth. His jaw stiffened. "Puabla is leaving the act," he announced.

Not surprised, I looked at Ameen. At my feet lay Jeff, my bulldog. He had traveled with us from the day I bought him. When Ameen lowered his vicious frown on me, spat out those words, Jeff sprang to his feet and growled.

"*Harram!*" Ameen cursed, throwing his cane at the dog. Jeff yelped, jumping into my lap. The iron cap of the cane tore a gash in his front leg. With the yellow shirttail of my costume, I wiped the blood. Nobody spoke. I got up, my back to Ameen, and began packing.

When I turned, I saw the others packing. Ameen, who had been glaring at the floor, cursing to himself, looked up.

"What's going on here?" he asked.

Gloomy Gus said, "We're leaving with Puabla."

"Ha! You'd better get unpacked before I fire you. Then you *will* go with him."

They continued packing.

"Stop this stupid joke," Ameen ordered.

Long John looked up. "We're not joking," he said.

Ameen rose. "How dare you threaten to walk out on me? Puabla, you started this. I command you to leave these men here."

"You ordered me to leave, Uncle. I'm leaving. I'll make my living without help from you." I started toward the door. The others followed. I faced them.

"Nobody's going with me," I said. "This is Uncle Ameen's troupe and it stays here." No one listened. "Good God, have you guys gone crazy? You'll starve to death in a week." Silence. "Nobody's going with me, that's that."

Pete Cazzazza spoke up. "He fired you because of what we did to his stepson. That means he fired us, too."

"If Puabla goes, we go," Gloomy Gus said.

Ameen lumbered to the doorway, confronting his men. Deep lines creased his forehead, his mustache barely bristled. "We are booked, right now, for five weeks. No one would be fool enough to walk out on five weeks' booking." A strange look came into his eyes. "Besides, you couldn't do this to me. My reputation would be ruined."

"We made more money for you than any troupe you ever had," Long John said. "You didn't want the act in the first place."

Ameen swallowed hard, his insides apparently twisting. "Puabla, you plotted thievery. You plotted to steal my men when I was away."

"You know that's not true, Uncle," I replied. "You fired me – I didn't quit you."

A coughing fit seized Ameen. At the end, he wheezed, "Well, Puabla stays. I have changed my mind. Puabla can stay."

I looked at him coldly. "I haven't changed *my* mind. You told me to get out. I'm getting out."

I walked to the door. He grabbed my arm. "Puabla, my God, it's eight years. I brought you to this country. You can't leave me like this. Stay till Saturday," he pleaded. "If I cancel in the middle of the week, I'm ruined."

Angry as I was, I could not destroy Ameen. I deliberated.

"I'll stay," I conceded, "till Saturday. Get one thing straight, Uncle. I'm nobody's boss. Anything these men do, they're doing on their own. If they want to work for someone else, don't blame me for it…on Saturday, I leave."

I made plans, Shaheen wanting to know what I was doing. I told him I remembered an agent in Cleveland who could get me a job. Cleveland seemed as close as anywhere.

Saturday night came and I packed. Ameen sat in the dressing room after he paid us off – at the raised salaries.

"Puabla," he said, trying to sound commanding. "The men will not stay when you go. It might not be good if they stay because my back will not hold them much longer."

I could muster no sympathy. Two years' work without more than five layoffs. One hundred weeks in which he pocketed three-fifty a week. Thirty-five thousand dollars. I remembered Excelsior Springs – the parlor, the bedroom.

I picked up my little suitcase, walking to the door, Jeff at my heels. Long John took my arm, clasped my hand in farewell. The act was staying. Ameen beamed.

"Shaheen tells me you're going to Cleveland to see an agent," John said, his face breaking into a smile. "When you get there, tell him you have *nine* unemployed acrobats looking for work." Ameen's mustache trembled. "We can be rented at a terrific bargain."

"Long John, you've lost your head," I said. "I can't find you so much as a club date."

"Maybe so – we'll see you in Cleveland."

"Oh, God!" Ameen groaned.

"Uncle, for this I'm sorry." I said. "Not for anything else. I wish you good luck. Goodbye."

Ameen did not look at me. He sat motionless, his black mustache still. My costume in my bag, Jeff by my side, thirty dollars in my pocket, I left him.

Chapter 14
The Tumbling Terrors

By Monday, the others arrived. My agent friend offered me immediate work in a new act; nothing for my wards.

Meeting in our hotel, I said, "We can spread for ourselves or stick together as an act."

"We are an act," Long John declared. "A good one. I vote we stick together."

Agreed.

"I'll send wires to the bookers now." Someone suggested saving money with letters. "We'll lose 24 hours. It costs us ten dollars a day to live, only a dollar to send the telegrams."

"Puabla's the manager," Gloomy said.

"We need action in a week," I added. "That's our limit."

Days passed. No answers. We picked up forty dollars for one show in a private club. Momentarily saved, we returned for a late supper. A telegram lay in my key box.

"Can you make ball park Pittsburgh 6 p.m. Wednesday for 100 dollars? Confirm McLaughlin Agency."

The clock showed 12:30 Wednesday morning.

"What does the wire say?" the friendly hotel clerk asked. I showed him.

"How can we make it? If there is a train, we can't afford tickets after we pay you. Pittsburgh by six o'clock? Wow!"

"Hold it," he said, making a phone call. "You have no chance." He outlined his plan.

I assembled the troupe. "We can get a booking at six o'clock tonight, in Pittsburgh. It must be Rafferty. He holds music rehearsal at six. Miss it, we're out."

"He should know all we need is two marches and a gallop," Cazzazza said.

"It makes no difference with Rafferty. The interurban trolley leaves in four hours. With two changes, we hit Pittsburgh at 4:30. What do you say?"

Nobody said anything. "What do *you* say?" Long John asked.

"We'll starve here. I guess it's no worse to starve in Pittsburgh."

"Try it," Long John concluded.

"Wait," I warned, "you might as well know the whole story. After paying our bill here, we'll have ten dollars. I'll buy six boxes of Graham crackers and save the rest for emergency. It's Graham crackers till tomorrow night. If we make the rehearsal, we get dinner. It not, who knows?"

Shaheen paled. "We just did a show. I don't think I can stand a day of crackers."

Gloomy Gus shoved him. "I can." We packed, checked out, bought the crackers and boarded the trolley. Heading toward Pittsburgh, I dozed. George Simon snored till morning, Sweeney never slept.

By sunrise, my body ached. I opened two boxes of crackers for early breakfast. At eight-thirty, we changed cars. The little exercise removed the pins and needles from our limbs.

All morning, the sun beat on the second trolley, scorching the very air we breathed. We munched two boxes of crackers, changing again at one-thirty.

The final tram was prehistoric. Rickety, dirty, originally orange, now blackish brown, it jiggled through the heat; stopping where it was suppose to, just as frequently where it was not suppose to. At four o'clock, twenty-five miles from Pittsburgh, it broke down.

"What's the matter?" I asked the motorman.

"Son, I wish I knew," he answered. "They should have junked this crate long ago."

I agreed. "What about us? We *must* get to Pittsburgh by six o'clock."

He pulled some levers. "Take it easy. All I do is fiddle with the guts of this thing. Sooner or later she starts. Luck, I suppose."

A motionless half-hour passed. With a roar, a motorcycle wheeled alongside the reluctant trolley. The rider laughed, wisecracking to the motorman.

"This is our last chance," I said, grabbing Long John. "Here's a buck. Get them to the ball park as soon as you can. I've got to make the music rehearsal."

I jumped from the trolley. "Hey, kid, where you going on that motorcycle?"

"Who you calling kid?" He looked my own age.

"Never mind. Are you going to Pittsburgh?"

He shook his head no.

"How much do you want to take me there?" I asked.

He thought. "Ten bucks."

"I've got five. You take it?"

"Nope."

The motorman butted in. "Don't believe him, mister. That nut would drive you to Philadelphia for five bucks."

The cyclist frowned. "Well, since *he* can't get you there, I might as well."

"I'm going to Forges Field. You know where it is?" I climbed on the rear seat.

"Yeah, the other side of town. Cost you an extra buck."

The motorman intervened. "Listen, fellow, if this man is crazy enough to ride with you, take him where he wants to go."

My chauffeur kicked the pedal and the motor roared. In little more than an hour, we needed to cover twenty-seven miles. Bouncing, along the dirt road, only a tight grip held me to the seat. I feared my end had certainly come, as we darted between motor cars. While I was wishing myself back on the streetcar, eyes closed, my chauffeur pulled up in front of the ball park. Our cycle screeched to a stop.

"Some ride!" called my driver over his shoulder. I couldn't confirm or deny as my foot groped for the sidewalk.

"Here's your five dollars," I gasped. "What time is it?"

"Twenty-five of six."

I sighed, wavering toward the gate. It was Rafferty all right.

"Hello," he said. "Seems I remember you."

"Sure, I used to be with the Sons of the Desert."

"That's right. Ameen Hamid's act. This act of yours any good?"

"Wait till you see it."

"What's the name?"

I realized we had no name. We got one in a hurry. "George Hamid's Tumbling Terrors," I said.

"Ow! It better be good. How about your music?"

"Two marches and a gallop," I said.

"Perfect."

"Where's the rest of your bunch?" He asked.

"Eating," I lied. That's what they would like to be doing.

"The show's at eight. Make sure they get here."

I agonized. Six-thirty. Seven. Seven-thirty. At twenty to eight, my acrobats straggled in.

"We ate the Graham crackers," mumbled Shaheen, admitting a sin. "I think I'm too weak to go on."

"The show starts in fifteen minutes," I told them. "We close the program; no leaving now."

Gloomy Gus looked Shaheen in the eye. "We lasted this long. We can go another hour. Besides, you'll tumble better on an empty stomach."

We worked the act to perfection. Rafferty ran over. "Hamid, that's a great bunch!"

"Thanks, Mr. Rafferty," I said abruptly. "Glad you think so." I wanted to find the nearest restaurant. Rafferty insisted on introducing me to the manager of Pittsburgh's Victoria Theater.

"Sun books my house," the manager told me. "He asked me to take a look. I can use you for a week starting Saturday. How about three hundred?"

His offer startled me. "We'll take it."

I relayed the good news as we ate a huge, happy dinner, found ourselves a cheap hotel, and waited.

On Saturday we opened at the Victoria. The manager, a friendly man, complimented us, wiring a first-rate report to Sun, whose circuit included Ohio, plus most of the Middle West. By Tuesday,

Sun wired back, asking confirmation on the next three weeks. I promptly okayed it.

On Wednesday, we caught our first big break. The manager of Snyder's Burlesque, seeing the show, walked backstage, offering us fifteen weeks at three-fifty. I took the offer, telegraphing Sun to cancel his booking.

I still shudder at the result. If I had not been a greenhorn, I'd have wired Sun first, asking for a release. I didn't.

Next day, the manager of the Victoria was ordered by Sun to stop our pay. Snyder's Burlesque was notified that Hamid's Tumbling Terrors were blacklisted.

Our world collapsed.

We expected our Victoria pay, if we never worked another date in the Middle West. We finished the week. Saturday finally came. After the matinee, the performers were paid, all except us. I walked through the darkened theater to the manager's office, where I discovered Long John, Gloomy Gus and Habash, the understander. In a corner sat the manager.

"Hamid," he called. "For God's sake, control these maniacs. Three more of them are outside blocking the doors. They've already smashed the crown."

The pride of the theater, a gold-painted replica of Queen Victoria's royal crown hung over the inner doors.

"Who did that?" I asked Habash.

"The boys are mad, " he replied. "One of them heaved a club that hit the crown. An accident."

I explained that the manager tried, even wired Sun to relent. Sun tied his hands and he couldn't help us.

Long John shook his head. "We worked, we want our pay. We owe hotel and food bills. No pay, we wreck this place."

To the manager, I said, "My hands look tied, too."

The manager eyed Habash. "How much will you take to clear out of here?"

"Enough to pay what we owe and get to New York."

"How much is that?"

"Ask Puabla," he answered.

I figured, stating a hurried amount. Too quickly, it turned out.

"How do I know they'll leave if I find it?" asked the manager.

"We're not crooks!" Long John announced. "We worked a week. Give us at least part of what's coming to us. If we say all right, it's all right."

The manager believed him. From a safe, he produced the money, counted it, handed it over.

I thanked him. "I'm sorry about the crown. If we ever get on our feet, I'll send you a couple hundred to fix it." He shook my hand goodbye. "Don't worry, I'll tell the boss it fell. He'll get another one made. Someday, give him a week at a cut.

Returning to the hotel, I sent the men to pack while I gathered the bills. They totaled more than my estimate. I paid, counting the balance.

"What's the exact fare to New York?" I asked the clerk. After five minutes, Long John joined me. "This," I stated, holding out my fist, "is enough to buy three full fares and six halves."

"What are we going to do?" he asked.

"Do?" I answered. "What can we do? Buy three full and six halves."

"Who's the halves?" he asked.

"Who looks youngest – Shaheen, or Gloomy Gus, or Pete Cazzazza?"

Long John frowned.

"You're going full," I explained. "Naturally, I'm going full because I have to do the talking. We need one more full and the other six go halves."

"Then you want to know which looks oldest, not youngest," he corrected. "Let's see. Shaheen is twenty, but with his heavy beard he looks thirty. Gloomy must be forty, but he doesn't look over thirty-five. Cazzazza – by the way, how old do they have to be?"

"It says on the ticket 'twelve or under'," I muttered.

He shook his head. "I'd pick Habash. He's the biggest."

"You, Habash and I go full."

"What about Jeff?" asked Long John. "Should I tell the conductor to put him in the baggage car?"

"My God, no. The less we say to the conductor the better."

"You're not going to leave Jeff?"

"Of course not. I've got it all figured out."

I sent Shaheen upstairs for an old dress I'd noticed in a cleaning closet.

"Here," I said to Long John.

"What's this?" He pulled his hand back as if he burned it.

"A dress," I told him. "You wear it. We'll put Jeff between your legs. The conductor won't dare touch a woman's legs."

Gloomy Gus looked at Long John. "Not an old woman like him, anyway." He grunted.

"No sir," wheezed Long John, backing away. "I'm not putting that thing on."

"I'm sorry," I told him. "You have to – for Jeff. Anyway, we'll look more believable with a woman along. The conductor won't know how tall you are. Maybe he'll feel sorry for you when he sees your family."

The troupe congregated. "Puabla is boss," grumbled Gloomy. "We all agreed."

Giving in, Long John glared at me.

"Everybody, not Habash, roll up your pants. Roll 'em on the inside," I directed.

"What!" roared Gloomy.

"You heard him," growled Long John. "You're little boys. Roll up your pants."

As I surveyed the results, Long John gasped. "Not him," he pointed to Shaheen. "For God sakes, he's got legs like a bear. The hair's an inch long."

I agreed. "Shaheen, roll 'em down. Sit next to a window. Keep looking out."

I instructed, "Get to the station early. We'll turn back two seats, across the aisle from each other. Long John, you and I sit on the aisle. I'll give the conductor the tickets."

The B & O train was to leave at midnight. Through the gloom we trudged. The shadows of the station fortunately hid us. The railroad car, dimly lit, provided further obscurity.

We pulled back the seats, settled ourselves according to plan, and waited. Twenty other passengers wandered into our coach. The train rolled forward.

Five minutes, ten minutes passed. The door opened. "All tickets, please."

The conductor inched through the dreary car. My heart pounded. He pulled alongside.

"Tickets!"

I handed him nine stubs, the three full on top. I looked away.

He thumbed through the stack.

"What's this?" he asked.

I looked up. "Tickets. Nine of us."

"Yeah, I know. Who's the six halves?"

"Them!" I pointed vaguely to six.

The conductor felt Gloomy Gus's cheek. "What're you trying to pull? This bird's thirty-five if he's a day."

"Oh, no," I assured him.

"And this guy...." Continued the conductor, turning to Shaheen, innocently staring out the window. The conductor reached for Shaheen's bare arm. He yanked out a hair.

"Ouch," shouted Shaheen. "You...."

"Quiet, dear," Long John cautioned.

"Who's this?" asked the conductor, "Your mother?"

I nodded.

"Well," he growled, "she doesn't look like she's shaved since yesterday." He paused, then, "Have you, Mom?"

Long John nodded yes, then no.

"How old is this fellow?" he asked, pointing at Pete Cazzazza.

"Twelve and a half," grumbled Long John. I nudged him.

"She forgets sometimes," I apologized. "She means eleven and a half."

"This has gone far enough," shouted the conductor. "If you guys are in trouble, that's one thing. Trying to pull a fast one like this is another." He looked at Long John. "You're no more a woman I am."

He lifted Long John's skirt.

Jeff lunged. The conductor jumped back, wringing his hands.

"A dog. A damned dog."

"You," he hollered at me. "get out of here. Take that dog to the baggage car and wait for me."

I ran to the rear with Jeff.

Alone in the rumbling baggage car I sank down on a trunk. Jeff licked my hand as tears rolled down my cheeks.

The conductor entered. I wiped the tears with my wrist.

"Come clean," he said. "What's going on?"

"I," I sobbed. "I…"

"You're crying?" He queried.

I sniffed.

"By golly, you *are* crying. You look like a gang of crooks to me. I never saw a crook cry."

"We're acrobats," I stammered. In stumbling phrases, I related our story.

He whistled. "You have a trunk full of troubles." He scratched his chin. "I'd like to help you, but I work for this railroad. My duty, my loyalty…"

"Listen," I interrupted. "Two of them would have bought a half fare anyway. That leaves four that shouldn't. Four halves means we're two full short. I could have bought those seven tickets on the Pennsylvania."

He eyed me quizzically. "I'll do the figuring. You're better when you just sit. I get off at Cumberland. I won't say anything. I'll write the next conductor a note. I can't make any guarantees for him."

We trembled through Cumberland. Conductors changed. The new one walked by without a glance.

Chapter 15
Little Top

We reached Hoboken in the afternoon, ferrying to New York.

Long John still had friends in Brooklyn. He found lodging for himself, Habash and Mustafa. Cazzazza, a former citizen of South Brooklyn, provided for Sweeney. Gloomy Gus managed his housing and George Simon's. Shaheen and I, never considering a call to Uncle Ameen, decided to inhabit the park for a couple of nights.

I beat the paths to the booking offices. For two days they turned me down cold. On the third, as quickly as I'd been chilled before, an agent handed me three weeks, opening in Fay's Providence, even lending me railroad fare.

The clan entrained. I thought of a few novel tricks, as did Habash. We rehearsed before the show, fitting them into the act. Show time came and we wowed 'em. Deep down inside, a performer knows exactly how he has impressed his audience.

We were destined to make a score.

Next day it happened. Into our dressing room walked John Quigley, owner of the Great (according to him) John Quigley Circus.

He asked if we would finish the season with him.

Circus! Our dreams that would not die – more important to an Arab troupe than the rest of show business put together.

"Starting when?" I asked.

"Next week."

I shook my heard. "Sorry, we're booked for two weeks."

A prim, authoritative little man, Quigley rose to his full five-foot-three. "You're going to give up three months in my circus for two weeks in a couple of tank theaters? Cancel."

"No," I cried. "We're outcasts in the Middle West for doing that."

Quigley walked across the room. "You don't seem to know how big a man I am. I can get you released in five minutes. Then will you join me?"

The boys nodded. I warned him, "You get us a written release. I'll call the agent to make sure. If everything is clear, we'll go."

"Well," huffed Quigley, "you insinuate you have to check on the Great…"

"That's the deal," I interrupted. "I'm not insulting you. If the *East* exiles us, we're done."

Quigley clicked out of the room.

The next afternoon he reappeared, displaying a telegram from our agent. The agent confirmed that he'd released us to John Quigley's Circus.

"You pick up my circus next Tuesday in Bath, Maine. Sign here."

I checked the contract, signing it – on top of the world.

The train chugged into Bath. We stepped off to find Bath a small town, which didn't surprise us. Some of the largest circuses played their best dates in hamlets.

A wiry old man chewed a cud of tobacco. Gloomy Gus walked to him. "Where's the John Quigley Circus?"

Two glassy eyes looked through him

"Never heard of it."

"Why, you numbskull," grumbled Gloomy. "It's playing right here in…"

"Come on," I called. "Stop wasting time. We can tell in a minute from the paper."

Circuses in those days (even today) blanketed a town with three sheets, displays and window cards collectively called "paper." With Buffalo Bill, one was smacked in the face with bright yellow, red and blue advertising.

We walked a quiet block. Long John observed, "I don't see much stuff out."

"What do you mean 'much'?" I growled. "You mean you don't see any."

"Do you think we're in the right town?" asked Shaheen.

Piped Pete Cazzazza, "There's a Bath, New York, a Bath, Pennsylvania, maybe a Bath in Iowa for all I know."

"It's Maine in the contract," I insisted.

A kid sat on a red stoop. "Where's Quigley's Circus?" we asked. A kid would know.

He laughed. "Circuses never come to Bath. When we want to see a circus, we…"

Shaheen grabbed my arm. "Do we have the right date?"

"The contract says August…" I read him the dates. "John Quigley's Circus under the auspices of the Odd Fellows."

A group of men stood on the corner. "I'm sorry to bother you. Where are they holding the Odd Fellows Circus?"

The townsmen exchanged puzzled glances until one spoke up. "Oh yeah – I saw them putting up a tent, but yer at the wrong end of town. It's a lot, a quarter mile outta town, that way."

"What's the catch?" wondered Long John.

"I wish I knew."

We soon found out. A quarter mile outside town we discovered the tent. I groaned. Sagging, dirty, full of holes, it wasn't fit for livestock.

We ventured inside. Sun streaks slid through gashes in the "top." Unpainted, splintery benches for four hundred surrounded the chipped ring curb.

I recognized Hip Raymond, the clown.

"Puabla! How are you?"

"I don't know. What's this Quigley Circus all about?"

He shrugged his shoulders. "Don't you know?"

"Where'd you play last week?" I asked.

"Last week? No place last week. I don't think this circus played anywhere yet."

I got angry. "Where's Quigley?"

"Nobody's seen him. I don't even know him."

"Who's on this show besides you?"

"I've seen Ajax, the strong man, Dedeo's dogs and ponies."

I shuddered. Dedeo's mangy, flea-bitten mongrels – as decrepit as ever pulled into a whistle stop.

Ajax, I didn't know. "Who's Ajax?"

"He's good. From England."

"A strong man?" I queried. "From England? They usually come from Borneo."

"This one's from England and he's plenty strong."

"Hmm…," I pondered. "Any music?"

"Vancini's here. Says his band's gonna play the show."

"How's he?"

"I did a show with him Fourth of July. The worst band I ever heard. I'm a guy who's heard some stinking bands."

"I suppose it's no use talking about the menagerie." All circuses carried a menagerie; a traveling zoo, where animals used in the show were displayed for an extra admission.

Hip frowned. "Dedeo's got his chimp, his dogs and ponies. Unless another animal act comes along, it won't amount to any menagerie. Besides, there's not a tent for it."

We looked at the tent top. "Lord help us if it rains," muttered Long John.

Next day we were to open.

At noon, the boss showed up. He wasn't the same boss we had met. "Are you Quigley?" I asked.

"I'm Quigley's brother. Anything I can do for you?"

"Plenty. He sold us on his great circus. What's his game?"

The brother looked me over. "If you're worrying about getting paid, and I don't know what else you got to worry about, forget it. He'll take care of you."

I scratched my head. "This show won't start unless somebody gets it rehearsed and gives us the lineup."

"What do you mean 'line-up'?" asked the brother.

We stared at each other. "The running order," I explained. "who goes first, what act goes second, third, so on."

He gave me a glassy look. "Can't you people figure that out yourselves?"

Dedeo stumped forward. "I'll be your equestrian director," he puffed. "I've had a lot of experience." An equestrian director routines the program. Dedeo couldn't routine his own act.

"Fine," agreed the brother.

If he didn't worry about my pay, I did. "Say," I suggested, "I've, got nine men. I'll do the butchering."

"The what?"

"Butchering. Peanuts, popcorn, lemonade. Every circus has butchers."

"Okay with me."

Ordinarily, the butchers paid a fortune for the privilege.

At no cost, I wasn't sure I'd gotten a bargain. We should be able to pick up some change to live on.

"How about rehearsal?"

"Go ahead. Rehearse," said the brother. "I won't stop you."

"Oh, no," groaned Gloomy Gus.

"Listen, Mr. Quigley," I told him, "we can't just tumble around the ring. Somebody has to practice our music. Otherwise, your show won't be a show, what little you have."

"What's your idea?"

"Three o'clock. Opening time's seven-thirty. It shouldn't take an hour. From what I hear about your band, better allow the whole afternoon."

What I heard about it couldn't possibly match what we saw. At three-fifteen the band dragged in, woebegone Italians and Italian impersonators unlike any musicians I had ever seen. Vancini himself resembled a gangster more than a bandleader.

They slumped to their chairs and burped out a march. I have forgotten its name, although I don't know how I could. It's the single song they played together.

I passed out our sheets. They barely hinted at our gallop and two marches.

I threw up my hands, wandered downtown, and laid in a supply of peanuts, popcorn, lemons, sugar and some ice – five dollars.

John Quigley arrived on the evening train to watch the first show.

What a first show! Quigley delayed the start twenty minutes for the "late comers." Late comers and all, eighteen people showed up. My acrobats peddled their "delicacies." Nine vendors, eighteen spectators. We grossed one dollar and thirty-two cents.

Dedeo set the running order the only way possible; Hip Raymond, Dedeo's dogs, Ajax, Dedeo's dog and pony circus, one other act, Hip again, then closing with us.

The audience suffered through long stalls, stuttering announcements and slow acts performing to fiendish music. Six patrons remained.

We were the biggest, carrying more people than the balance of the show.

At the finish, I grabbed John Quigley. "Tomorrow, send us money. This outfit won't make enough to pay our move out of here."

He brushed his neat lapel. "Son, don't worry. You're dealing with a man who is rarely wrong. The tent will be jammed before the week's out. It's building. I can feel it."

Business "built" to a Friday peak of seventy-five paid admissions. My butchers grossed thirty dollars on peanuts and popcorn. What we didn't sell, we ate.

On Saturday, the awaited letter arrived from Quigley. It contained tickets for our move out of Bath. Nothing else.

The second week duplicated the first. Dedeo's role of equestrian director went to his head. He annoyed everybody with useless orders.

The band! When it played, it drove us crazy. When it didn't play, the musicians took our chairs and stole our shirts. Ajax alone, because of his terrifying strength, was spared their shenanigans.

John Quigley reappeared on Friday with a hundred dollars. As we grumbled, he announced, "Next week we get rich. Lewiston is a big town. The people love circuses. The Shriners are our sponsors. They already have a four thousand dollar advance sale."

Lewiston was indeed an enthusiastic circus town. Even so, we would have bolted from Quigley had our resources not dried up. Only the relentless butchering job kept us going. We climbed in the train with the others.

Lewiston turned out to meet us. People swarmed over the lot looking for the horses, seals and the herds of elephants.

I trailed the others. Looking sheepish, I explained to as many as I could that the rest of the circus would be on a later train. Much later.

A Swift, an Armour, and a local refreshment supplier looked at me. I didn't dare fool with the Swift or the Armour man. The local dealer I called aside. "We need twenty dollars worth of ice right away."

"What about hot dogs and peanuts?"

I shook my head. "Feel this weather. It's ice cream. You have to let me have it on credit."

"I don't even know you. How can I sell you ice cream on credit?"

"Bring it and stay here. The first twenty dollars we take is yours."

He hesitated, looked at the swarms of people, then accepted. "Don't forget the scoopers and cones," I called.

We sold out with little trouble. Net $25.00. We could eat.

Quigley's confidence was founded on the Shriners committee, my misgivings on the same thing. No such circus-wise business men would pay Quigley a plugged quarter for his sad conglomeration after they saw it.

That evening as I moped in the tent, the promoter who dealt for Quigley approached. "Quigley isn't here, is he?"

"No," I answered. "I phoned Boston (collect). His office man says he's out of town."

"What a chiseler!" grumbled the promoter. He took a seat near mine. "You know he'll never get paid when the Shriners see this."

I nodded.

He added, "I'll let you in on something important. Tomorrow, after the parade, they're to make a twelve hundred dollar payment. They'll make it to you as well as anybody when I tell them you're authorized."

"After the parade, you say?"

"Yeah."

"This circus has never paraded in its life. It wouldn't dare show itself on a public street." I paused. "By God, it'll parade tomorrow!"

For four dollars, I rented nine local steeds. Each of my acrobats would ride a horse. I told Ajax, Hip Raymond and the other act about parading, then argued Dedeo into it. Even though Dedeo rejected any ideas except his own, he agreed to this, provided his animals could follow behind the acrobats. I took Ajax with me to convince Vancini. His band would *not* parade, he insisted.

"Just play your one march," I told him.

No amount of persuasion budged him, though the parade meant as much to the band as to the rest of us.

I turned to Ajax. "Without the band, we're sunk!"

"Really?" replied Ajax. He faced Vancini, grasping his arm in his iron fingers. "Puabla says we might acquire twelve hundred dollars tomorrow. I must insist that you join."

Vancini nodded his head and ran.

Next day, we gathered at the head of the main street. I discovered an old outfit from my Buffalo Bill days. In full Arab regalia, with hood and cape, I pulled up behind the band. Half a block ahead rolled two carloads of Shriners. They hadn't looked behind them any farther than the band, as I knew they wouldn't.

The band began its march, walking forward. Although my horse didn't want to march any more than the others, we managed a haphazard trot. Behind my horsemen straggled Dedeo's indifferent animals, Hip Raymond, Ajax and the five remaining performers.

We might have carried it off anywhere else, or even in Lewiston, if we paraded down one street, up another. Not Lewiston. We trod down the main street, circled, returning up the same street again.

Going down, we sneaked by the thousands of watchers before they realized they had witnessed the entire parade. What would happen when we faced them a second time?

My horse decided to get thirsty. He loped to a trough by the curb. A kid recognized him, calling, "Hey, Ribbon!" Ribbon raised his dripping snout as the kid petted him. I kicked, spurred and slapped the horse's flank. Ribbon refused to move.

I ignored the chiding till the kid asked who I was suppose to be.

"Buffalo Bill," I growled. "If you don't let go of my horse, I'll shoot you."

"Buffalo Bill. Ho, ho, ho. Look what says he's Buffalo Bill."

I yanked my horse's rein away, spurring him up the street. Too late. From all sides, people jeered.

The Shriners stopped their cars to investigate the howling. They stood along the curb like a reviewing stand, then directed us to the lot for a private performance.

Afterward, the head man called Dedeo and me aside. "You're not to blame, but this is no circus. Only five acts on the whole bill. Yours, kid (meaning me), is the only authentic troupe here. We had you perform once for us. Here's a hundred bucks. Pack up, we're canceling, and notifying anybody else with this Quigley to cancel, too."

Our "weary" circus conferred in the center (the only) ring. "This money will buy tickets as far as Portland."

"Why Portland?" somebody said.

"Quigley told me if anything happened to his circus, he'd book us in his vaudeville houses," Dedeo said, "in Boston."

"What makes you think he's got vaudeville houses?" I countered. "I wouldn't believe he had measles without seeing the spots."

I phoned Stuart Collins, Quigley's Boston man, telling him we were stranded. "Does he control any vaudeville time? He promised everybody two week's work when they reached Boston."

"Hamid," answered Collins, "haven't you had enough of that four-flusher yet? All he controls is a desk and a phone. He skipped town yesterday without paying his phone bill. I couldn't find him if it meant my life. I'll tell you what," he continued. "If you get to Boston, I'll line up a week for you. As for the rest of those dilapidated acts, except for Hip Raymond, I couldn't get them work if I *owned* a vaudeville house."

No Quigley, no money, no work. We trained to Portland.

If it hadn't been for the S.P.C.A. reporting Dedeo, for Dedeo cursing the Shriners out loud, and the Shriners wanting us out of Maine, we might be in Portland yet.

The Portland Shriners, inheriting us from the Lewiston Shriners, herded us, fully ticketed, onto the overnight boat for Boston.

In my pocket remained two dollars and twelve cents. I crossed the cobblestones to a store, where I purchased two dollars worth of Uneeda biscuits and sardines. Back on the dock, I doled out one biscuit and one sardine at a time. Poor Hip, Raymond's wife, a consumptive, teetered bleakly by his side. Each time she saw a sardine cracker, she paled. Each time, Ajax crept to her side, pilfering her ration.

On the boat, Long John and I found the captain, told him our story, offering to present our whole show for his passengers in return for a decent meal for all of us.

The captain thought it over. "How many?"

"Thirty-two or three."

"Oh, Lord, no. Maybe a couple, not thirty."

"Will you feed one free? Without a show?" I explained about Mrs. Hip Raymond, how the very sight of sardines sickened her, how she needed milk and vegetables. The captain wrote out a note for Hip to give to the dining room steward.

I thanked him. "You don't mind if our band gives a concert for what we can get out of it, do you?" I added.

Long John jabbed my ribs, whispering, "*That* band? A concert?"

"Anything we make," I urged, "will return to your boat for food."

The captain consented. "Can't hurt, I guess."

Toward the rear of the boat, the three decks ovaled around an opening. A person on any level could gaze onto the bottom deck. Ajax corralled the reluctant musicians into the improvised band shell.

"You can keep half of the take," I tried to explain to the band. "You'll make more out of this than anybody."

I stationed Ajax alongside the band to prevent any of them from disappearing.

Vancini raised his arms. The concert began. For some reason, he selected a number other than a march. Curious passengers gathered at the inner rail to find if such squealing could possibly be coming from musical instruments.

"Folks," I announced, "you're listening to Vancini's great circus band. Along with twenty of us, they were stranded in Lewiston, Maine."

"Why didn't you leave them there?" someone yelled.

I continued. "These grand troupers have decided to give a concert, free of charge. Anything you care to toss will be appreciated." Aside to Vancini, I ordered, "Play the march, you fool."

Giving Long John six of my twelve pennies, keeping the other six, we dashed to the upper deck. I crowded to the rail.

Fat Alfredo puffed the big horn – oomp ah, oomp ah. I aimed a penny, plunking it into his horn.

Alfredo jumped, shaking his fist. Two drunks alongside me howled with laughter. One aimed a fistful of coins at the horn, the other followed and missed.

Livid, the bass player waddled from the bandstand.

"Ajax," I yelled. Ajax walked him back to his tuba.

"Now, everybody," I shouted. "Let's fill it."

Coins flew toward the big horn, most of them clinking home.

The excitement subsided, so I terminated the concert.

Ajax guarded the horn as my Arabs gathered the loose coins. We dumped the money on the table and counted. The performers cheered the final figure – -sixty-four dollars!

I handed the band their half. The rest of us each cleared two dollars.

Ajax kissed me. "By jove," he declared, "I love you Americans." Me, eight years in this country.

Chapter 16
Coney Island Courtship

Back in Boston, broke, I wondered how long we would stick together. I blundered in Pittsburgh, then turned down a Boston arrangement for the Quigley fiasco. I sought Stuart Collins, hoping for a booking to pay our way to New York.

Collins came through with Norumbega Park for four hundred!

"After working for Quigley," he said, "you can keep my commission."

Norumbega, though only one week, restored our confidence. I warned it might take our every cent to stay in New York. They didn't care. Before long, an agent would snap up a great act like ours.

Interesting suggestions surfaced. Mustafa offered to double our wealth with shooting craps. Every day, Shaheen whispered the name of a horse. I hoarded every cent, paying only expenses.

Doors slammed faster and tighter than before. Each rebuff fired my determination. I hounded bookers until they sickened at the sight of me. Resources dwindled. One agent said, "Don't you know the East is sewed up for acrobats?"

"I have to try," I said.

"You're wasting your time," he replied. "The only acrobats nowadays are Ben Ali's."

"Who is Ben Ali?" I asked.

The agent laughed. "Your biggest competitor." He scratched the address on a slip of paper – Coney Island.

After a long subway ride, I found the Surf Avenue address – the office was in a fashionable hotel. The door said, simply, "Ben Ali."

Behind the desk sat a beautiful woman.

"I'd like to see Mr. Ben Ali."

Her blue eyes looked steadily at me. "You cannot. I'm Christina Ben Ali. Can I help you?"

"I don't think so. When will he be back?"

"Hassan won't be back. He died last winter."

"I'm sorry," I said. "would you tell me who handles his business?"

"I do. Who are you?"

"George Hamid, owner of the greatest acrobatic act in show business."

Mrs. Ben Ali laughed. "What does this great act want from me?"

"I came to ask your departed husband to find me work," I admitted.

She laughed, a shining, pleasant laugh. "You aren't short of gumption, are you? Do you suppose that I would turn any of my routes over to you, a competitor?"

Silence followed. She continued.

"If I should lose my head and give you work, what would you pay me?"

"Naturally, you'd get ten percent commission, as my agent."

"Of everything for a year?"

I thought. "If those are your best terms, I agree."

She called to the next room, "Bessie, bring me a route file."

A younger girl appeared, not quite so tall, a little plumper, with a good looking, impudent face.

"Bess," said Mrs. Ben Ali, "I'd like to present Mr. Hamid. My sister, Bess."

With a curt, "How do you do", she lifted her chin, marching out of the room.

"She doesn't like Arabs," Ben Ali's widow explained.

"I'm not an Arab. I'm Lebanese."

"You're an acrobat. As far as she's concerned, you're an Arab."

Mrs. Ben Ali examined her file and turned to me. "I *might* have you a twelve-week tour to the West Coast at three-twenty-five for nine acrobats. Have you that many?"

"Sure I have. That's low pay, wouldn't you say?"

"It will be lower after I get my ten percent."

The acrobats averaged twelve dollars a week with my uncle. I pay over twenty. That leaves me one hundred and thirty. "I'll tell you what I'll do. If you can get me four weeks on the way back, I'll do you a favor and take this."

She paused, smiled and handed me a letter.

"What is it?" I asked.

My eyes soon absorbed the precious words from Alexander Pantages:

"Please accept my heartiest congratulations and good wishes on the manner in which you are preserving the fine business of your late husband.

"Kindly assist me if you are able. An old fox named Ameen Hamid operated a splendid acrobatic troupe, which he called 'Sons of the Desert.' I am told that one of his nephews revolted against the wild old devil; the performers leaving with the nephew."

"I would like to play the act for two reasons. One, because it is a standout; two, because I admire a boy with the courage to defy that tyrant of an uncle.

"Since you, my esteemed lady, rule the Eastern acrobats, I feel sure that you can locate Mr. Hamid.

"Wire me at once for transportation if he needs it. Knowing the uncle, he will.

"I offer three-twenty-five for twelve weeks, plus one-way transportation. This may sound like a steal for nine people, maybe it is, but go no higher. He will accept it.

"Thank you for your kindness. Sincerely, A. Pantages"

The letter overwhelmed me. I exited the Ben Ali office in a daze, hardly hearing the lady say, "Keep the letter, George, to look back on." The pendulum had swung again. We were employed, had a slick agent, discovered the great Pantages wanted us, and most important, I was attracted to a lady….not Mrs. Ben Ali….her sister.

We received our train fare, set our departure for the following afternoon, and taking no chances, I bought the tickets. Shaheen and George Simon met me at the station.

"There's something we have to do before tomorrow," I said.

"What?" asked George Simon.

"Go to Uncle's house and pick up the rest of our things."

George objected, "You go. What if he's there?"

"We'll all go," I said. "Don't worry. We're not his property any more."

Nearing the red brick house, we felt the power of his old spell.

"I hope Uncle lost his cane," Shaheen mumbled.

We climbed the steps, I touched the bell. The door opened and my aunt motioned us inside.

"We came for our belongings," I spoke softly. "We'd like to say hello to Uncle."

Anger clouded her face. "Your Uncle is gone."

"Where is he?"

"Lebanon. He took his money with him."

"For good?" I queried. "What about you?"

"For good." Her words dropped like stones. "He left me here. He didn't want me."

In our old room, our home for so long, we reminisced, we packed, and bidding it goodbye, we left.

The tour opened in Minneapolis, played through Western Canada, the Mountain States, California, then back to Texas. In California, I learned to know Alexander Pantages. He loved George Hamid's Tuzaneens.

He admitted buying us at an indecent price, saying, "To make up for that, wire me anytime you're in trouble. I'll book you on my circuit."

I grinned. "You don't owe me a thing. You offered – I accepted."

Mrs. Ben Ali found three weeks, not four, going East. She held our price, squeezing four and a quarter from one date.

Nearing New York, we outfitted ourselves – I in spats, a suit coat with braided lapels, a bright green shirt, plus a scarlet tie; my acrobats assembling similar atrocities. "Fashionably" clad, we invaded lower New York; mainly Southern Brooklyn.

We agreed to a two-week layoff, during which I visited Coney Island. My objective since August had been Mrs. Ben Ali's impossible sister, Bess. I visited the office three times in two weeks. Mrs. Ben Ali, wonderful as ever, offered three weeks of local work in January. Not one glimpse of Bess.

When the layoff expired, I told the troupe, "We have bookings for January. Take it easy till after Christmas. Meet every other day at the gym."

Long John called me aside, a strange look on his face.

"What is it, John?"

He hesitated, "I've decided to retire."

"What?"

"I met my old girl," he explained. "She still loves me. Maybe I'm crazy, but I love her."

"What are you going to do for a living?"

"Bordens has a job driving a milk truck."

"An acrobat," I gasped, "running a milk route?"

Long John nodded. "That's right."

I stuck out my hand. "By God, Long John," I cried, "I'm going to miss you…sell milk to everybody in Brooklyn."

"Thanks, Puabla. If you ever need an acrobat, don't forget the Brooklyn dumps."

Since the Brooklyn dumps provided few acrobats in December, I headed for Coney Island. To my delight, sister Bess presided over the desk.

"Where's Mrs. Ben Ali?" I inquired.

"Away."

"When will she be back?"

"I don't know."

"Are you running the business?"

"If it's any concern of yours, I am."

I removed my hat and sat down. She shuffled some papers.

"Your sister has a monopoly on all the Arabs around here." I complained. "I want to buy one."

"That will be fifty dollars," she stated.

"Fifty dollars!"

"Any week you fall behind, we take him back."

"Not when I'm not working!"

Mercy tempered her voice. "No, not when you're not working."

"Listen," I fumed, "you've been nasty to me since we met. Now, when I want to buy an acrobat, you hold me up. I'll be back tomorrow to tell you if I want him."

All night, I alternated between a growl and a smile. I told her off; smile. She held me up; growl.

Next day, I subwayed to Surf Avenue.

"Okay, okay," I scowled. "I agree to your terms. Fifty bucks, and he'd better be good."

"I'm sorry," she said, near weeping. "I spoke to Christina on the phone. We're out of fifty dollar acrobats. We have one left, at sixty-five."

"Sixty-five dollars!"

"He's a Moroccan," she purred, "very good."

I yanked the paper from her hand. "I'd better sign it before the price takes another leap."

"You won't regret it," she assured me.

I regretted it already.

"Now, we're business associates. Will you let me take you home tonight?"

"No. When I'm working for my sister, I don't go home. I stay here."

"Aha!" I thought. A good sign. She was defending.

"While your sister's away, you have to eat. I'll be happy to take you to dinner."

"Where?" she asked. "To Feldman's?"

"A good idea!"

She tossed her head, "Thank you, no. I have already accepted a gentleman's invitation to dine."

"I'll be over tomorrow night. Five-thirty. No excuses. Good-bye."

I spent next afternoon in Coney Island. A friend of mine named Sam Gumpertz wanted to interest me in a *Streets of Cairo* sideshow. This seemed as good a time as any. By five o'clock, we looked over the site – 8th Street and Surf Avenue – discussed the talent he required, how long I needed to break it in, terms, and opening date. From five to five-thirty, I rechecked Surf Avenue. I sauntered toward the office at five–thirty-one.

"Ready?" I asked.

Bess looked up. "My heavens! I forgot about you. Don't wait. I'll be at least a half hour."

"I've got lots of time, I'll wait."

She shrugged, then excused herself. After an hour and a half, she returned. I sizzled.

On Surf Avenue, we turned left. "Where are we going?" she asked.

"Feldman's."

She slowed. "That place!"

"You're lucky I'm even taking you out. A half hour, huh?"

At Feldman's, she ordered plenty, then picked at her food. "Peter takes me to Sheepshead Bay."

I said, "Look at me." She raised her eyes. "You're no kid, you're a good seventeen."

"I'll be eighteen in February."

"I'll be nineteen. You should know my business. You're in it. I work hard for what I get. Regardless, I'll take you anywhere Peter, whoever he is, does. If where you go means everything, maybe I had you figured wrong from the start."

"The right person is important, too," she said.

"Am I to infer that you're not satisfied with me? For your information, I come from the first Christian country in the world. If you expect me to apologize for my race, you're mistaken. I am Lebanese. Your sister married an Arab. We both come from the same part of the world. From what I hear, he did mighty well by her."

"Don't you talk about Hassan that way. He was the finest person who ever lived."

I took her arm and steered her from the restaurant.

Next afternoon, I was again at her office.

"You coming?" I asked.

She nodded. This time, she kept me waiting forty-five minutes. As punishment for such a wait, I steered her toward Feldman's.

Her mood changed. She chatted and laughed. Ordering a sensible dinner, she ate what she ordered. She finally admitted, "I shouldn't dislike you because you're an acrobat. Where would Christina be without acrobats?"

I wanted to hold her hand. My other dates were with "show worshippers" – girls who hung around stage doors. They had provided my only baptism.

We talked. She marred the conversation only once. "George," she inquired, "where did you get those braided lapels?"

I beamed, "Spiffy, eh?"

"Honestly," she said, "I won't complain where we go. I'm certainly agreeable being with you, but for heaven's sake, get rid of that jacket."

"*This* jacket?" I couldn't believe my ears.

She nodded, "And those braided spats."

That ruined a half-hour. Otherwise, the evening was the nicest in my life. We walked through new snow. At her door, we shook hands.

After Christmas, she allowed me to escort her from Coney Island to Jersey City, where she lived. Not a long trip as the crow flies; the subway, the ferry and the trolley consumed three hours.

We eventually stopped in front of a big gray house. I asked, "Should I come in?"

"I guess so."

"Will I shock somebody?"

"I don't think so," she answered. "My mother doesn't even know I know you."

"My father doesn't know I know you," I declared. "I don't worry about it."

"Don't be fresh. When we get inside, say no more than you have to. Whatever you do, don't mention that you're an acrobat."

"What's wrong with…."

"Shh," she interrupted. "Do as I say."

Once inside the full living room, Bess tried to smile. "Mother," she said to a stern looking woman, "I'd like you to meet George Hamid. Father," to a large, Prussian type man, "I'd like you to meet George Hamid. George, meet my mother and father. This," her wave covered the balance of the room, "is my family."

I stared through vague mumbling. Her family! I recognized Christina. One by one she spoke the names of five brothers – Jupey, Aug, Emil, Tom and 'LaLa.'

"LaLa?" I asked.

"Short for George," she explained. "He's the youngest."

"Leave the room," ordered Mrs. Raab. On the door, I noticed a name plate, "von Raab". The "von" had disappeared.

"Young man," demanded Mrs. Raab, "why have we never met you before?"

I didn't know. Bess rescued. "Christina introduced us. Mr. Hamid travels quite a bit. Doesn't he, Christina?"

Christina confirmed my comings and goings. "George is a fine boy."

Mrs. Raab doubted. She asked questions. Christina explained she had known me quite a while, that I traveled for a firm she knew well.

"Papa" halted the interrogation. "Bessie, please play for us."

Bess smiled, moved to the big piano, fingered the keys, then entertained with songs I had never heard. Occasionally, her mother pierced me with her eyes. By the last number, I ached to get away.

Fortunately, Papa insisted on leaving us with Christina till ten o'clock. At 10:01, I left.

At the door, Bess turned her eyes to mine. A tear wet her cheeks. As she threw her arms around my neck, crying, "You're so brave," she kissed me.

I stumbled down the steps, glided to West Side Avenue, took the wrong streetcar, wound up in Bergen Point, changed to another car, and hours later reached my flat in New York.

Our dates increased. Although she refused to grant me an exclusive on her free time, I declared my love. She admitted a warmth of her own.

We dined, mostly at Feldman's although I splurged once at Sheepshead Bay. She let me take her to Jersey City.

Things progressed smoothly – too smoothly, with my luck.

Bessie announced, as we neared her Delaware Avenue home, "You can't come in."

"Why can't I?"

"You've been banned. Mother doesn't think you're the right person."

"That's a hot one. Why not?"

She lowered her eyes. "Mother says I'm Jersey City aristocracy and you're just an Arab."

"I'm Lebanese," I insisted.

"Arab, Syrian, Lebanese – they're all the same to her."

"Jersey City aristocracy," I repeated. "Boston aristocracy I've heard of. Good God! Jersey City aristocracy?"

"She found out you're an acrobat, and as far as she's concerned, it's over."

"Well," I stormed, "I can tell her a thing or two myself." I marched toward the door.

Bess restrained me. "That won't help. She'll only get angrier. If you go in, she would make my brothers throw you out."

"Let them try."

"There's five of them. The older ones are pretty big."

"I don't care how big they are," I scowled. "I'll knock their heads together and pile them in a corner."

"Oh no you don't," Bess answered. "Not if you ever expect to see me again."

I apologized. No sense antagonizing the one I took the abuse for. I left.

Throughout a working week in a Manhattan theater, I didn't call. (Incidentally, her acrobat, Absalom, was a whiz.) I suffered as long as I could, then called.

"I'm glad to hear your voice," she cried.

"Yours sounds good, too," I confessed. "I'll be down at six. Feldman's for chowder."

"Not tonight," she stammered. "I promised to spend the evening with my brother, Aug."

We hung up. I remembered Aug; big and good-natured, but not about to trot to Coney Island to entertain his sister.

I rounded up Shaheen. "We're going to Coney Island," I said. "I'm getting the business from somebody."

We crept to Feldman's window. I seized Shaheen's arm. "Look, there she is. If that's Aug, I'll eat my hat."

"You know who he is?" Shaheen asked. I shook my head. Shaheen continued, "Peter Dingle, the butcher's son."

"So that's her "Peter." Too good for an acrobat, but dates a butcher's son."

"He's a good-looking guy," Shaheen observed.

I could see that. We waited on the boardwalk. "What are you going to do?" Shaheen asked.

"Shh! They're coming." I dragged Shaheen behind a stand.

As they sat on a bench, I sauntered by. I remembered a popular song and sang it. "Somebody's getting it where the chicken got the axe."

Bess ignored me. Pete scratched his head. I walked to where Shaheen was hiding.

"Shaheen," I called, "hold my coat."

I sprang into a row of flip-flaps, polishing them off with three backs. I landed inches from Dingle's feet.

"Oh," gasped Bess. "Peter, don't touch him. He's a madman. He'll kill you."

I laughed. "I wouldn't hurt your butcher's son." I donned my coat.

"Come on, Shaheen. Let's get out of here."

I don't know what else I accomplished, but I sure scared Dingle.

Three days later, Christina phoned. Bess broke her kneecap.

"That's awful!" I cried.

I sulked. "After her double-cross, I shouldn't even see her."

"Don't be silly," Christina laughed. "I'll tell her you're coming."

Next day, I entered the hospital carrying two boxes of candy, flowers and a basket of fruit.

Bessie beamed, then winced. Dressed in her fancy bed clothes, she looked rather well, except for her leg, which was caked in plaster.

She giggled, "Nurse, help him. I can't see him behind those packages."

I unloaded and sat beside her.

"George," she cooed, "it's so nice of you to visit me."

She explained how she'd hit her knee on a lamp post as she slipped on a piece of ice; how it broke in six different places.

I wrung my hands. "Terrible! What a shame!"

She smiled. I melted. She pouted. "You were ungentlemanly to Peter the other night."

"He deserved it," I grumbled. "Anyway, it was your fault, not his or mine!"

She nodded, "You're right. The Lord must be punishing me."

I re-melted. "Don't worry. That's over. Forget it ever happened." She took my hand.

One day, I decided to ask her, point blank, to marry me.

She recoiled, "I don't know if I'll walk again." That was true. The doctors refused to predict.

"You'll walk," I assured. "That's not the point. I want you to marry me."

"What will we tell my mother?" she asked.

"We are married."

"Oh, no!" groaned Bess. "That would kill her. We must keep it a secret."

"Then you'll marry me?"

Her brown eyes met mine. "If you'll keep it a secret, yes."

"Certainly I'll keep it a secret," I shouted. "If you and I know, what do I care about the rest of the world?"

"Quiet," she whispered, "or it won't be a secret long."

Bess tried her first step. The doctor let go of her arm. Her knee, shaking, held. She hobbled two steps and collapsed to the bed. I kissed her. "You'll walk, and run, and dance."

My visits purposely avoided the family. Bessie's friend, Mary MacMillan, stood guard, escorting me in and out of the hospital. When unavoidable, I bumped into Mr. and Mrs. Raab. I nodded hello. "Papa" smiled pleasantly, Mrs. Raab gave slight recognition. Mary explained that the hospital couldn't close its doors to me, and after all, what harm could a little visit do their invalid daughter?

What could I do? To defy them meant losing Bess.

We set the wedding for March 17th, Saint Patrick's Day, a neutral date since none of us were Irish. We went to Union City, New Jersey.

In the eyes of God, the preacher, and two witnesses, we married each other.

After the shortest honeymoon on record – an afternoon in Manhattan – I took Bessie to her house. She led me down the opposite side of the street. "You can't come in," she whispered.

"Why not?" I asked. "We're married."

"That makes it worse," she answered. "They'll suspect."

"Well, I'm all for…

"Remember your promise," she interrupted.

"Oh, all right." A strange man climbed the front steps. The door opened and he walked inside. "Who's that?" I asked.

"A friend of Au…" she started. "He's one of Mother's favorites."

"Favorite what?" I demanded.

"Favorite boy friends of mine."

"Favorite boy friends of yours?" I gasped.

She blushed. "Yes, his name is Freddie Plummer. I think she's planning for me to marry him."

She kissed me. "Good night, I'll call you tomorrow."

She crossed the street, mounted the steps and rang the bell. The door opened. Freddie Plummer reached for her arm, kissed her cheek. Through the window I saw him lead her to the parlor. She walked to the piano and sat down. Plummer stood beside her as she began her song.

I waited and watched. The door opened as Plummer departed. I looked at my watch. Ten o'clock. Bess's mother was at least consistent.

Bess's mother, Mrs. Raab, would be my mother now. Wait till she heard that!

For weeks, I spent afternoons and evenings with Bess, taking her to Jersey City and releasing her across the street from her house to walk up the steps to her fiancé.

Christina met a Spaniard named Juan Rabassa. He liked me and Bess. He worshipped Christina. His Spanish sights focused on her, keeping her under steady bombardment. One night, he invited Bess and me, Christina, Bess's mother and brother Emil to dinner.

Aside from Mrs. Raab's stony silence, the table rang with laughter. Mrs. Raab suspected Bess and I were together more than she knew.

Juan's voice addressed the group. "You know," he winked, "I wouldn't be surprised if Bess and George are secretly married."

"Oh, no," I assured him, "not us."

"What do you think, Christina?" Juan continued.

"Juan, I don't want to hear another word of this nonsense," Mrs. Raab ordered. "Not another word, do you hear?"

Christina laughed. "Juan, I don't think George has the nerve. But if they are married, it would be all right with me."

"Christina, you're trying to tease me," I said. "You know I've got the nerve."

"George, by golly, I think you're foxing people," Juan said. "Tell you what. If you and Bess are married, I'll give you living room furniture."

Great!

Christina took my hand. "I'll furnish your dining room."

Mother's eyes scalded them. "Emil, get the car."

I stood up. "Wait a minute, Mrs. Raab."

Bess tugged at my arm. "Sit down, please. George, sit down," she urged.

"Mrs. Raab," I went on, "it's about time we stopped this foolishness. Juan and Christina have made us wonderful offers. I wish I had your blessings, too. Anyway, Juan's right. Bess and I are married. We've been married since March."

"I don't believe it!" she stormed.

"If you'll come to my apartment, I'll give you the certificate."

Mrs. Raab disappeared out the door.

Juan drove to my apartment, after which we proceeded to Jersey City. Inside the house, I produced our marriage certificate. Mrs. Raab sat in a chair. When she saw it, she burst into tears.

"Poor Freddie Plummer! What will I ever tell Freddie?"

Papa spoke, "George is a fine young man. Freddie will live."

Bess pouted, "I wouldn't say so. How can he?"

Christina whispered, "Put your arm around her and call her 'Mother'."

"Oh, no," I gasped. "I shouldn't have listened to you and Juan to begin with."

"Go ahead," urged Christina. "Win her over now."

I tried, gingerly touching my hand to her shoulder. "Mother," I croaked.

She gasped and cried harder than before.

Papa seized my hand. "Son," he advised, "she'll collect herself by morning. You and Bess go to your room."

I lay exhausted on the bed, Bess sitting on the edge.

Twenty minutes later, the door burst open. Mother, with Jupey in tow, wailed, "Look what he's done. Do something!"

Jupey smiled, scratched his head and closed the door.

Ten minutes later, the door widened. In she popped with Aug. "Augie," she cried, "do something. Look what Bessie married!"

Aug, good-natured as usual, grinned. "Hello, George," he greeted. "Congratulations."

Emil and Tom followed. Finally, she brought LaLa. "Oh, look what he's done to your sister."

Only LaLa, about twelve, rose to the occasion, striking a fighter's pose.

"Get out of here, you," I roared. He ran.

Bess sobbed.

"LaLa!" I mumbled. "What a nickname for George. Lawrence or something, but not George." I put on my coat.

"It is George," murmured Bess. "His nurse called him LaLa when he was a baby." She looked up. "Where are you going?"

"Out the window," I answered, climbing to the sill. "I'm going to my little flat. If you want me, you'll find me there tomorrow." I dropped to the alley.

Next day, I waited, alone. Toward evening came a tapping on the door. I opened it.

A smile forced its way to my lips. "Hello, Bess."

"Hello, George."

I remember her outfit – dark gray suit, black shoes, boyish hat. "It's getting late. Won't you come in and make me supper?"

Chapter 17
No Blow-Off

Once my marriage calmed, business improved. Sam Gumpertz' *Streets of Cairo* opened to ample attendance. Luna Park wanted a similar show for its Oriental Midway. I divided the original act in half. Satisfied? Not me. In the back of my mind, I longed to create a circus like Buffalo Bill's, my first and best. Owning a couple of acts was merely a stepping stone to a full-fledged circus.

As Bess and I sat in Luna Park, Leon W. Washburn, owner of Washburn's Carnival, walked up and introduced himself.

As a circus man, I scorned making a living exploiting deformed animals, freaks, fat ladies, midgets, giants and misshapen unfortunates. I preferred performers, acrobats, trapeze artists, horsemen, clowns, high-wire cyclists and daredevils – entertainers who entertained.

"I hate to tell you this," Washburn started. "You're wasting your time."

"What do you mean?"

"You produced two great *Streets of Cairo* here and all you net is a small fee and commission."

"What's wrong with that?" I asked.

"Why," bellowed Washburn, "you should own your own sideshow."

Bess nudged me, "Let's go."

"How can I?" I asked Washburn. "I don't have the money or even the tent."

"What difference does that make? You could hitch up to a carnival like mine. To bring one of your shows on my midway, I'd supply you with a tent, wagons, a front, seats and everything. I'd transport you

135

from town to town. You'd be independent. All it would cost you would be a small percentage of your take."

Much as I disliked carnivals, it sounded attractive.

"What do you think, Bess?" I asked.

She frowned. "We're doing well enough right here."

"I'd like to get details, Mr. Washburn," I said.

"Meet me in my office tomorrow morning." He handed me his card. "No time to lose."

Next day, he outlined his proposal. It sounded even better. Still, I hesitated, until he mentioned Gyp, the elephant.

"Gyp's famous because she survived the Dreamland Park fire in 1906," Washburn said. "His trunk's half burned, but he's gentle as a lamb. You can use Gyp as a ballyhoo."

"I get the elephant, with no strings. Is that right?"

"We'll put it in the contract," he assured me.

I had two and a half weeks to set up my third *Streets of Cairo*. I spirited three performers from the Gumpertz show, two from Luna Park, as the Luna manager fumed and threw out my remaining acts, buying replacements.

With my nine Arabs back from Coney Island, courtesy of the Luna Park manager, my new *Streets of Cairo* would be the most elaborate in history! To make sure, I added four specialty dancers, six line dancers, four sword fighters, flageolet players and tom-toms – courtesy of Sam, who stopped being mad now that he, not me, would be getting commission. The costumes and production surpassed anything in Washburn's Carnival, or any other carnival, for that matter.

We were to open in Waterbury, Connecticut. I lined up three ticket sellers instead of the usual one. When the spieler described what went on inside, the crowd was sure to rush the box office.

The opening "tip" consisted of all the roughnecks and loafers in Waterbury. (A tip is the crowd a barker gathers to listen to his spiel.) They listened. When my barker finished, they booed him!

"Where's Fatima?" someone yelled.

"What about the blow-off?" another shouted. (A blow-off is a private "after-show" for men only, costing an extra quarter.)

I jumped to the platform. "There's no blow-off in this show," I yelled. "Anybody who's looking for that kind of stuff can go someplace else.

"We will," roared one of the men. They marched off. Never again would I invite an audience to leave.

The first day, we sold a hundred tickets. I fired the three cashiers. I kept the spieler – he and I alternating between the platform and the ticket box.

At the end of the week, I confronted Washburn. "Listen," I said, "remember the sales talk you gave me in Luna Park? Well, I'm giving the best show on the midway. I didn't take in enough to pay my own act."

"I can't understand," muttered Washburn. "I've got nothing to gain by your flopping. Don't worry, it's only the first week. No carnival breaks records the opening week."

Next stop, Meridean. Crowds improved, but my *Streets of Cairo* starved. I let the barker go and sent for my oldest brother, Saleem, now in America (the one who in childhood began the hand-me-down process.) He would sell tickets. I would spiel.

From morning till night, I stood on the platform coaxing, imploring, painting the most inviting pictures. I hollered, I whispered. The customers walked on.

"I can't understand it," moaned Washburn. "Nobody's breaking records. You aren't even making expenses." He paused. "Tell me, how's your blow-off doing?"

"My blow-off?"

"Yeah."

"I don't carry one," I spat.

"What's the matter with you?" Washburn asked. "No wonder you're broke! Everybody operates a blow-off."

I yanked him to his feet. "You never mentioned a blow-off in Luna Park."

"Hamid, let go of me," he sputtered. "Anybody knows that. You've been around, haven't you?"

I dropped him into his chair. I said, "If you think I'm starting a strip-tease, you're crazy. I wouldn't get into that racket if you gave me Washburn's Carnival."

I stormed out.

I dropped two sword fighters and two specialty dancers. We moved on. The next week everybody would pull out of the hole. Fourth of July – South Norwalk.

Bess wanted us to leave in Waterbury. She hated the carnival. Now she watched my spring surplus drain away. After Meridean, I borrowed what little money Saleem had. I determined to cut my nut to the bone to somehow make back the money I'd lost. The best of the season lay ahead.

Gyp, the elephant, kept us afloat, just as butchering kept us from starving with Quigley. The pennies he earned riding kids in his *houdeh* (riding harness) paid for his feed, his groom, a colored boy named Ambrose, and fed Bess and me. Gyp, tied at our entrance, attracted a crowd.

On the evening of the Fourth, I put Roman candles and a tom-tom into the *houdeh* and climbed aboard to produce my most spectacular pitch.

Ambrose pulled Gyp in front of the entrance.

"Hurry, hurry, hurry!" I yelled, beating the tom-tom. "The greatest, the wildest show of all times. See Fatima, The Wonder Girl, in her original Asiatic dances. See the sword fighters defy death with their razor-like blades. More thrilling than fire works!" With that, I set off three Roman candles.

Through the shouting and drum beating, Gyp had been standing calm as a cow. When the balls of fire puffed from the candles, he roared. People scattered, screaming.

"Oh my God!" I remembered. "Dreamland Park – 1906. He's scared of fire!"

I was thrown to the bottom of the *houdeh*. People raced in all directions. Ahead stood a candy tent.

"Look out!" I screamed senselessly to Gyp, who pounded straight through the tent, spraying lollipops and chocolates.

Only the padding saved me from breaking my bones as I huddled in the wildly rocking houdeh. The light began to fade. Gyp slowed. Looking up, I saw only stars and sky. The elephant lumbered to a stop. I pulled myself cautiously to a sitting position. We were in a cabbage patch of a small farmyard.

In the distance, I heard voices. Frenzied calls came closer. Marshals, sheriffs, constables and assorted deputies surrounded us in a half-circle. "Take aim!" someone commanded.

I jumped to my feet, my wits suddenly awake. "Hold it," I screamed. "Don't shoot! I'm up here."

A small dark figure raced across the field.

"Ambrose," I called. "Ambrose, come here." Ambrose ran over and petted Gyp's trunk.

"Nice Gyp," he soothed. "Come with Ambrose."

"We ought to shoot the devil."

"Don't shoot him," I urged. "He couldn't help it. He got burned once before. My Roman candles frightened him. Otherwise, he's gentle as a kitten."

The constables debated, then ambled off.

Ambrose, Gyp and I retraced his four-mile flight. At the carnival, we saw the devastation. Gyp had smashed three shacks, several small trees, and five stands on the midway. Luckily, no patrons were hurt.

At *Streets of Cairo,* no one. Business had stopped at the height of the evening! Inside I found Bess weeping.

She was convinced that I was dead. She rushed up, throwing her arms around my neck. We stood there till Bess started to cry again.

"I can't stand it," she sobbed. "This awful carnival. We've lost all our money. Next thing we'll be dead."

"There, there," I comforted her. "Everything will be all right." I couldn't blame Bess for hating *Streets of Cairo.* I told her to go home if she wanted to.

She shook her head. "I can stay as long as you can."

In South Norwalk, the show netted enough to pay salaries. Gyp, with a repaired *houdeh,* did a brisk passenger business, paying our expenses.

We moved to Torrington. Business died.

On Thursday night, I mounted the platform as usual, to grind in a few customers. I surveyed my tip – thirty to thirty-five people.

"Ladies and gentlemen," I began, dismissing my brother Saleem who had drummed up the tip with a tom-tom. "Inside this tent, you will witness, for the first time in your lives, the greatest, the most tremendous...." My words caught in my throat. From the corner of my eye, I noticed two ladies stomping through the midway – Christina and Bess's mother. I looked at the crowd and gulped. "Right over here for tickets," I groaned. "Step right up for the tickets."

I leaped from the platform. "Hello!" I called, as cheerfully as I could. The ladies' greeting was non-existent.

"So this is how you make your living!" Bess's mother exclaimed. "Where's Bessie?"

"Inside."

"We've come to take her home," Mrs. Raab announced.

"Wait," I said. "There's a show going on. I'll tell her you're here."

I ran backstage and sat down beside Bess. "Listen, Dear," I said, "are you expecting anyone?"

She looked puzzled. "No, unless it's the sheriff for you."

"Well, Christina and your mother are outside."

She paled. "Tell them I've gone to Bridgeport."

I shook my head. "They've come to take you home," I said. "How in the world did they find us?"

"Christina," Bess said. "She could follow Washburn's route in Billboard. The rest would be easy."

"I guess so," I admitted.

"She probably spilled the beans to Mother," Bess continued, "or Mother forced her to."

On the midway, the three exchanged kisses. "Bessie," ordered her mother, "get your things. We've come to take you away from this, this...."

Did she mean me or the show? "Listen here....," I began.

Christina restrained me. "George," she implored, "don't interfere. This is no life for a young girl and you know it. Let Bess go home. When you straighten yourself out, send for her."

"You know what your family will do," I grumbled. "They'll turn her against me and she'll never come back."

"No, they won't," she answered. "I'll see to that."

"You promise?"

"I promise," said Christina.

While Christina and I spoke, Bessie defied her mother. I cut in.

"Your mother's right, Bess. As soon as I clean up this mess, we'll be together."

"Do you want me to go?"

"No. For now, yes."

Things had been tough enough together. Now I had to face it alone.

After Torrington, I re-borrowed the fifty from New York and released one of the two sword fighters. Saleem doubled at selling tickets and sword fighting. Twice, his opponent's "razor-like blade" clipped his arm and once, nearly stabbed him in the leg.

We survived Bridgeport, then Derby. Saleem and I conferred. "Sam," I said, Sam being the nearest American name to Saleem, "we'd better think up something good or I'm done."

"Brother George," he spoke with his slight accent, "quit this thing now. You got your Tuzaneens somewhere like Cincinnati. Go join them."

"I can't leave everybody flat."

"Give them the week's notice," Sam said. "I'll run the show till Saturday."

"What'll you use to pay off?"

"I tell them you're broke."

"No," I said. "If I stay till Saturday, I can grind in a little business to make payroll. Besides, how would I get to Cincinnati – on Gyp? I can't raise carfare to New York City."

Sam, a roly-poly fellow, shook his head, saying, "Okay, I help."

It tied me in knots to do it, but I gave the performers and Washburn their week's notice.

By Saturday, things took a last nosedive. Receipts totaled less than payroll. I needed another forty to get to New York and Cincinnati.

Sam and I conferred Saturday morning.

"You're a fool," grumbled Saleem.

"Why?"

"Washburn tells you to work a blow-off. Why don't you do it?"

"Never!"

"Then forget blow-offs. Do a midnight show instead. Sell tickets all day. Fatima's one good girl. I bet she'll take a little off. No dirty blow-off. Enough to make everybody happy."

A smile crinkled his face. "This is your last night. You have nothing to lose but maybe a little reputation in Derby, Connecticut. In fact, it might help your reputation in Derby, Connecticut."

"You think we can get away with it if Fatima only strips half way?"

"Sure," encouraged Sam. "Take chorus girls out of silk skirts, put them in shorts. That's all. It's no good for every night, but once, try it."

"Get Fatima." I forgot this feature dancer's name, but by this time everybody referred to her just as Fatima.

I explained the idea, the need, and the procedure of the show to Fatima. "Don't take off too much – just enough so they'll get the idea. When you reach the vital parts, I'll start dimming the lights. Do a lot of wiggling and make all the movements with your hands.

"I'll turn the lights so low, the audience will never know whether you're undressed or not. Then I'll black out and that's the finish."

It sounded fine to Fatima. She agreed.

I plugged the midnight show all day and all night. Every roughneck in Derby, it seemed, bought a ticket at seventy-five cents a head.

By eleven o'clock, we peddled three hundred dollars' worth. Deducting Washburn's thirty percent, which he did on the spot, it left me two hundred ten, plus about twenty-five we'd netted during the day.

Saleem and I rejoiced. I could pay off and clear out with a clean slate – except, of course, what I owed him and what I owed New York.

While we were still congratulating each other on the plan, in walked Fatima's husband, towing Fatima.

"This is an outrage," he stormed.

Saleem looked from him to me. "Every Fatima in the world travels alone," he grumbled. "Yours has to have a husband."

"This midnight performance, it's vile and you should be ashamed."

"Don't be silly," I said. "I've explained it to Fatima and we have it all worked out."

"You can do what you want," he cried. "My wife will not appear in lewd shows."

"Wait a minute," I warned. "This is no lewd show. Your wife's under contract to me and you're not, so get out."

"No wife of mine makes a public spectacle of herself." The man screamed.

I pushed him on the chest. Into a corner he sprawled. "Oh!" cried Fatima. "How dare you hit my husband! He's right. I should never have worked for you."

Mr. and Mrs. Fatima disappeared.

The audience had assembled. They whistled, stamped their feet, and shouted. I yanked a girl out of the line, instructed her as best as I could, and started the show.

The customers howled, "We want Fatima! We want Fatima!" The line girls went on first, then the sword fight.

"That's the bird who sells tickets," someone yelled, spying Sam.

"Yeah," called a different voice. "I hope the other guy kills him."

"We want Fatima!"

Now my chorus girl wiggled on stage. I dimmed the lights. She bounced in a semi-circle. After her opening wiggles, she removed her skirt, revealing legs as skinny as they were bony. I winced.

"Boo!"

She removed an upper garment, which she should have kept on.

Somebody shouted, "You call that a human body?"

The dancer stopped mid-stage, facing the audience. Jeers and laughter replaced the booing. The audience stamped angrily. My makeshift Fatima bolted.

I leaped to the platform. "That's it," I shouted. "Show's over. Everybody out."

"Oh, no you don't," called an enormous customer in the front row. "We paid for a midnight show, and brother, you better give us one."

"Don't get tough," I warned. "You broke up the show yourselves."

"If she can't take it," the giant growled, "send out a real Fatima who can."

"I'm trying to be reasonable," I answered. "Anybody who thinks he's gotten gyped can have his money back."

"We don't want our money back. We stayed here all night to see the real thing. Bring it on."

I ducked a flying chair.

"Wait a minute!" I pleaded.

Another chair. "Get him, guys!" Four hundred roughnecks surged toward the stage.

A clatter erupted beside me. The oncoming mob halted. There stood Saleem, in full costume; sword in one hand, shield in the other. Bang! He slammed the sword against the shield. "Stand back!" he commanded. The crowd hesitated. He motioned me away.

I ducked into the dressing room and listened. "We don't want you!" they shouted. "We want that Greek."

Wham!…went the sword on the shield.. "Out!" ordered Saleem. "Out, everybody, before I cut you up."

"Mister, the Greek, not you…"

Swish! The sword whistled through the air.

"Wow – that was close!" someone yelled. "Let me out!"

"Get out, you…." Saleem growled. "Get out before I slash you good."

Chairs splintered. Men stumbled. Saleem beat the shield. They scrambled from the tent.

"Ha!" Saleem spat. "That teaches these loafers to call my brother 'Greek'!"

Chapter 18
Terrible Turk and the Forty Thieves

Washburn hid me in his wagon till morning, urging me to catch the early train to New York. Handing Saleem twenty dollars (all I could spare), I embraced him.

New York bound, I noticed two other refugees from Washburn's Carnival – One Lung and Fat Face.

One Lung, a geek, carried no known name. He wasn't short a lung, but suffered from asthma with its characteristic wheeze. With Washburn, he geeked in the snake pit. His half-naked body painted horribly, he rolled with the snakes (de-fanged), "charming" or "fighting" them by turn, always deadpan. Most geeks were human derelicts – alcoholics, dopesters, or demented. One Lung differed in that he was none of these and had some intelligence. At least he had the brains to fall in love with Fat Face.

Fat Face started her career as a hoofer with the carnival's "girlie" show, traveling with Washburn for many years. As she grew older, turning off even the Washburn audiences, she was converted by a process still a trade secret to a half-man, half woman.

Before love descended into his life ("descended" is the right word according to the story), One Lung's visage expressed nothing. One day, as he zombied by the rear of the freak show tent, Fat Face stumbled off a platform and rolled under the tent flap at the feet of the geek. Their bleary eyes and broken souls met. Thereafter, they sought each other late at night, sitting together, wordlessly. Gradually, One Lung learned to smile. At Washburn's, I'd talk to him, which no one else did. I enjoyed his return to life, his happiness so complete when

145

he left the snake pit to coil next to Fat Face.

Before I departed so unceremoniously from the carnival, I encountered One Lung behind the snake pit, tears soiling his cheeks.

"You crying?" I asked. He sobbed on. "What happened to make you cry?"

He might not have answered anyone else in the carnival. "I lose my job," One Lung wheezed.

"Lose your job?" I queried. "Why?"

"They say geke shouldn't look happy. I grin, so they go to find new geek."

Great heavens! I thought. Imagine firing someone because of a grin.

"Maybe," I suggested, "you'll get better work."

A picture of total defeat, he shook his head. "No, I leave Fat Face. Never get work."

"Take Fat Face with you," I suggested.

The overwhelming impossibility smothered him. One Lung rose slowly, color drained from his face, his eyes dull, shoulders sagging and dragged away to the snake pit.

The morning I fled the carnival, while Washburn and I were exchanging farewells, Fat Face broke into a freak show strong-box, helped herself to the hundred dollars she found, then kidnapped One Lung. They boarded the train without Washburn's detection, easy though they were to identify.

They asked where I was going. I told them, "To join my tumbling act."

"Does tumbling act need geek and Fat Face?"

I paused, "We've had strange performers," remembering Long John. "I don't think we can use your particular talents."

Impulsively, I scribbled Sam Gumpertz' address and number. "Promise me you will call him."

Fat Face tried to kiss my hand. I withdrew, not knowing which half would do the kissing.

I phoned my dismal *Streets of Cairo* report to Gumpertz, finishing with, "By the way, Sam, you'll be hearing from two of my friends."

"Who?"

"One Lung and Fat Face."

"George, are you daft?"

"A geek and a half-and-half. Find them work on a Coney Island sideshow. Be sure to keep them together. I know you can do it, Sam."

"Of course I can," he laughed. "Who gets the commission?"

"You get it on the half-and-half, I get it on the geek."

I directed the lovers toward Coney Island, myself to Jersey City.

I told Bess we were leaving for Cincinnati. She balked. "I won't like Cincinnati. I know it."

"That's okay. We won't be there long."

"We'll be traveling, won't we?"

"That shouldn't surprise you. Your sister booked it."

"Give me time to think."

"No, Bess, but I want you to hear a story about two lovers who stole to be together."

"What's their names?"

"Promise not to snicker?"

"I promise."

"One Lung and Fat Face."

She nodded a serious nod.

"Tell me."

I did, ending with, "I don't know if they'll live happily ever after. They will sure try."

She asked, "Do you think we have a better chance than they do?"

"We can discuss it on the train to Cincinnati."

We worked west to Chicago, landing thirteen weeks of fairs with Ed Carruthers.

In Salt Lake City, I met Danny Odom.

"I like your act," he announced, after shaking hands. "Ever been in a circus?"

"Brought up on them," I answered.

"Ever hear of Howe's Great London Hippodrome Circus?" he asked.

"You mean Mr. Mugivan's circus? Of course, who hasn't?"

"I'm Mr. Mugivan's agent," he declared. "He happens to be looking for an act like yours. Give me your route and your price. Make it a good one – we feed and transport, don't forget."

I asked and got four hundred for nine acrobats.

Alexander Pantages happened into town. "Watch out for Mugivan," he warned, as we chatted in his Salt Lake theater office.

Late in March of 1916, we joined Howe's on a fairground outside of Montgomery, Alabama. We had no sooner arrived when a man approached.

"Ever ride a horse?" he asked.

"Most of us have," I said.

"Come with me."

We followed him to the race track, joining thirty others sitting nervously on jittery steeds, half untrained colts, half unridden since Fall. A man in the center barked orders, which we tried to follow.

He stopped. His voice crackled through the air. "Take those elephants back!"

We all turned toward a heard of elephants crossing the field. Our horses sniffed, then whinnied. As though on cue, they bolted, reared and bucked, taking off in every direction. Riders were thrown on the track, in the paddock or on the wooden stage.

Five horses and three men lay on the ground. The fallen horses were promptly destroyed, two of the men carried to the hospital. The third, a young boy, lay dead.

I walked to the leader. "You should be shot, putting novices on horses like these."

"Shut up!" he shouted back. "Mind your own damned business! If people don't know how to ride, they got no place in a circus."

"I lived in circuses all my life," I snarled. "We didn't kill people to tame horses." I strode away.

Within an hour, a roustabout came for me. "Mr. Mugivan wants to see you."

"What for?" I asked.

"He says get to his car, and get there fast."

I was about to meet Jerry Mugivan, an Irishman known to everyone in the circus world as 'The Terrible Turk." In his elaborate, private railroad car, Mugivan, a large man, sat in a plush chair. Two associates hovered in shadowy corners. I'd been told of his "forty thieves." These looked like two of them.

Mugivan's fingers, feeling the beads of a rosary, bore no resemblance to the owner's voice. "I hear you're criticizing the way I run things."

"Not exactly, sir," I answered. "Your riding master used bad judgment, putting novices on untrained animals."

"He did?" His hands worked up and down the prayer beads.

"You ought to know," I said. "It cost you five horses."

His eyes widened. He beckoned to one of his men. "Find out what this crazy kid is talking about. You'd better be lying," he said to me.

"That isn't all. A boy died, too," I added.

"Regardless, Hamid," he said, "you learn to mind your own business. I run this circus. If you don't like it, that's too bad. Next season, hitch up with somebody else."

The man returned, bent down and whispered. Mugivan's eyes darkened. "Get him in here." To me, "Get out before you see something that will really upset you."

We never again saw the riding master.

None of us ate dinner. Soup, sweet potatoes and bacon. Nor did our appetites improve as the days passed, and the menu did not vary. Breakfast – oatmeal, a slice of sowbelly, a cup of black coffee. Lunch – baloney and grits.

The performers, old timers with Mugivan, swallowed it without much trouble. "You'll get used to the stuff," they advised. "Nobody died from it yet."

After two weeks, I looked for the 'Turk." Between the maintop and the menagerie stretched a twenty-foot section of tent called the "privilege room," with a full assortment of dice and card tables. Three thugs guarded each of two entrances. Only performers and accredited locals had access to this space. I found Turk inside one of the entrances, watching the games. Across his fingers moved a small nail file. Through his open shirt collar, I saw the beads.

"Mr. Mugivan," I said, "may I speak to you?"

A guard sidled up. "Turk, is this guy bothering you?"

Mugivan shook him off. "What's on your mind, kid?"

"Well," I gulped, "it's the food."

He kept filing his nails. "What about the food, kid?"

"Mr. Mugivan, sowbelly, bacon, grits and oatmeal – it's hardly fit to eat."

"Don't you like it?" he asked.

"I'm sorry to say I don't."

"And your boys don't like it either?"

"No."

Mugivan led me outside. "Mind your own business." His eyes hardened. "I warned you before."

As he started away, I spoke again. "Just a minute, Mr. Mugivan, this is serious."

He stopped. "You believe in religion?" I spoke quickly.

"It's the most important thing in the world." His fingers touched the beads.

"Well," I pleaded, "my boys have their religion, too."

A puzzled expression filled his face. "What about it?"

"All your cook house serves is pork. A Mohammedan isn't allowed to eat pork. My men are starving."

"Is that true?"

"It's part of their religion," I told him.

He spied Odom and called him over.

"Danny," he asked. "What do you know about Mohammedan?"

"Not much," he answered, "except that they're mostly Arabs."

"Do they eat pork?"

Danny scratched his head. "As a matter of fact, I don't think they do."

Mugivan instructed, "Put Hamid's troupe at a special table. Tell the cooks to prepare whatever he says they're allowed to eat."

The other performers' eyes popped seeing our meal that night – and thereafter. Lamb, beef, veal. I never explained.

During the first two weeks, we received no pay. Mugivan held back two weeks' pay as a deposit until the end of the season. That way nobody defied his discipline or ran out on his show. At the end of the third week, I headed for the pay car for my four hundred dollars. The cashier handed me eleven dollars, plus a white slip of paper with some figures on it.

"What's this?" I asked.

"Your pay."

"Eleven dollars?"

"That's your four hundred, less what your men lost in the privilege car."

I'd seen Absalom, Mustafa, and sometimes Shaheen and George Simon lurking in the privilege room. "They can't use my money for that!" I roared.

One of the guards walked over. "This guy giving you trouble?"

"Get him out," growled the cashier. "He's holding up the line."

Something hard pressed my ribs. "Move," ordered the guard.

Counting my eleven dollars over again, I departed.

Bess waited for me in our little compartment on the train. She took one look.

"What's the matter?"

"Here," I showed her the eleven dollars. "Our pay."

"That's awful."

We exchanged unhappy glances.

"Get out some paper," I instructed. "Write what I tell you, and make an extra copy for me."

Dear Mr. Mugivan,

This is to inform you that I object to your deducting from my pay the money lost by my employees in your privilege car. I am not, and never have been, responsible for their gambling debts. Please, in the future, do not reduce my pay for these purposes. Also, kindly restore what has been taken out.

Yours respectfully,

Bess handed me the original and copy, beautifully penned in her smooth secretarial scroll. I signed both, attaching the cashier's slip to the copy, which I ordered Bess to hide in a safe place.

Her eyes widen as I turned toward the door. "What are you going to do?"

"I'm going to give this note to Jerry Mugivan."

"Don't," she pleaded. "He won't hesitate to send his thieves after you."

Though everyone referred to Mugivan's henchman as the "Forty Thieves," I never counted. Everywhere I turned, I bumped into one. They operated the gambling games, acted as guards, bouncers, muscle men, fixers and thugs. Several carried guns.

Bess spoke the truth. If I overtaxed Mugivan's patience, he'd turn a couple loose on me. I would come back, if at all, with a broken head.

"Don't worry, Darling," I said. "He won't touch me."

I walked to the private car. The guard passed the word to Mugivan, then let me through.

Mugivan's eyes followed me to his desk. They turned to a small ivory crucifix.

"I expected you," he growled. "You apparently don't like our method of paying off."

"That's right, I don't, Mr. Mugivan." Though everyone on the show addressed him as 'Turk," I never called him anything but Mr. Mugivan.

"What do you plan to do about it?"

"Here," I answered, laying my note on the desk.

Mugivan read the letter, raised his head and laughed. "What are you trying to do, kid me?"

"No, I'm not," I answered. "I pay my boys in full. What they do with theirs is not my business. They can sleep in your privilege car. They can break your dice bank, for all I care!"

"That'll never happen," he laughed.

"I know. They have no right to gamble my money."

Mugivan slammed the desk with his fist. He rose slowly, leaned over the desk, stuck his chin in my face. "Nobody makes the rules around here but me," he said slowly. "On my books, your nine men make four hundred a week. The nine of you have that much credit in my privilege car on the train or the privilege room on the lot. One signature is as good as another." He sat down. "Whether you like it or not, Syrian boy, you're going to be deducted accordingly."

I boiled. "Then," I declared, "I'll keep my people out of your privilege car."

He muttered, "If you think you can. Those Moroccans of yours" (meaning Mustafa and Absalom) "wouldn't stay away from the dice if you jailed them."

I marched out, saw Habash and ordered, "Bring everybody to my car."

"They won't come," he scowled. "They're shooting craps."

"That's what I thought," I snapped. "You tell them I said *NOW*! Tell them anyone who hesitates will regret it, for real!"

Twenty minutes later, Habash appeared with five. "Mustafa and Absalom said they'd be down later."

"Did you give them my message?"

"Yeah," answered Habash. "They laughed."

"Wait here," I ordered, running through the jouncing train to the privilege car, where I headed for Mustafa. Seizing his collar with my left hand, I drew the right and smashed his jaw. Absalom shook. I drove a right to his face. They whimpered in opposite corners.

The game ceased.

"Get on your feet," I commanded. They struggled from their hands and knees. "Now, back to my compartment, fast."

As they entered, the others gawked.

"George," gasped Shaheen, "what did you do?"

"Nothing," I said, "compared to what I'll do if I catch anyone in the privilege car again."

"What?" Shaheen cried. "You're kidding. That's the only fun around here."

"See this!" I threw the eleven dollars at him. "That's all that's left after you guys had your fun."

"Aw, but George…"

"Forget the 'buts.' Mugivan says he won't stop your credit. I'm warning you. Don't gamble with my money. That's final."

Bess stared out the window. "George," she pleaded. "Stop your defiance. Mugivan will kill you."

I shook my head. "If I don't end it now, we won't wind up with a quarter."

"We don't owe anybody anything. We have our little bank account in Jersey City. If we don't make it this year, we'll get it next."

"No," I disagreed. "With a payroll of a hundred and ninety, I should be netting close to two hundred. Thirty-two weeks means nearly six thousand dollars. It's ours, not Mugivan's."

My orders reduced the gambling, but didn't end it. If I left the lot, they'd sneak to the privilege room. When I slept, Absalom and Mustafa, often joined by Shaheen and George Simon, crept to the dice table.

I threatened, I punched, I held long practices. I bruised Absalom's jaw again. The gambling stopped, then silently resumed. The Forty Thieves devised a spy system, a whispered detailing my every move.

My "persuasion" had a partial effect. Each week my pay was cut – now a somewhat tolerable seventy, eighty, ninety dollars.

Each payday, I wrote my same note to Mugivan, saving the copies, plus the cashier's slips.

Mrs. Mugivan, meanwhile, became fond of Bess. For hours at a time, while we were traveling, she visited with Bess in our compartment. A beautiful woman, devoutly religious, she never uttered an unkind word to or about anyone. Bess and I worshipped her.

Mugivan adored her. He set her totally apart from his circus life. A special cook prepared her meals. One of the more gentlemanly thieves attended her needs, saw that no one disturbed her. Where possible, Mugivan arranged for the town priest to visit her.

She cautioned me about her husband. "George." Her voice settled through a room like snow. "You are young and impetuous. Control your anger with Jerry. He is set in his ways and you can't change him."

"Mrs. Mugivan," I answered, "your husband has pushed people around for years. Thank heaven he's religious, or Lord knows what he'd wind up doing. It's not fair to someone who only wants to earn an honest living."

"But that's Jerry," she whispered. "He's fervent about religion. When it comes to his business, he's like stone. Bess keep George away from Jerry. George, be sensible. You're not fighting one man, but dozens."

I steered clear of Mugivan till the middle of July, when I began to sense trouble. Habash, my understander, sulked. The two Moroccans avoided me like a leper.

Shaheen approached me. I hadn't spoken to him for three weeks.

"George," he said, "I've got to talk to you. Even if you are mad at me, you have to listen. I shouldn't have sneaked off to shoot craps."

"So what?" I snapped. "You did. You're still doing it."

"You've got to know this. Habash and the Turk are planning to take the act and throw you out."

"Ah!" I said. "I suspected that!"

"Habash promised to let us gamble our hearts out. Besides, Turk knows he can handle Habash any way he pleases."

I didn't say anything to Bess. She worried enough already.

In Ephrata, Pennsylvania, I pocketed my little notes and pay receipts.

"Where are you going?" Bess asked.

"To attach the show," I announced.

"Oh, no," Bess gasped. "They'll shoot you!"

"Don't worry," I told her. "The law is bigger than Mugivan."

The law might be bigger than Mugivan, but not in Ephrata. My lawyer phoned the sheriff. He hung up, shaking his head.

"The sheriff won't touch him with a ten-foot pole," he told me. "Says he'd rather serve the mayor. Mugivan must be dynamite."

"He is," I admitted. "He carries forty thieves and I guess they fix every town. What should I do?"

He studied my notes. "It's good paper." He remarked. "Should be able to make any attachment stick. Here's an attorney in Harrisburg. Tell him I sent you. I suggest he get you an attachment outside Harrisburg. For heaven's sake, forget the pay wagon, forget equipment. Get a lien on the train. Anything else, and this monster will walk out from under."

I thanked him and shook hands. "If you collect," he said, "send me fifty."

"Glad to," I agreed. My slips showed over two thousand due me.

We played Harrisburg. Early in the morning, I visited the attorney. He evaluated my plan, agreeing to meet me in Homestead three days later. His fee – two hundred if we won, fifty if we lost.

The attorney, his first name was Fritz, met me in Homestead. I led him to the compartment.

"It looks tough," he stated. "This town is really under wraps."

"You brought the papers?" I asked.

"A hundred percent legal attachment on the entire train."

"Let's go," I said.

Bess sat by the window. "George, be careful."

"I will," I assured her. "I've got the law on my side." The law…Fritz.

At the sheriff's office, Fritz threw the paper on his desk. "I want this served."

The sheriff adjusted his glasses and began to read. He pronounced the name Jeremiah Mugivan. He dropped the papers. "No sir, not me. I'm not serving him."

"Look at the dateline." Fritz ordered. "Harrisburg. This is a Commonwealth document, not county."

"Nope."

"You know what this means?" warned Fritz. "I'll have you impeached for neglect of duty and you'll be cited by the Commonwealth for contempt."

Whether or not Fritz could do these things, he impressed the sheriff.

The old man trembled. "Will you go with me?"

"Sure, Sheriff, we'll both go with you."

The sheriff trembled as we walked into Mugivan's car.

"Here, Mr. Mugivan," the sheriff croaked. "This is for you. I'm sorry, I'm sorry."

The sheriff ran toward the door. Fritz grabbed him.

"What's this thing?" Mugivan demanded.

"It's – it's an attachment," the sheriff stammered.

"Forget it," Mugivan grumbled. "I've been attached before."

"You can't forget it," choked the sheriff. "This attachment's on your train."

"The train."

"That's right," Fritz broke in, "and, you can't move an inch till you've satisfied it."

"Who's stopping me?" Mugivan wanted to know.

"Mr. Hamid."

"Let him try it."

"Mugivan," Fritz said, "you are no longer playing local politics. You're involved with the Commonwealth of Pennsylvania. If you move against this court order, state troopers will haul you in for contempt."

"Grab 'em," Mugivan yelled.

Three henchmen sprang at each of us.

Fritz calmly confronted Mugivan. "This violence will do you no good. As long as Mr. Hamid and I can testify, as long as the sheriff served you, strong-arming won't help. Besides," he added, "I've already notified the railroad."

"Well, you unnotify the railroad," Mugivan stormed. "Sheriff!" The sheriff stumbled toward him. "You never saw this paper, did you?"

"No sir, if you say so, Mr. Mugivan, I never saw it."

"Now…" Mugivan turned on me, "you are about to learn a lesson. Unfortunately, you'll never profit by it. You won't live to."

"As for you," he spat at Fritz, "there's a river running by Harrisburg. If I ever hear a peep out of you, you'll find yourself rolling along its bottom."

I knew Mugivan respected very little, but I never dreamed he'd disregard state law.

"Now, by God," Mugivan shouted. "I'll notify the railroad."

How Fritz maintained his poise was a mystery. He laughed in Mugivan's face. "My secretary warned the railroad you might try that. Only she, or I, in person, can clear you."

"Well, then," he cursed, "I'll call in the engineer and we'll run without clearance."

Whether he would have or not, I'll never know, for at that moment, Mrs. Mugivan, followed by Bess, burst into the car. Mrs. Mugivan fell to her knees.

"Jerry," she begged, "stop this. For the love of God, stop what you're doing."

"Leave the car, woman."

"No," Mrs. Mugivan sobbed. "I love you, Jerry, but if you go through with this, I'll leave now and you'll never see me again."

Mugivan, red with fury, now paled. He sagged to a chair.

"Get out!" he ordered his henchman. They hesitated. "Get out, I say!" They left.

Fritz spoke softly and carefully. "Mr. Mugivan, I don't know how far you would have tried to go, but you can thank that little crucifix that your wife stopped you. Railroads and state governments, not to mention murder, are dangerous things to fool with."

Bess clung to my arm. "Release the train," she whispered. "Please, for my sake, release it."

I spoke up. "Mr. Mugivan, I've got the say on when and if your train moves. I want to make a fair offer. You pay me what you owe me. In turn, I'll settle with my men in your presence. Whatever you have coming, I'll make them hand you – limited, of course, by what they have earned. If one of them owes you more, I'll see that you get it week by week. From this day forward, my paycheck is not to be reduced to cover their obligations."

Mugivan was silent.

"One more thing," I said. "Habash leaves the show. I'll send for an new understander."

"What if you don't find a new understander?"

"Then I'll do the understanding myself. It won't take me long to learn."

Mugivan's eyes narrowed. "I'll make *you* a proposition. I'll pay you, exactly as you specify. You think you're good enough to take over Habash's job. I say you're not. Two nights from tonight, I'll pull Habash off the stage. If you can hold the seven remaining men in 'tukul' (where the understander holds all the men on his shoulders) " and keep 'tukul' for fifteen seconds, then Habash goes, and I'll pay you for eight the same as you now get for nine. If you can't do it, Habash takes over the act, you pack up and leave."

"No sabotage?" I asked. "Nobody kneeing my neck, swaying the pyramid?"

"Nothing but guts. To satisfy you, my wife and your wife will be the judges."

"You're on," I said. "Fritz, write the agreements just as I outlined, plus Mr. Mugivan's twist at the end."

Mugivan's cashier entered with money and his deduction slips. One by one I called in my Arabs, Mustafa and Absalom collecting nothing, still owing Mugivan. Shaheen and George Simon settled with some to spare.

We signed the agreement. Mrs. Mugivan, Bess, Fritz and one other person witnessed it. I insisted on Mrs. Mugivan's signature to forestall Jerry's possible doublecross.

As we began practice, Bess regretted my decision. She said, "Mugivan knew you couldn't resist his challenge. Now you'll lose the act, or break your back saving it." I suspect she secretly hoped I'd lose it and get away from the hated Howe's Great London Hippodrome Circus.

I sweated and strained. For two days we practiced, not telling the acrobats, even Habash, the terms. They knew I worked on tukul for a purpose; to hold seven. Five came easy. I struggled with six. Absalom, the sixth man, slipped and the formation collapsed. His face told me he'd slipped deliberately.

I yanked him to his feet. With my open hand, I cracked his face. "One more trick out of you and you'll wish you'd never been born." Discipline became no problem.

Before the evening deadline, I sent Sweeney (number seven) to the top of the pyramid. It held, until my left leg bowed, collapsing the formation. We tried again, same result.

"That's all," I yelled, wandering back to the compartment and stretching out on my back.

"Bess, rub my left leg," I said. "I've got to rest for a while."

Her fingers worked into my thigh muscles. "Do you think you can do it?" she asked.

"I don't know. Maybe."

At the door, Shaheen.

"I'm rubbing George's leg," she informed him.

"Which one is it?" he asked. "Here, let me." His strong fingers massaged the knots in my thigh. "Puabla," he said. Nobody had called me that for ages. "I'm changing places with Pete. I'm going to do middleman."

"Can you?"

"Sure, and Pete knows my old position better than I do. Besides, I can do more good as middleman."

I didn't argue.

I ate little supper. Show time came. In the dressing room, I waited for our turn. I told Mugivan I'd explain the story to my men immediately before the show. I talked, they listened in silence.

"Tomorrow," I concluded, "you may be working for Habash."

The call came. We began the performance.

"Tres-flutes," I called. We executed the easy one. I looked at the box. Bess and Mrs. Mugivan sat beside Jerry, an ugly smile on his lips. Behind Mugivan sat Habash.

"Burge!" I called. In seconds, we accomplished it. Although for once I couldn't care, the crowd approved.

Three more formations. Then I faced Bess, who held the watch in her hand, and set myself. She tried to smile. She couldn't.

"Alley-oop," I called. "Tukul!" First Shaheen, then one by one the others, George Simon, Pete Cazzazza, Gloomy Gus, Mustafa, Absalom, and finally Sweeney.

Fifteen seconds, the longest period of time in the history of the world. 1 – 2 – 3 – 4 – 5… Bess held her hand outstretched, her eyes on the watch.

My arms strained, my back pulled with the great weight on my shoulders. This I could stand. 8 – 9 – 10… But my leg, my left thigh, ached. Pain stabbed me. The leg started to give.

Shaheen looked down, "Hold it, Puabla." He groaned. Slowly, somehow, in a way I'll never know, he swayed the entire pyramid, straining the seven men's weight off his left foot, away from my left side.

12 – 13 – 14… The leg held.

"You did it!" Bess screamed across the tent.

Down leaped the acrobats. No bow, nothing! They pounded me on the back. I kissed Shaheen as we ran off stage.

Habash left the show the following morning.

Mugivan stuck to his agreement. No more run-ins until the final day of the tour. After we were paid our last week's salary, for some unknown reason, the engineer began backing the train. The pay car, now at the very end, overlooked a deep gorge.

A roustabout walked through the train as it stopped. "Last pay," he shouted. "Everybody collect your two week's holdback."

"Well, this will end our tour with The Terrible Turk," sighed Bess. "Thank the Lord it's over."

I wandered to the end of the train. One of the thieves yelled, "Hamid" and the name of another performer. He admitted us into the car. Mugivan sat at a table, nail file working over his fingers, an open door on each side of center, baggage car style.

I watched as the cashier counted out two weeks salary for the other performer.

"Over here," Mugivan commanded him. "You owe two hundred and ten."

"But, Turk, I…"

"You heard me, two hundred and ten."

"Honest, Turk, I don't think…"

With a flick of his wrist, Mugivan motioned to two thieves.

"Out!" yanking a handful of bills from the man. The two thieves shoved the performer across the car, through the right hand door. A scream cut the air.

My stomach muscles tightened.

"Take a look," Mugivan said to me, grinning.

I peered through the right door, looking out over a fifty-foot embankment. The man lay in a heap at the bottom.

"Don't worry about him," Mugivan said. "He'll live. Now, look over here."

Two henchmen clamped the right door shut. I peered through the left to see a hundred-foot drop to a roaring, rocky river.

"He wouldn't have lived," Mugivan snapped, "if he'd been shoved out the left side.

"What's that got to do with me?" I asked.

"Go get your pay and we'll see."

The cashier counted out seven hundred and fifty dollars, the proper amount.

"I changed things around just for you." Mugivan growled. "Your agreement, dated July 18th, says no more deduction. I'm not deducting. I haven't touched your earnings since." He paused. "What you've got in your hand is April earnings. I have here three hundred and eighty-four dollars worth of privilege car notes from your men, these last two weeks. I gave them credit. Our agreement says nothing about April earnings, so pay."

I leaned toward the table. "Jerry Mugivan," I said, "you knew what we meant when we signed this agreement. Technicalities don't change…"

"Here's the agreement," he snarled. "You signed it. Now live up to it."

The henchmen shifted from their corners. The rapids roared below. I peeled off three hundred and eighty-four dollars. I looked into Mugivan's eyes. "Remember that amount," I said. "Three hundred and eighty-four dollars."

His laugh rang across the hollow car.

At the exit, I turned. "Turk, mark my words. A circus can be run by decent people. You think your prayers clean you out every night. You push people, steal and connive, washing the evil away with religion. You're all wrong, Turk."

"I'm taking a circus out next year. It won't be as big as yours, maybe not as successful. But by God, the Lord will be able to look on George Hamid's circus without being ashamed."

A strange pallor tightened his face.

"You!" he crackled. "If you go on the road with a circus, you won't last four weeks. Now get out!"

I walked away happy to be leaving by the same door I came in, his taunt ringing in my ears.

Chapter 19
Mine – All Mine!

I laid plans for my circus, placing the act (now the Abou Ben Hamid Troupe) in the casual hands of Shaheen, whose indifferent management of the troupe resulted in no reports. I hopped a train, tracked him down, and collected both report and money. Otherwise, I operated out of Bess's house in Jersey City, going from bleacher dealer to canvas dealer to straw dealer.

Mrs. Raab finally accepted me, not as her son (she had plenty of them) but herself in the role of mother. I told her stories of my childhood, of Uncle Ameen, of last summer with Jerry Mugivan, and also our plans to build our own circus.

"Good!" she exclaimed. "Run Mr. Mugivan off the road."

We laughed. Two years before she'd never heard of the "road."

My funds insufficient to swing the new venture, I borrowed from Christina. Instead of trains, which were expensive, I decided to use trucks and wagons. The heavy equipment, tents, bleachers and poles would move on trucks. The performers, animals and costumes would travel on the slower wagons.

One night, sitting at home, I cried, "I've got it!"

"You've got what?" Bess asked, startled.

"The name of the circus," I said. "Hamid's Oriental Circus, Wild West and Far East Shows Combined."

Bess responded, "Sounds too big for a small circus."

"No, Dear," I declared, "the bigger you think, the bigger you get."

Bess shrugged. "If you can survive that title, you're made forever."

Warren, Ohio, became winter quarters. We bought trucks and wagons. For my special tournament mount, I acquired the shiniest jet-black stallion I had ever seen. Bess named him Demon. I also purchased the daintiest of white ponies, pink-eyed with black eyelashes. Even a white mule.

Unbelievably, I came upon a rare golden bear, "Jim". He had been trained to box. He boxed gently and loved it. Jim and I became boxing pals. When I was worn out, I would walk to his cage, pet him and in return, he stroked my shoulder with his paw.

Organizing a touring circus created problems I'd never encountered – routing, set-up, tear-down, and estimating costs. I learned to hire roustabouts and riggers, workers almost beyond control.

Roustabouts drank. Riggers caroused. They wasted a day and a half setting up the tents, another day and a half tearing them down. Being only twenty-one, I punched only scant obedience into the crew.

To open in Warren, we needed to move four miles from the winter lot to downtown, where I'd schedule our first performance. I allowed plenty of time – two days. A week-long rain turned the winter lot into mud. I wallowed through the ooze to the tent. Lifting the flap, I ducked inside. Liquor bottles littered the ground. Five drunken craps games roared.

"Hold it!" I shouted. My voice didn't dent the tumult.

I waded into the biggest crap game, picked up the ringleader, and knocked him out. Nobody batted an eye. They kept right on.

The men gambled the morning away before afternoon work began. I battled the crews all night. By morning, we had the show loaded. As the wagons pulled away, a groom ran to me.

"Come quick!" he cried. "It's Demon – he's hurt."

I ran after the groom to the stable. There lay my black pet, wide eyes looking at me. He had broken his foreleg, the bone sticking straight through the skin.

All I could say was, "Go get a policeman." I sent another groom for a nearby vet.

The vet confirmed what had to be done. The policeman placed

the muzzle of his pistol at Demon's forehead and fired.

After a sick and sleepless night, I assembled my people on the new lot. My loafers had barely unloaded the equipment. Show time was eight-thirty. No chance.

I worked the men until three in the morning, finally raising the tent. I staggered to the hotel room and fell into bed. Bess took off my boots and socks.

"Well," I said, "we set a record."

"Go to sleep," she whispered. "What record?"

"The first circus in history to miss the opening performance in the town where it wintered. Looks like we condense a two-night stand into one."

Next morning, I was on the lot by eight. A dozen minor things required attention – cashiers, ticket-takers, change, sweeping, sawdust.

Although we played to fewer than four hundred people, I'll always remember the thrill of leading the tournament at the opening performance in my own circus. More nervous than my mount, I bowed to the audience, inhaled the smell of sawdust and horses and swelled with pride.

The audience liked the show and that evening the crowd doubled. If business doubled in one, it would be tripled or quadrupled in two. The lost day could not be reclaimed. We moved on.

My wagon/truck theory failed. Either the trucks moved too fast or the wagons dragged. If I traveled with the trucks, the wagons arrived late. If I traveled with the wagons, the truck men headed for a saloon, the trucks still loaded.

Though I had held off my opening till late April to beat the weather, it rained, then froze. One night brought snow.

At week's end, I nearly collapsed. We fell behind our paper on Thursday, played our Friday night town on Saturday, skipping the Saturday date altogether. By the end of ten days, my bank account emptied.

Matters worsened. The crews, untrained and unwilling, caused me to miss most matinees. Cashiers, ticket-takers and grooms grumbled. Some walked out. Only the performers remained loyal.

At the end of the second week, in McKeesport, Pennsylvania, W. H. Bean, head of the W. H. Bean Carnival, introduced himself.

"I've been watching that golden bear of yours," he said. "I'd like to rent him and have him box on my show."

"No," I replied. "Not Jim."

Bean persisted. "I'll give you a good price. Fifty dollars a week." He surveyed the mangy tent crew. "Besides, the bear certainly can't do you much good here."

"Your carnival reputable?" A silly question. Would Bean say no?

He peeled off fifty dollars. Though I hated parting with Jim, I figured he would probably be better off. Jim licked my hand as I bid him farewell. I scratched out a receipt for Bean, giving him my route.

I had hired two of the best advance agents I could find. One was Harry Thurston, brother of Howard Thurston, the magician. Without my realizing, both figured I'd fail and that when the crash came, the show would fall in their lap. Instead of beating the drum for the Hamid Circus, they spread gloom in towns we hadn't yet reached. Bill posters, printers, lot owners pounced, whether payment was due or not.

Attempting the two-fold job of hiding from creditors and running Hamid's Oriental Circus, I rarely slept. By now, I drove a wagon. When a stranger approached, Bess took over as I crept inside. When the stranger left, I crawled out.

My head spun. My eyes bulged. I set-up, staged the show, shipped my shrinking crews over the road. I had borrowed every cent I could lay my hands on, mortgaging the equipment to the last dime. The performers kept me alive by accepting half salaries, taking notes for the balance.

We battled and struggled, somehow keeping up with our paper. When the weather broke, we did business. Occasionally, we squeezed in our matinee – late, but still a matinee.

The money fled as fast as it came. I now dodged sheriffs as well as creditors. Bess invaded the box office, took the receipts, stuffing wads of bills into her dress to pay for our hotel, buy food for the cook house, plus a few of the un-sheriff bills.

End of the third week, we were scheduled to play Rochester, Pennsylvania; nineteen miles from Pittsburgh. It rained – not our usual downpour; but a steady Spring rain. I sat on the wooden wagon seat, black raincoat over my shoulders. The wagon clacked on the cobbles as we reached the outskirts of town.

My eyes rested on the wet rumps of the horses. They had become swayback in three weeks. Gradually, the bobbing heads of the animals blurred. Though I blinked, the blurring increased. A pressure seized my chest. My arms weakened, the rain falling as I blacked out.

The wagon stopped on the spot. Bess, lying inside, came to join me on the seat. I wasn't there. "George!"

The wagon behind halted. Two performers jumped to where I lay in the gutter and lifted me to my wagon. As Bess screamed, one of the performers covered me with a blanket. "Don't worry," he said, "your husband isn't dead, just asleep."

I woke up on a small hotel bed, sunshine streaming through a window. Bess sat in a chair.

"Rain over?" I asked.

She nodded.

"Better get going," I mumbled. "Show time must be close. We missed the matinee, didn't we?" I rubbed my eyes. "What the devil happened?"

"You passed out."

"Why the dickens didn't you wake me up?"

She sat erect. "George, let's give this thing up while we can still salvage a few dollars."

Sleep hadn't improved my temper. "Are you out of your mind? Quit now, after going through all this?"

"Things aren't improving. They're getting worse." She continued. "Find Shaheen, rejoin the act. In a few months we'll be out of debt."

"Not a chance," I snapped. "I'll go at least one more week, if I carry the show on my back."

"What's one week got to do with it?"

"Jerry Mugivan," I answered. "He swore I wouldn't last four weeks. I'll make sure he's wrong if I never do another thing."

Bess walked to the bed. "Can't shake Jerry Mugivan, can you?"

"It's not only Mugivan. We're going to survive this. My circus will pull itself to its feet."

I looked out the window, "What's the sun doing in the middle of the sky? Shouldn't it be setting by now?"

Bessie turned away. "I suppose you'd like to run the heavens, too!"

"No sarcasm. Am I cock-eyed? Shouldn't the sun be going down by now?"

"That was yesterday."

I narrowed my eyes. "How long did you let me sleep?"

"Twenty-four hours."

"Where are we?"

Her voice moved evenly. "Rochester, Pennsylvania."

"Where's the circus?"

"Here."

"How much did it take in last night?"

"Nothing. We didn't show last night. They couldn't get up in time."

"That's what I thought."

"It's set up now," Bess continued. "We should do business this afternoon and tonight."

"This afternoon and tonight," I said, "we are scheduled to be in Greensburg. Do you know what you've done? You've got us behind our paper."

Bess spoke. "Yes, and saved your life."

I trudged to the lot, mud everywhere. In the office wagon, I poured over the maps to figure how to make up the day.

We opened the fourth week, twenty-four hours behind our advertised schedule, to scattered crowds. We played Tuesday's town Wednesday, skipped Wednesday's town, landed on schedule late Thursday naturally missing the matinee.

I paid the performers a quarter salary, gave them notes for the rest, emptying our coffers.

Luckily, being a day late confused the sheriffs. Friday they caught up. A sheriff dug me out of hiding and handed me a summons. A printer in Pittsburgh, to whom I owed seven hundred and fifty dollars, attached the wagons and the trucks. The show couldn't move.

Mugivan's words burned my brain, "Four weeks."

Bess grabbed the summons. "You've come this far," she snapped. "Don't quit now!"

"There it is," I choked. "If I can't move my equipment, I'm through."

"James T. Carberry, printer." She read. "His address is printed right here. We'll go see him."

I shook my head. "What can I offer him? We don't own five dollars worth of anything that's free and clear."

"That's what I mean. Even what Carberry's attached won't bring him anything."

"You're right. We open at Heinz's lot, almost in his back yard, on Monday. If he lets us move, he has a chance."

We rode to Pittsburgh on the interurban. Carberry ushered us into his little shop.

"Remember me?" I greeted. "I'm George Hamid."

Carberry's smile went into hiding. "What are you doing here?"

"Asking you to let me move."

"I won't do it."

I explained his attachment was worthless, about the forthcoming two days on the Heinz lot, and the glowing possibilities of the coming week.

"No sir!"

"But, Mr. Carberry, you'll get first money." He shook his head.

"Listen," I took a shot. Everybody in the world wants to own a circus. "You can have ten percent of the entire show for two years." A sparkle lit his eyes, though his head shook no.

"By golly," I declared, "you'll make a fine partner – twenty percent."

"You're on," he agreed.

We signed a makeshift agreement. Carberry phoned the sheriff, releasing "his" show.

"One more thing, Mr. Carberry, " I announced. "Since you're my partner, advance me two hundred till Monday so we can move the show."

"What?"

"I owe you seven-fifty now. Two more will still be under a thousand. Don't weaken at this stage."

Carberry ruefully counted out two hundred dollars. I handed back fifty. "This is for straw and sawdust, partner. Have it on the lot Sunday afternoon. We set up Sunday for the Monday matinee."

Bess and I danced out of Carberry's shop. "The fifth week!" I cried. "We made it!"

Bypassing our Saturday night spot, we moved directly into the Heinz lot. Sunday noon, Carberry delivered the straw and sawdust.

Townspeople straggled through the grounds as the tent went up. Bess opened the ticket office, selling over a dozen seats for Monday's matinee.

Carberry snooped everywhere. By nightfall, he knew the name of every performer, making no secret that he owned an interest in the circus.

I worked till early in the morning, fell asleep in the office wagon until Bess woke me.

"Look out the window, George. Look!"

I pushed open the shutter. Men, women and children crowded the grounds. Two long lines queued from the ticket office.

I sighed, "It can't be. I'm dreaming."

"You're awake," Bess smiled. "They've been buying tickets for an hour. The matinee's selling out; maybe the night, too."

I jumped to my feet. "What am I lying here for?"

"Take it easy," Bess cautioned. "Carberry and Mrs. Carberry are selling tickets. I'm gathering the money every half hour and putting it in the safe. I've given Carberry two hundred and promised him the next two hundred he takes in. He's happy."

Both performances sold out. We kept one-third of the money, allotting the rest to back debts. We loaded up with steaks, strawberries, cream and cake for the cook house. We celebrated with the performers and the Carberrys.

I made a little speech, "Friends," I said, "you've stuck by through an awful run of luck. This banquet is the best that Bess and I can do. Things are looking better." I motioned to the lines at the ticket boxes. "This looks like another great day. There are great days ahead for all of us." I sat down.

The performers didn't respond. I was too hopeful to notice.

As I bit into my strawberry shortcake, a stranger crossed the grounds. He walked straight to the head of the table and flashed a badge. "George Hamid? Here are fourteen summonses and a box office attachment."

"Fourteen summonses?" I gasped.

Bess quickly leafed through them. Her gaze ran down the table. She dropped the sheets in front of her.

"They're from the performers," she gasped.

Tuesday's receipts went to the show people. Fortunately, Bess hid a hundred dollars on her person. The hundred would barely pay for the move to Duquesne Hill.

Tuesday night, while the crews tore down, Frank Bodeen, owner of the flying act, knocked on my wagon door.

"I got the performers together," he said. "We're lifting the attachment.

"Are you?"

"Some of us don't feel good about what we did. We chipped in a hundred to help you move to Duquesne. Here."

Badly as I needed the money, something inside me rebelled. "Keep it!"

On Duquesne Hill, my world collapsed. The S.P.C.A. condemned my still healthy animals The next day, strangely, the "condemned" animals brought respectable prices at a surprisingly quick auction.

By Thursday, the sheriff had more attachments than he knew what to do with. He closed Hamid's Oriental Circus, Wild West and Far East Shows Combined. I couldn't even enter my own office wagon.

I told Bess she'd have to go home to her folks till I settled things.

"On what?" she asked. "I have a dollar and a half, and I know you don't have that much."

"I couldn't match half of it," I admitted. "Should I wire Mother?" she asked.

"No, not that! I won't let them think I can't transport you from Pittsburgh to Jersey City!"

Who could I borrow from? I already tapped everyone I knew.

Suddenly I remembered. "Bess, do you recall in March I sent a shipment of baggage to Warren? I bought three railroad tickets and had them punched, thinking we were going to use them. We never did. Where are they?"

"We gave one to Aug," (he had visited us in winter quarters) "the other two are in the wagon."

"Where?"

"In a cigar box in the center desk drawer. I put them there in Warren and haven't touched them."

"I'll get them," I said. "One of those tickets would take you to Jersey City."

On Duquesne Hill, a deputy guarded the steps of the office wagon. I explained the situation.

"Can't get in," he decreed.

I pleaded, "All I want to do is send my wife home."

"Nope, orders is orders."

Burning inside, I wandered toward the Duquesne cliff overlooking the city, trying to devise a solution. I felt a hand on my arm.

A hooded monk from the college smiled at me. He shook his head and pointed toward the precipice. "Don't do it. That never solves anything."

"No thanks, Father. They offered me one with a rapids last fall. If I didn't take that one, I certainly won't go for this."

"I've seen you around that circus for two days," he observed. "I don't blame you for being discouraged."

"That's not all," I grumbled. "They won't let me in my own wagon to pick up a few personal papers." I explained about Bess and the railroad tickets.

"Where did you put the tickets, my son?"

I told him.

"Wait here," he said.

The monk walked off to the steps of the wagon. He spoke in a low voice for several minutes. The deputy rose, unlocking the door.

The monk reappeared, thanked the officer and strolled toward me. "Here are your tickets," he smiled. "I wish your wife a pleasant journey; for you, a happy conclusion to your troubles."

I thanked him profusely. Next morning I put Bess on the train, wondering how to pay the hotel bill and gather train fare to Chicago.

For four and a half weeks with the circus, I'd paid little attention to Shaheen and the act. He had sent no reports, no money. He rarely did. Where was he? A collect wire to the last address came back undelivered. I had to reach Chicago. There, I felt certain, the booking offices would give me his whereabouts.

No money, no Chicago. Without street corner tumbling, I couldn't even walk there. I stayed to see if I could salvage anything from the equipment.

On the fourth day after Bess left, a man strolled up to me in the lobby. "You Hamid?"

"I'm Hamid."

"Ever hear of a bear named Jim?"

I jumped to my feet. "Jim!" I cried. "That means W. H. Bean." I had, in the furor, forgotten about my bear. Bean hadn't paid me since the first fifty dollars. He owed me a hundred and fifty. "Where is he?"

"The bear's in McKeesport."

"Good. Is Bean with him?"

"I don't know who Bean is, but if you're Hamid, I have a warrant for your arrest." He handed me a summons.

"Arrest? What for? I owe some money, but I haven't committed any crime."

"Cruelty to animals. Some kids found the bear abandoned in your cage in a field, starved and dying."

"I can't believe it," I cried, horrified.

"I'm a constable. If you don't come, I'll put the cuffs on you."

"Where is he, Constable?" I pleaded. "I must go to him."

"I'll take you to the County Court House. The bear's wild. Nobody can get near him, least of all you. Tomorrow he'll be dead anyway."

I explained that I'd rented Jim to Bean's carnival almost four weeks ago.

"Tell it to the judge," he said.

The hotel clerk intervened, "Listen, Officer, this guy's not anybody who'd leave an animal in an open field to die."

The constable spoke, "What can you do if I take you to the bear?"

"He'll take food from me," I said. "I know he will. You think he's savage. He's not. He's as tame as you are."

"We'll take the other street car," the constable agreed. When we boarded the trolley, I told him he'd have to pay my fare. He frowned and produced another nickel.

At McKeesport, we climbed from the trolley. "This way," called the constable.

I stopped, "I need a dime for a quart of milk. If anything saves Jim, it'll be milk."

The constable reluctantly handed me a dime.

We bought the milk, walking from the town to a scraggly, rocky field. I spotted the cage. My circus color, chapped, battered, all the same, my colors. We approached the cage from the back. Only the words 'Hamid' and 'Oriental' could still be read.

We rounded to the front and I knelt down. "Gruff," came weakly from Jim.

The bear was slumped in a corner, his golden coat turned to a sickly brown. Sores covered his big paws. Foam dripped from his jaws.

"Jim," I called. "What happened to you, Jim?"

His glassy eyes rolled. I yanked the door.

The constable yelled, "Don't go in that cage. Are you crazy?"

I snatched the top from the milk bottle, lifted Jim's head from the corner. His paw fell across my shoulder. I touched the bottle to his mouth and poured. His tongue reached into the white milk.

Jim inhaled, shivered, and died in my arms.

After a while, I crawled from the cage. "Where to now, Constable?"

"Court House, I guess, Mr. Hamid. Was he really a nice bear?"

"Finest bear that ever walked this earth," I said.

Side by side, we ambled to the Court House. The judge had his overcoat half on as we entered.

"This is Mr. Hamid," announced the constable. "Here's his warrant. I don't think he should be put in jail."

The judge removed his coat and scanned the warrant. "Did he do this to a bear?" he asked.

"No, he leased it to a man who left it in a field."

"He'll have to put up bail or spend the night behind bars. I don't make laws; I only enforce them."

I'd never been in jail in my life. "But, your Honor, I...."

The constable interrupted. "Listen, Judge," and he repeated the story just as I'd related it to him.

"I know exactly how you feel," the judge agreed. "I can't do anything about it. The law is the law."

"Judge!" the constable's face lit up. "Suppose he gives the body to the Carnegie Institute. The bear's dead, and I'm sure he'd be glad to."

I nodded.

"If the Carnegie Institute accepts it, we can let Mr. Hamid go."

"Please call them," urged my constable.

The judge lifted the phone. I described Jim and he passed the description to the institute. He listened, then hung up.

"They'll take him, but you've got to keep him on ice for four hours till they pick him up."

"How much ice will it take?" I groaned.

"Fifty or sixty cents worth, if it's a big bear," answered the judge.

I turned back to the constable. "You've gone this far. Will you spring me to fifty cents worth of ice?"

"I don't know why I should," he grumbled. "Here it is."

I shook his hand. At the door, he stopped. "Hey, you."

"What is it?" I asked.

"You need to get back to town, don't you?"

I nodded.

With a sheepish grin, he tossed me a final nickel, saying, "Make sure you don't take the wrong street car."

Chapter 20
Desertion, Revenge and Epidemic

The despicable Bean was beneath my hatred. Jim's cruel death obscured my other troubles. Because I had forgotten him, Jim died and now belongs to a museum.

Breakfast had been my last meal. I couldn't make myself go to the hotel clerk. As I wondered where or when my next meal would come, the phone jingled. I managed a weak, "Hello."

A voice rasped, "You the gent who runs Hamid's Oriental Circus?"

"I am," I admitted.

"By any chance are you missing a white mule and a white pony?"

The gears of my brain meshed. The mule and pony disappeared ten days before Pittsburgh. I'd forgotten about *them* too.

"Your right," I answered.

"Well," crackled the voice, "they're here, right outside of Rochester. They ain't no use for ploughin'. I've tried it. If you want 'em, come get 'em. All you'll have to do is pay me for the feed I fed 'em." He gave me the location of his farm.

"I'll see you in the morning." I said.

I eyed the clerk. "Frank, looks like you're going to have to lend me another quarter. I've got to go to Rochester."

I couldn't afford supper, so I went to sleep. At six a.m., my stomach woke me up. I headed for the interurban.

By the time I reached the farm house, my hunger and despair almost did me in. I knocked on the door. A woman answered.

"You want my husband," she said. "Won't you please come in?"

She motioned me to a living room chair. I almost didn't make it, due to the aroma of recently cooked ham. I licked my lips. A tear rolled out of my eye.

"Young man, you look hungry," the woman said. "Haven't you eaten breakfast?"

"I haven't eaten since yesterday morning," I told her.

"My heavens!" she exclaimed. "You come right with me."

She fried me a huge slice of ham and three eggs. By the time I finished, I'd have scrubbed her floors. Meantime, her husband came in from the fields.

"If you're the feller who owns them animals, pay me the fourteen dollars I spent fer feed and you can take 'em."

"I'll have to owe it to you," I said.

"Nothing' but cash, son. I know you circus fellers."

His wife rocked back and forth in her chair, tapping her foot on the floor. "This boy hasn't money to feed himself, Pa. How can he pay you for the hay?"

"You believe he'll send me the money?"

"He will, when he gets it," declared his wife.

In a state of doubt, but not wishing to contest matters with his wife (for fourteen dollars), the farmer turned them over. I rode my white mule all the way to Pittsburgh, leading the pony. I headed straight for Riverside Stables, site of the suspect S.P.C.A. auction.

"I want ninety-six dollars for this pony and this mule," I told the owner. "They cost me over five hundred. You've got them for ninety-six."

Train fare, hotel bill, plus the farmer's feed and what I owed the clerk totaled eight-eight. I wanted a spare eight to insure against the now ever-present "unforeseen."

"I can't use them for anything but coal mines," declared the stable owner.

I gasped. "These beautiful animals in the coal mines?"

He nodded. Though it sounded phony, I was desperate.

"Even in the coal mines," I snapped, "they're worth fifty apiece."

"How do I know they'll work in the pits?"

"I wouldn't worry about it. The pits is the last place you'll put them."

"Eighty dollars," he offered.

"Ninety-six," I demanded. "Ninety-six is the price."

After half an hour, he paid me ninety-six.

Through a Chicago agent, I located Shaheen in Davenport, sent him a stinging telegram, in return receiving a twenty-dollar money order. I joined him.

"I never expected to see you tumbling again," Shaheen said. "What happened?"

"I lost the circus," I said, telling as much as I could bring myself to repeat.

"What're you going to do now?" piped Sweeney.

"What have I always done?" I answered. "Run an act. I can still do acrobatics. The attachments will take care of themselves. I'll pay back what I borrowed. Any better ideas?"

George Simon had one. "There are nine of us. We'll attack the constables, take back the circus, pitch in, and we can all run it."

The war had started in April with George Simon becoming "attack"conscious.

"You could enlist," suggested Gloomy Gus.

I laughed. "Fat chance paying off on a private's wages. Anyway, everybody says it'll be over by Christmas."

Talking about the war gave me an idea. I sent Harry Begar, a new member of the troupe, to find one-and-a-half by two-foot flags of nine countries. I sewed them across the fronts of our blouses, saving the American flag for my own.

We tried them in Davenport. The audience loved it. I sent wires to all the Chicago agents, requesting work for "Hamid's International Nine." Bookings poured in. We played eleven fairs, then theaters. By Christmas, though the war hadn't ended, I retired my debt.

Nan Elliott, manager of Pantages' Chicago office, sent for me. I asked if Pantages had forgiven me for joining Mugivan against his advice. He had. "Mr. Pan wants you to bring him an entire unit for twenty weeks, starting in February. You're to feature the International Nine, starring with Hamid's Tuzaneens. People still ask for the Tuzaneens."

"What type of unit does he want?"

"Circussy," she explained. "An hour and a half. He says you know his theaters as if you had built them. You can figure out what will fit and what won't."

"That shouldn't be hard."

"Go to it," Nan said. "Thirty-five hundred a week, and he knows he'll get his money's worth."

I constructed the theaters in my mind. Bess suggested certain acts. We composed shows, tore them apart, did it again, eventually evolving a program that would excite people, at the same time fitting the mechanical limitations of each theater.

We signed our acts, instructing them to meet us two days ahead in St. Paul. Aside from my circus, I had never attempted such an undertaking.

Our work paid off. Pantages delighted in the reports from his theater managers as we toured Western Canada, the mountain states, down to San Francisco. I settled my debts and, to Bess's delight, deposited several hundred dollars in our bank.

Danny Odom paid me a visit. We congratulated him on taking over the Hagenback-Wallace Circus. Mugivan, Odom and a few others had organized the American Circus Company, combining Howe's Great London, Hagenback-Wallace, and Sells-Floto circuses.

Bess and I declined Odom's dinner invitation. Shaheen didn't.

We closed the week in San Francisco, packed and trooped to the station. As the train moved, a shout rang through the car.

"Look!" cried Bess. On the station platform was Shaheen, plus four of my acrobats, waving good-bye. Running back, I found that only the new boy, Begar, Gloomy, and George Simon remained. The train rolled toward Los Angeles.

George Simon explained. "Danny Odom convinced Shaheen to take the act. He offered them a big salary and the run of the privilege car. He told Shaheen you didn't need the act anymore – you being a producer."

"Why didn't he ask me?" I snarled, furious at Shaheen. "He'd find in a hurry how much I need the act."

"That's probably why he didn't." There we sat. Next stop, Los Angeles. Command performance before Alex himself.

I impressed three athletes from the parallel bar act and two grooms from a pony act into my International Nine.

Within five minutes after our opening, Alexander Pantages entered my dressing room.

"George, I love you almost like my son, Rodney. Thank God you do the nicest tinsicas in the world, otherwise I couldn't stand these Tuzaneens. Do me one thing. Put your patched up Tuzanens second. Close with the bar act."

"By gosh, Uncle Alex," I said. "That's the solution. Why didn't I see that?"

Three weeks later I heard from Shaheen. "Dear Cousin," his letter read, "I know you hate me for stealing the troupe on you. I don't know what else to say, Cousin, except I'm sorry." If he used "Cousin" once more, I would find him and execute him.

"This circus is worse than Turk's. Everybody gambles all of the time. Odom cuts the pot more than Turk did. Besides holding back two weeks' salary, I've only been paid seven dollars."

"Please, I'll give you the two weeks hold-back if you let us come back. We play Rock Island next week. Please, we'll never leave you again. Shaheen."

"Throw it away." I told Bess. My fury holding fast. Every week produced a new letter from Shaheen. The boys added their pleas. In Chicago, Bess begged me to answer.

"Bess, if I answered one of those letters, Shaheen would be sunk. Don't you think the thieves go through every piece of in-coming mail? They do. He'd never get out if they got wind I planned to help him! If I do help him, it will be my way."

I had Bess phone the American Circus Company office in Chicago to find out which circus Mugivan traveled with. If it was Hagenback-Wallace, he and Odom together would be too much for me. Bess confirmed he wouldn't be near Dubuque, where Hagenback-Wallace closed a half-week stand the following day.

Bess wrote a few notes for me. I stuck them in my pocket,

boarding the train for Dubuque. Next morning I headed for the lot and found Shaheen in the dressing tent.

"Puabla!"

"Mr. Hamid, to you."

"Gee, George, I'm so happy I could kiss you."

"Spare me," I responded. "Get the men, fast."

When in five minutes they were assembled in the tent, I asked, "Do you want out of here like your letters said?"

They nodded.

"And give up your two week's holdback?"

"Sure," volunteered Mustafa. "We've blown most of it, anyhow."

"Sign these," I ordered. The notes Bess had written lay on the table. When signed, they would show that the acrobats owed me three hundred eighty-four dollars. "If you want to get out of here, sign," I said. They signed.

"Now listen, I'm only explaining this once. Get it straight. I'm avoiding you because I don't want anyone getting suspicious. See that woods over there? Empty your trunks of whatever you need. Wrap your stuff in bundles. One by one, casually carry them to the woods. After the matinee, meet me there. I'll have a car to cover the ten miles to the railroad station."

I left, wandering around the lot, then asked one of the thugs, "Where's Odom?"

Danny sat at his desk – not as big as Mugivan's, but quite a desk.

"Danny Odom," I declared. "I should sue you for stealing my act."

"I didn't steal them. I made your guys an offer. That's not stealing."

"When those so-called acrobats ran off, they owed me three hundred and eighty-four dollars. All I want is the money I have coming."

"I can't give you any."

"Oh yes you can. You manage this circus. You're holding back two weeks' pay – over five hundred if it's a nickel."

"We hold out pay so acts don't run out."

"So, hold back their next two weeks' salaries." I leaned over the desk. "There's a lawyer in Des Moines drawing up papers. I'll tie your train up so it'll never run again. If I did it to Turk, I can do it to you. What'll Turk say when you miss tomorrow's stand for a lousy three hundred bucks?"

"If you're pulling anything, Hamid, you'll be sorry."

He drew a checkbook from his desk. I wanted cash. If I insisted, he might suspect more than he already did.

I pocketed the check and walked downtown.

At five, I drove to the wooded section. Through the trees, I could see the tent emptying. One by one, two by two, the acrobats joined the crowds, ambling to the woods. Each picked up his bundle. Within five minutes, we were on our way to Chicago.

I still had to devise a way to cash the check. At eight the next morning, I entered the lobby of the American Circus Company building in Chicago. To go to the bank would be silly. Odom would certainly have stopped the check whether or not his acrobats had skipped.

"Has Ed Knupp arrived?" I asked the guard. Knupp ran the Chicago office.

"Hello, Hamid," he greeted. "What are you doing here?"

"Danny's in trouble."

"That's funny. I didn't hear about it."

"It's not the kind you'd hear about. He bought my act and says he can't use them without new costumes."

"So what? I don't have any costumes."

"He says you're to cash his check as soon as possible."

Knupp took off his coat, walked to his office. On his desk lay letters and telegrams. "The bank will take care of you in twenty minutes."

"No good. He told me to catch the morning train, or else. I'm to deliver the costumes by the night performance."

He sat at the desk. I threw the check. "Some costumes!" he whistled. "Three hundred and eighty-four dollars."

"Danny wants the best."

"Aren't you in an awful hurry?" he asked.

"Maybe," I admitted. "Think what's going to happen if I miss the train."

"Okay, okay. Take it easy." He pulled a steel drawer out of the wall, counting out three eight-four. I thanked Knupp, strolling through the door.

His voice rang out. "Hamid, come back here. This telegram…."

Down the stairs I flew, disappearing into the Clark Street rush-hour crowd.

Despite my previous woes, I now owned two acrobatic troupes. Each played a fair route. I disbanded one because the draft cut into both. Although I fell into the "married" classification and Bess now carried our first child, my turn could not be too far away.

Far enough, however, for me in September of 1918 to accept Alexander Pantages' invitation to create another major presentation – forty-five hundred dollars a week, starting in October.

Bess naturally remained in Jersey City while I recruited thirty-five performers. In twenty weeks, I would net ten thousand dollars, enough to send my son through college, or my daughter through boarding school.

We met in Chicago and entertained for Minneapolis, our opening.

I couldn't budge the theater doors, I scrambled for the manager.

"Influenza. The theater's closed," he said.

"Good heavens! I have thirty-five people. What'll I do?

"Wish I could help you. Folks are dying all over town. Others are worse off than you are." I wired Bess for the few thousand in our bank. Pantages sent money from the coast.

Accomplishing nothing in Minneapolis, we moved to Winnipeg. Things worsened. People donned masks, walking in the middle of streets to avoid each other.

In Calgary, we checked into the Windsor Hotel, finding that the theater had been shut down for three weeks. Pantages could no longer advance funds.

Next morning, a knock on my door. "You own this big show in town?" a man asked.

"Yeah," I answered. "Do you want it?"

"I'm from the Vet's Hospital. We ain't seen a show in a couple of years. If we get the police to okay it, would you perform for us outdoors in the middle of town?"

"I don't think they'll let you."

"They'll let us. We'll pass the hat, take in a couple hundred dollars. You keep half and we'll keep half."

"You get the okay and we'll do the show."

He secured the clearance for November the 8th, three days hence. On November the sixth, the paper blasted a headline that if the show went on, the city physician would put the manager in jail. He didn't want crowds, even outdoors, until the flu epidemic ended.

I tried to cancel.

"No sir," declared my veteran planner. "I'll handle this."

On November seventh, two headlines appeared in the paper. "HAMID DECLARES SHOW WILL GO ON." Next to it, "DOCTOR DECLARES SHOW WILL NOT."

I called my sponsor. "What's the idea?" I asked.

"You're not giving in to a stupid sawbones, are you?" he replied. "It's become a matter of principal."

Next morning, November 8th, the doctor crowded war news, dominion news, and world news off the front page, declaring that if the performance took place I would languish in jail next day.

The afternoon came. The vets rolled their wheel chair and stretcher buddies toward the Hudson Bay Store, where we set up our "platform" – a section of street enclosed by our ring curb. All portable chairs in Calgary circled the "stage."

People appeared from nowhere wearing masks, some coughing – at least four thousand. The performers outdid themselves. The people, masked or otherwise, cheered.

The entire cast assembled in the ring for a finale. As they bowed, I sneaked down a side street to the back entrance of the Windsor Hotel. By pre-arrangement, the committee met me there.

I expected the collections would exceed the two hundred anticipated by my veteran friend. Our share of four hundred and seven dollars surprised even me.

Then I waited. I wondered which would arrive first – the paper or the police. The doctor needed to work up his charges. Naturally, the newspaper came first.

I opened the paper, November 9th, 1918. "Armistice," screamed the headlines.

My show was forgotten, including the doctor, even including influenza.

Anguish followed that false declaration. Two days later came the real armistice. People threw off their masks and danced in the streets. Restaurants, clubs, theaters opened wide. Curiously enough, the influenza waned.

On November 15th, playing Butte, Montana, I sat chatting with Shaheen and Sweeney when a messenger brought in a telegram. Shaheen slipped him a dime, tore open the envelope, handing me the yellow sheet. "Another George Hamid joined your act today. Love, Bess."

Chapter 21
Fair Business is Good Business

We worked all summer on county and state fairs. I created a second acrobatic troupe and made a deal for two fair routes.

Bess and I loved the fairs. We did one or two shows a day and lived in the outdoors. During July and August, we kept house in a tent where clowns and other performers played with the baby. They sat him on ponies and mules and gave him a puppy. Daredevils and acrobats competed to baby-sit.

I played the great Canadian National Exhibition for the second straight time. I met Frank Wirth, manager of his wife's famous riding act, who suggested he and I might become super fair bookers.

"After all", he reasoned, "we've played almost every fair in the East. We know the men who run them. We know the value of acts, owning three of the best."

A telegram from Alexander Pantages interrupted my contemplations. He wanted me West as soon as I could get there.

Early October found me face to face with Uncle Alex.

"George, you enjoy my theaters, don't you?"

I nodded.

"You have been like a third son for me. I want you to join my organization."

"What job could I fill, Uncle Alex?"

He smiled. "General Booking Manager for all Pantages Theaters."

My head reeled. This was a career, not a job.

"You know," I warned, "I've staged some better-than-average flops in my twenty-four years."

I asked him for two weeks to think. This could be my big chance. If I could succeed as Pantages' booking manager, I might rid myself of the obsession to own a circus, to be my own boss. The title, the responsibilities, the prestige, the association with Pantages, all appealed to me. One doubt remained: Ameen. My only other boss had left a bitterness that even Pantages might not be able to erase.

By the time I reached Chicago, the fears had melted. I phoned Nan Elliott in Pantages' Chicago office and told her the good news. I took her to breakfast. To my surprise, I found her almost brooding.

"What's wrong?" I asked.

"George, it's wonderful. Only...only...." She looked straight at me. "You love him, don't you?"

"Of course."

"Don't take his offer. He feels the same about you. Once you join his staff, that will all change. He'll drive you. He'll chide you. Your idol will crash. In his own business, he's merciless. Maybe it's what makes him great."

"Nan," I said, "you can't mean this!"

She nodded. "George, you can't take it. You've attracted devotion by your individuality, not your submission. Now you'll be forced to submit. In two years, you'll probably quit."

Her glance sought a nearby table. "There's John Robinson. Ask him."

John Robinson, a great animal trainer and circus man, had known Pantages much longer than I had. In a daze, I approached him and sat down.

"George, what's on your mind?" he asked.

"I can get a job working for Alexander Pantages. Should I take it?"

He frowned. "You've been a protégé of his, haven't you?"

"He's done more for me than anyone in the world – except Buffalo Bill."

"My opinion," advised John Robinson, "is you will suffer. My advice, drop the offer without giving it a try."

I returned to Nan, bewildered.

"I'm sorry, George, but you're saving yourself future anguish."

"Well, it proves one thing. If Mr. Pan thinks I'm good enough to book for him, I'm good enough to book for myself!"

"Don't be impetuous," cautioned Nan.

Nan composed a wire for me.

Dear Uncle Alex:

People have been talking to me, and although I tried not to, I listened. Before they got through, they had changed my mind. I can't take the job. I hope you don't feel quite as bad as I do. Love, George.

"Nan, while that's the straight truth, it won't do. Why hurt him? I would hate myself. Try this…"

Dear Uncle Alex:

Much as I would love to build my career with you, I must decline. Bess's family insists we keep our roots in the East. A divorced George Hamid would be useless to you.

My thanks are yours forever. George.

We telegraphed the second version.

I think of what happened next in terms of a railroad – naturally enough, since I spent half my life on trains. A switch was kicked, routing me to another track.

Same railroad, different roadbed. George Hamid, Acrobat, became George Hamid, Booker. With a flick of a pen across a check, I became one-third owner of a fair (and circus) booking office with Frank Wirth and a thrill act importer name Herman Blumenfeld.

By a two-thirds vote, the company was named Wirth and Blumenfeld.. By another two-thirds vote, I became official road man. Before I could catch my breath, I found myself launched into the hinterlands in search of contracts.

I learned fast. I had to or go broke, a condition quite familiar to me.

I jumped the gun. Fairs opened in the summer, but booked their attractions the previous winter. Most bookers started on the contract trail in November. Armistice Day found me in Hinton, West Virginia. By Thanksgiving, I'd stumbled through a dozen nearby fair towns, gasping to New York with five fair contracts.

As a reward, my two partners refused to honor my expense account – one thirty-five cent breakfast, a two-bit lunch, and one eight-five cent dinner, making it plain such extravagance would bankrupt our company. Besides, I'd better get back on the road in a hurry. I didn't argue. My welfare depended on it as much as theirs.

I drew a blank in the Carolinas, except for a horse doctor named Dorton who bought a high act. I changed my course for Lehighton, Pennsylvania. Starting at Lehighton, a series of unpublicized meetings would be held. I figured if I could get the jump on other bookers, I might steal a few contracts.

As I entered the lobby of the Carbon House, I found what I hoped I wouldn't: three bookers – John Jackel, Fred Murray and Anita Goldie.

We exchanged unenthusiastic greetings.

Anita spoke first. "Why in the world these new companies employ broken-down performers, I'll never know. They clutter up the meetings and annoy everybody."

"You'll tolerate me for the few weeks till we go out of business, won't you Anita?"

"It's a free country," she said. "I'll tell you one thing. I'd hate to be Mae Wirth or your acrobats if they have to live on bookings you deliver."

"Don't forget to pity Cedora's Golden Globe. We're Eastern representatives for her, you know."

Cedora rode a motorcycle in a cage-like globe; a beautiful act. Everybody in fair business knew of her.

"Hamid," John Jackel said, "you could be Eastern representatives for Rudolph Valentino and it wouldn't save you."

The Lehighton meeting started. One by one they called us in. I concentrated on my two features. Being a partner, I set the prices. In view of the heavy competition, I chopped the mark-up on the Wirth family in half, leaving the International Nine price alone. My prices startled the committee. They saw one other salesman, closed the doors and conferred. Thirty minutes later, the secretary called us together.

"The committee has decided to accept," he announced, "the program offered by Miss Goldie." Anita beamed, sliding a sneer in my direction.

He added, "We have eliminated three of her seven acts." He

named the three highest priced attractions in her book. "The committee wishes to purchase and feature the two acts submitted by Mr. Hamid."

I turned toward Anita and boomeranged her sneer.

In the lobby, I said, "Anita, let's bury the hatchet and be friends. You've had your own way in these woods. Don't resent a little live competition. Come over to Western Union. I'll help you send your telegram." Road sales people promptly telegraphed commitment to their offices to prevent other members of the company from booking the same act for the same dates.

"I've wired in more bookings than you'll ever make." She answered. "I don't need your help."

Jackel joined us. "George, you and I should get together," he said. "Why don't we have breakfast tomorrow?"

"That's nice of you, John. I'd like to."

"Eight-thirty okay?" he asked.

"Fine."

I wondered where the others would go from Lehighton. My next listed meeting left two days open. Maybe they'd loaf around a day, then move on. Maybe Jackel was pulling a fast one.

"Any trains before eight-thirty in the morning?" I asked the telegraph clerk.

"Yep. West bounder at six-thirty. East at seven."

Which way would they be headed, I wondered.

"Mind if I lay this down here?" I asked, laying my hard-pointed contract pencil on the counter.

He didn't mind. I ripped four sheets from the pad, throwing them away. I removed the company's soft pencil, sat down in a chair and waited.

Anita entered. "Hello, Miss Goldie," I greeted.

"You!" she said. "What are you doing here?"

If I annoyed her, she'd write hard. "Just thought I'd check so you don't write in the wrong acts. After all, Mr. Melville…" (she worked for Frank Melville) "would feel mighty upset if you made a mistake."

"Humph," she humphed. "The only mistake I made today is talking to you."

She picked up the pencil, digging her message into the pad. After she left, I tore the blank sheet from her pad, bid the clerk good-night and returned to my room. I easily read her impressed scrip. It ended with, "Port Royal tomorrow."

I slipped onto the train for Port Royal and hid behind a newspaper. Murray, Jackel and Miss Goldie boarded from the rear.

"Ho, ho," rumbled Jackel. "Wait'll that punk comes down for breakfast and finds himself eating alone! I hope he chokes."

"I'm glad you gave him the shake, John," Anita said. "He gets into people's hair. I want to keep him out of mine."

Fred Murray looked like a preacher. "I don't know," he drawled, "that's a dirty trick to pull on such a young fellow." The other two laughed.

I rustled my newspaper, stood up and sauntered toward the rear of the car, stopping at their seat. "Good morning," I beamed. "Enjoy your breakfast?"

"You!" screeched Anita.

"Hamid," grunted Jackel.

I smiled. "Who did you expect, Rudolph Valentino?"

I had them so rattled I got the Port Royal contract, too.

While I was signing with the committee, my rivals disappeared. Had we been in Harrisburg, Reading or Altoona, I might have lost them. From Port Royal, they could only move in two directions and very infrequently at that. I reduced their possibilities to three – one where the secretary had promised to see me. I phoned the first two. No meeting. I tried the third, my friend.

"Why yes," he told me. "They called and I said I'd get the committee together. I didn't think there was any harm in talking to them. I promised you we wouldn't sign."

"Alone," I answered him, "you'd be right. One of those cuties will talk your committee into signing, sure as God made little apples. What time is the meeting?"

"Noon."

"Hold it off till three. If I get there by four-thirty, they'll still be talking."

"I don't think I…"

"You're my friend. Please do it."

"Okay, if it's that important to you."

Next afternoon, as I entered, Jackel was talking behind the meeting room doors. Anita and Fred Murray sat in the small outer office.

Anita groaned at the sight of me. She followed Jackel, flustered. She might have saved her breath. With the help of my secretary friend, I won the contract.

The following day, Anita rallied, snaring a beauty. Proud as a peacock, she led the parade to Lebanon, Pennsylvania, her stronghold.

We each tried to be last to make our pitch, on the theory that the most recent presentation stays freshest. Any advantage lay with the last one in.

The secretary, a good friend of Melville's, and consequently of Anita's, greeted us when we assembled in the hotel lobby.

"Who's first?" he asked. "The committee's ready."

Anita started to say something.

"Mr. Secretary," I interrupted. "Isn't it common courtesy for ladies to be first?"

Anita began again, "I think…."

"Fred," I continued, smiling towards Murray, "what's the rule book say?"

"Well, I suppose ladies always go before gent…"

"Anita," I bowed, "we concede."

She dug a hole in me with her eyes.

I kidded Murray into going next and won a coin toss from Jackel, entering last. With the acrobats as my feature, I launched into my sales talk, spreading out a strong program. The committee responded.

Then, the secretary pointed out, "That's a decent program, Hamid, but I don't see any real outstanding thriller." He casually shuffled my pictures that I had laid out on the table.

I told him the high act would thrill anybody.

"I mean something unusual. Don't you handle Cedora's Golden Globe?"

I couldn't offer Cedora because she was booked in a big Iowa fair the week preceding Lebanon. I had boasted to Anita about the Iowa booking and she tipped him off.

"You wouldn't want that act," I answered. "It's not the…"

A big Dutchman interrupted. "Maybe ve vould. Show us pictures."

I fumbled for the pictures of Cedora. What act would jump from Iowa to Lebanon, Pennsylvania over the weekend? Suddenly I recalled that the Iowa fair closed on Friday. Lebanon opened on Tuesday. I would hire a baggage car to pick up Cedora in Chicago. She'd make Lebanon by Monday night. Knowing railroads, I figured the cost on the baggage car, mentally adding it to Cedora's price.

"Cedora's a very expensive act and…"

The secretary spoke coldly, "Mr. Hamid, I don't think you want to sell Lebanon a show."

I looked at him. "I planned to save your committee a thousand dollars and at the same time stage the greatest grandstand show ever." I turned to the Dutchman "With Cedora in it, I can't save you five hundred."

He slammed the table. "Ve vant the show with Cedora. Don't ve, chentlemen?

The Dutchman picked up his coat. "Ve all agree. Dat's better dan voting," and walked out.

Anita exploded when I descended the stairs, contract in hand.

I took a seat. Fred Murray had told me earlier they had no meeting the next day.

"Let's stop acting like children," I offered. "You have no place to go tomorrow. I have. If you'll agree to stick together, I'll tell you where I'm headed tomorrow."

Fred Murray sighed. "We'd better agree. You're going to find out anyway."

Anita refused. "It's a trick. If he had a meeting tomorrow, he'd die before he'd tell us."

I turned to Jackie. "John, do you agree? Fred does."

I'm not faking," Jackie agreed.

I named the town. Anita boarded the train with us, still

unconvinced. When she found out there really was a meeting, she accused me of losing my mind.

I hadn't. I knew of only two upcoming meetings. I didn't dare lose track of them in Lebanon, so I brought them along. They were, after all, giving me a guided tour of the circuit.

Chapter 22
Build a Better Pyramid

We booked more than fifty fairs our first year, not bad, except too little profit for our triumvirate. Dividing the earnings three ways, we made less than any of us did the previous year on our own. I insisted we refrain from inflating our prices. Profit, I contended, could grow by increasing volume. Blumenfeld disagreed.

The second season saw our volume rise faster than our profit. Blumenfeld bowed out.

Wirth and Hamid Fair Booking Co. fought on. Something drastic had to happen to impact the industry. In January, I headed toward Calgary to bid for the renowned Canadian 'A' Fair Circuit.

Western Canada offered two circuits of fairs. Operating in June, ahead of the regular season, eastern as well as western bookers bid for one or both. To win the larger circuit, the 'A' meant a fine income. More than that, it meant instant prestige. Ed Carruthers, the Midwest's largest booker, had controlled it for years.

In the lobby of Calgary's Windsor Hotel, I immediately spied Carruthers as he spied me.

"George," he boomed. "What in the world are you doing here?"

Tall, forceful, a naturally dramatic man, Carruthers drew admiration, even from competitors. "You here for the 'B' circuit?" He continued, "Good luck. They need a change."

"Not 'B,' Ed. I'm wondering if the 'A' doesn't need a change."

Ed's tone hardened. "Others have tried. You might as well get your wings clipped."

I went to my room and reviewed my program, which listed every hit we owned.

Next afternoon, the committee heard all proposals. After my

turn, I retired to the waiting room and sat next to Carruthers.

"You know what happens now?" he whispered.

I shook my head.

"They call back one agent, stall with him for ten minutes, then they call me in and sign up. Happens this way every year."

Carruthers was half right. They called back one other agent – me. After they called him, to his surprise and my delight, they asked for me again.

"Mr. Hamid," said the secretary, "the committee is impressed with your show. What we're skeptical about is the price. How can you sell for less than the others and deliver the show you claim this one is?"

"You see, we operate a…" I stopped. They wouldn't want to hear that we operated a small office, with low overhead, and wanted the business badly. This approach would toss the deal in Carruthers' lap. "We have a large office," I said. "We base our prices on volume. Since we offer our acts long routes, we buy right. We already book most of the eastern fairs."

I resisted the temptation to tell them that Carruthers had been giving them "the business" all these years.

More questions followed. Carruthers again, then me. By midnight, we were exhausted. The door opened.

"Gentlemen," announced the weary secretary. "The directors have reached their decision. Mr. Hamid is awarded the contract."

For a moment my eyes blurred. I could hardly believe my ears. The 'A' circuit! This *made* us. I thanked everyone and pulled out my contracts, even though the stenographer had her coat on.

"Do we have to fill that out *now*?" she gasped.

"Take it easy, Hamid," said the secretary. "We'll come down and type it in the morning."

"I'm phoning my partner tonight. He's got to get it to *Billboard* by early morning. That's okay, isn't it?"

"Certainly."

The president suggested everyone go out for a snack. I refused, especially since I couldn't afford to pick up the check.

Carruthers stood nearby. "To prove I'm still a sport," he flashed a big grin, "I'll do the inviting. There's always next year."

I phoned Frank the good news, sleeping with one eye on the clock. Not long after dawn, I rooted myself outside the office, contracts in hand. The stenographer ultimately arrived shortly after the secretary. He looked at me.

"By gosh, that's right," he declared. "Nobody told you, did they?"

"Told me what?"

"After you left, Carruthers persuaded the committee to see the error of their ways. They signed with him."

I staggered to my hotel through a bottomless world. A day later, they sheepishly awarded me the 'B' circuit.

Entraining for the East, I read the ironic Billboard headlines. Next week would come the correction.

A week later, at the Pennsylvania Fair convention, I picked up the new Billboard. To my horror, it featured the story of the 'A' circuit's unprecedented reversal. I felt like a fool.

As I entered the hotel, before I could duck away, I encountered two committeemen from Reading. "Good heaven, George. What happened? Tell us."

By the time I half-finished, a crowd of fair men and showmen surrounded me. Before I reached my room, I had told my story three times. Instead of being the fool, I became a hero. People I hardly knew offered sympathy. The Wild West couldn't treat Eastern boys like that. Between recitals, I sneaked committees off and signed. Frank and I nailed some majors we never could have expected.

The pattern followed in New York and Ontario. Billboard converted one of the most crushing blows into the breaks I needed.

The next year, we hired two salesmen. One, Larry Boyd, weighed four hundred pounds, three times that of his perky wife, and had the warmest laugh and the deepest voice imaginable. As our second salesman, I hired Stuart Collins of Boston, returning an old favor due him from the Quigley leaky tent fiasco.

In 1925, John and Charles Ringling invited me to Sarasota, Florida, where their circus wintered. They had bought our importations ever since we started in the business.

"George, we didn't ask you here on a social call," John said. "Charles and I are sick of searching all over the world. We want to know if you'll do our booking for us."

"Exclusive?"

"Call it that. Except for an odd thriller once in a while."

"You want to buy the circus through me?"

John Ringling answered "yes," introducing me to his new road manager, tough, gruff Sam Gumpertz of *Streets of Cairo* days.

"John, you couldn't do better," I said as as I virtually embraced Sam.

Sam grinned as he handed me an envelope.

"George, I don't think I ever told you. Remember the Geek?"

"How could I forget One Lung and Fat Face?"

"He lost his job," Gumpertz continued.

I frowned, "Not again."

Sam smiled. "They promoted him to tent sweeper, the best in Coney Island. Before that, like you asked, I got them each thirty bucks a week for a year. Maybe you were kidding, but anyway, here's your hundred and sixty buck commission on the Geek."

I answered, "Bess will love it."

The Canadian National Exhibition selected us to supply its variety acts. Luna Park in Coney Island asked us for a twenty-week small circus. Other parks bought a full season of thrill acts. Eleven years before, with Uncle Ameen, I'd played Atlantic City's Steel Pier. Frank Gravatt, its owner, chose me to create an over-the-ocean stadium circus. We swept the East.

In the fall of 1925 came an announcement by the Midwest booking powers Carruthers, F. M. Barnes and John Simpson, of the formation of the World Amusement Fair Booking Association, a combine of booking offices designed to cover the entire country. We were slated to handle the Eastern States.

I busied myself with our clients, filing away contracts with all the big fairs. Carruthers and Simpson set the meeting for the Astor Hotel. The combine would lock up the East, along with the rest of the country. It would crush any agency that refused to join. Carruthers and Simpson would set policy.

I settled in a chair as they wove their tale. Carruthers, persuasive as ever, painted a glowing picture.

I interrupted him once. "What's our share?"

Ed beamed. "It isn't hard to read your mind, Hamid. Fifty percent of the profits on all eastern business."

"I should thank you? Except for your six eastern fairs, we already keep all of the profit from the East. We have forty-seven of next year's contracts signed now!"

Carruthers' temper shortened. "Hamid, we're giving you a chance to join one of the biggest operations in America. Otherwise, we'll wipe you out."

I declined. "You better start wiping us out."

In setting up its eastern office, World Amusement pulled a surprise. An old man named Bottsford, head of the Plattsburg, New York Fair, reigned as president of the New York State Associations of Fairs. On the theory that Bottsford could swing New York fairs, World Amusement hired his son, Bennie, as a salesman.

I decided to strike at the core. I left the office early one night. "I won't be in tomorrow," I announced to everyone in general.

"Will you be home?"

I laughed. "It wold be one of the few times since I joined this office. No, I'll be in Plattsburgh at their meeting."

My secretary screeched, "That's Bennie Bottsford's own fair!"

"It's Bennie's father's fair."

"If Bennie can't sell his own father…"

Bennie did *not* sell his father. Gently needling his father in front of his committeemen, I embarrassed the old man out of buying from his son. Folding the contract into my briefcase, the World Amusement Company folded forever.

Our bookings mounted – hundreds of fairs, dozens of amusement parks, plus four or five circuses. We branched to London, Paris and Berlin to scout European acts. We imported more than the remaining American offices combined.

Our name became synonymous with circus and thrill acts as we discovered the Zacchini family of human cannonballs, the Wallenda high-wire walkers and hundreds of others. For the Steel Pier, we perfected Carver's high-diving horse and a dozen more circus features.

We opened Pittsburgh and Norfolk branches. We entered a new field through a working agreement with Ralph Hankinson, the outstanding auto race promoter of the day. Through the years that followed, Ralph became one of my closest friends.

Wirth and I made money, and a lot of it. Frank invested his in a yacht and the golf course. I put mine in a theater in Queens and White City Park in Worcester, Massachusetts.

Chapter 23
Tumble

At the top of a business pyramid, I should have remembered how easily a pyramid can topple. Frank Wirth and I used the profits of our booking business to build another pyramid – one we didn't understand – an indoor theater.

We bought a plot of land at what promised to be "The Times Square of Queens", and built a gawdy, palatial vaudeville theater. Through no fault of our own, the Queens sewer scandal erupted, meaning the new Queens Boulevard would not curve past our door as planned. Then, *The Jazz Singer* appeared – talking movies pushing vaudeville toward its grave. We had counted on vaudeville acts with silent movies to draw Roxy-sized crowds. The crowds didn't come. The Great Depression did.

Wirth and I had depleted our cash. We mortgaged our business, our families and our futures to finish the Queensboro Theater. The debt harassed me for years.

Tension increased between Wirth and me until we split. I bought his share of the booking business – and he agreed to keep out of the business for seven years. Larry Boyd left me and went to a relative of Frank's, Phil St. Leon, who promptly changed his name to Wirth. That meant tougher competition than I had ever faced. I sued Frank Wirth for breaking his contract. I won the decision, but lost the battle. The court said he violated the contract; nevertheless, I still had to pay him.

I came within an hour of losing White City Amusement Park in Worcester, Massachusetts. By setting the park clocks back to Standard Time, I gained enough time to barely scrape together the cash for the late payment.

These troubled years were not without gratification. I had been able, before they began, to buy the home for Bess that we had long dreamed of. Although twice on the verge, I didn't lose it. A beautiful daughter joined the family. Staunch friends stuck by me through every crisis.

Most of my fairs stuck by me, too. The Depression knocked some out for good, shook the credit of a few more, but rural America and its major fairs remained.

In the spring of 1933, I received word that North Carolina had decided to abandon its state fair. This would be a body blow to fair business everywhere. I piled into my car with Max Linderman, a carnival operator, and drove south to see what I could do.

Max, the finest "carney" I ever knew, was no competitor of mine. He produced one of the three basic parts of any fair: the carnival midway. I handled the grandstand shows, with clowns, acrobats, animals, and now extravaganzas under lights. In the third part, the exhibits, lay the true value of a fair to its state. Prizes for agricultural displays stimulated greater yield and better farming.

Max and I both knew the North Carolina fair had deteriorated because it was riddled with gypsies and every part of the midway crawled with crookedness and corruption. The result – attendance dropped until the fair had lost an enormous thirty thousand dollars.

The Commissioner of Agriculture asked me to address a key luncheon attended by every important man connected with the state fair. I detailed the entire story – what was wrong with their fair and how to correct it by driving out the gypsies and crooks.

The results stunned me. They decided to hold the state fair, provided I would run it myself. It was a tremendous job, yet I knew it could be my road to recovery. Years ago, I had determined to own my own circus. I still planned to. Why not operate my own fair?

I signed a lease and agreed to run the North Carolina State Fair.

My first break came within a week, though not a good one. The *Raleigh News and Observer*, in headlines and editorials, screamed its objection to the fair being turned over to private interests, worst of all, Yankee interests. The poor Carolinians, the paper said, were being carpetbagged.

Back to Raleigh I went. Josephus Daniels published the paper and

I was determined to talk to him. I had met him years before, when Franklin D. Roosevelt (with my partisan help) stumped North Carolina for Al Smith's presidential campaign. As producer of the grandstand show at the fair, I helped Daniels escort Roosevelt on a tour of the grounds.

I pricked his memory, gaining an invitation to his office. Daniels explained that he knew the fair had been rotten and crooked in the past. He thought it would worsen with an "outsider" at the helm.

"If we Carolinians won't protect our own interests, how can we expect you to? If there's no one in our own state who can run a fair as it should be run…" Daniels said.

I interrupted. "But there *are* men in this state who can run good fairs. Over at Winston, they stage a wonderful fair. Down in Shelby, there's a horse doctor named Dorton who can operate rings around most of the fair men in the country. That's not it. By a strange sequence of events I did not initiate, I now have a lease and an obligation."

I voiced my determination to operate a clean, honest and entertaining fair. He believed me.

"Don't worry any more," he conceded in his slow, southern drawl. "My paper will boost you all the way, Sir."

As fall approached, papers all over the state featured our plans. Interest grew.

On Sunday of fair week, I arrived in Raleigh, drove to the grounds, and got the shock of my life. A dozen gypsies were firmly tented. I stormed to the office. The sheriff, of all people, had permitted them to set up.

Obviously, the "law" was not about to evict the gypsies. The office staff, a few tough performers and I tossed them bodily off the lot. Then, Max Linderman, who had an exclusive on the midway concessions, startled me with the news that fifteen of the worst left-handed "lucky boys" in the business had erected fixed wheels and dice where he was suppose to put his midway, again the sheriff's work.

We led Max's elephant, Ginger, to the row of concessions, where I gave the thugs fifteen minutes to clear out. In the face of jeering defiance, I pronged Ginger, who demolished the first tent. The owner rushed me. My experienced fist flattened him, convincing the others to depart, pronto.

When I returned to the hotel room, Bess looked worried. "Don't fight them. Let them operate," she said.

"How do you know about this?"

"I've had two phone calls. They said to tell you if you don't wise up, you'll be a corpse by tomorrow night."

I wasn't as concerned about my life as much as my commitment.

Next morning, I drove to the grounds early. In twenty-four hours (Tuesday noon) we were to open. I checked the gates, the concessions, every inch of the fairgrounds.

The exhibits looked beautiful. The midway sparkled. At the grandstand, my acts had arrived.

A little building caught my eye.

"What's that?" I asked the grounds man.

"The coroner's office. He and the sheriff take the bad boys in there. Sort of a jail right on the grounds."

I met the coroner and the sheriff, who greeted me with the warning that I was running the fair all wrong.

"You can't be partial," the sheriff said. "One concession's as good as another. You open the gates and let them poor gypsies back in – and them poor fellers you heaved out yesterday."

"They don't come back on these grounds – for you or anyone else!" I said.

"Now, now. We don't like violence," the coroner replied. "We understand you got a few threats already."

"How do you know?" I asked. "Nobody heard of them but me."

"WE got ways of knowing. You got to cut out bein' partial or we'll have to close the whole fair."

I laughed. "You're off the deep end. The State Fair Charter is a lot bigger than either of you."

The coroner's eyes darkened. "It ain't bigger than the law. We got a law on the North Carolina books allows us to close this whole fair tighter than a drum."

He tossed me a sheet of paper; a law passed in 1827.

"Yes sir, 1827. Ain't never been used, but it's as good as if they passed it yesterday."

In a daze, I returned to the office. If I didn't submit to their tricks, I'd be closed. If I did, I'd be ruined operating a fair no cleaner than last year's.

When I told Josephus Daniels, he could scarcely believe it. If the sheriff and coroner were taking graft from the gypsies and the gamblers, that ought to be easy to prove, he reasoned. I shook my head. They were much too clever to take fix money. I described the little jail on the grounds; how a thug would be brought in for some trivial offense; posting bail, the size of which depended on the crook's profits.

It was now too late for Daniels to accomplish anything through newspaper stories. He made an appointment for me with Superior Court Judge Harris.

The judge listened.

"This sounds fantastic. The two gentlemen are waiting in another room. Suppose we invite them in."

The coroner and the sheriff entered. The coroner became spokesman. "Good ev'nin', Judge. What can we do for you?"

"Mr. Hamid says you've got a little courthouse set up on the fairgrounds. Is this true?"

"Yep. Need it, too. Lots of fussin' goes on around there."

"How would you feel if Mr. Hamid keeps out the trouble makers?"

"We told Mr. Hamid to mind his part of the fair, so we'll mind ours."

"I see. Did you suggest to Mr. Hamid that you might close the fair for any reason?"

"If he keeps on discriminatin', we told him we'd be forced to do somethin' about it. Judge, you can't have no discriminatin' at a fairgrounds."

"By 'do something', I imagine you mean close the fair. On what authority?"

"By this law. I thought you might want to see it, so I brought it along."

The judge scanned. "This law is valid, all right, even though it couldn't be sensibly applied to modern amusements. Why didn't you enforce it other years?"

"Didn't have to. Nobody discriminated."

"I wouldn't say this law makes specific reference to discrimination. It merely provides the power to close amusements under certain conditions." He smiled. "From the list of conditions, you could close a church picnic."

"That's right, Judge. Prob'ly meant to give us law enforcers the idea to use our own judgement."

"That, Coroner, is where you presumed wrong. Do you imagine this law, or any law, was enacted to protect wrong doing?"

"No, Judge, but...."

"Is it an evil to prevent a criminal from executing his crime, a thief from thieving?"

Judge Harris' voice rose. "Is the whole banishment of petty thieves from our state fair a violation of a person's rights? Is it a conceivable form of discrimination?"

"Judge, you gotta look at it from..."

"You'll be looking at it from behind bars, both of you, if I ever hear of you molesting or threatening the state fair again – or Mr. Hamid, – or anyone else who operates it. I'll have you impeached, publicly disgraced and thrown into jail."

They stumbled over each other through the door.

"Mr. Hamid," Judge Harris said, "I believe you can forget about those two devils." He offered his hand. "I wish you the most successful fair in the history of our great state."

Bess rejoiced at the news. I fell into bed beside her and eyed the window.

"Nothing but rain to worry about for the rest of the week."

Tuesday dawned clear. Wednesday it showered a bit, but by evening it cleared. On Thursday, the traditional big day, cars blocked the highways for miles around. Thousands of people jammed the grounds.

By eleven p.m., with all receipts in and counted, I joyously drove downtown, announcing to Bess we had crossed the hump. "From here on, it's gravy!"

We talked for over half an hour in bed. Just as I dozed, Bess nudged me.

"What's that funny glow in the skies?" she asked.

I lifted the window shade. "Fire, I guess. Holy smokes, that's the fairgrounds! Call the fire department!"

All I needed was the fairgrounds to burn.

Bess spoke into the phone, learning the big exhibit building at the fair was afire.

I jumped into my clothes, while Bess called Max Linderman.

The two main exhibit buildings were built end-to-end, a thirty-foot arch between them. Beyond the second building stretched the tents, rides and shows of Max's midway. Exhibit building number one blazed wildly.

"Oh," moaned Max. "Oh, I'm ruined. Dis is de end of Max."

I grabbed a fireman. "Why don't they put the hoses on the other building?" I yelled over the thunder of the blaze.

"Can't. No water pressure."

"Can't the city give you pressure?"

"They're trying."

"Then chop down that arch," I screamed. "The fire will hop the arch to the second exhibit building. It's good-bye midway, good-bye fair."

"We couldn't chop that arch in two hours."

Except for the orange coloring, people's faces shown like daylight. To my horror, no one made a move. Back in the crowd, I caught a glimpse of a smiling sheriff and grinning coroner.

"George," cried Max, "I think I saw it leap to de arch! Look!"

I grabbed Max's arm. "Where's Ginger?"

"I don't know. Vot you vant to do, play with elephants?"

"Get Ginger over here fast with one of your long chains."

Max returned with Ginger and her trainer as the arch sparked. I grappled with the chain.

I called to the trainer, "Back up toward me."

With only a twenty-foot chain, we had to bring her within ten feet of the arch. I held my breath while the trainer pleaded with Ginger.

"Hold it," I finally yelled, climbing eight feet to the hub of the arch. "Max, hand me the chain."

I looped it around the upright, knotting it so I knew it would hold.

"Let her go," I yelled to the trainer.

He prodded Ginger. She moved forward. The chain clanked taut.

"Come, Ginger," called the trainer.

She slacked the chain, then surging, she hauled it taut once more. Creaking and groaning, something yielded. I prayed it wouldn't be the chain.

Ginger trumpeted. In a roar of sparks, the arch tumbled.

A cheer burst from a host of firemen, state troopers and carneys. The firemen dug a trench to halt the fire. Water pressure slowly rose so that by dawn the firefighters smothered the blaze.

Friday drew crowds as large as those of big Thursday. The blaze, with the news of Ginger's accomplishment, fascinated everyone.

On Saturday, I tabulated my figures. Not only did the receipts exceed my most optimistic hopes, I had another reason to be happy. I had finally made friends with an elephant.

Chapter 24
Upswing

North Carolina reestablished me financially. The legend of Ginger even helped to swell my booking business to the levels of the twenties. I discovered or created some of the greatest thrill acts in the world.

My closest, daredevil friend was "Lucky" Teter, idolized by millions. His career began as a test driver for manufacturers. He perfected stunts and organized an automobile "thrill show" crashing cars, rolling them, broad jumping them. Lucky gave me an exclusive.

One day, in Trenton, a sudden downpour slopped the race track before Lucky's rollover. The trick worked by running the left wheel up a ramp and throwing the car over to the right. Four times Lucky tried, unable to develop the needed speed as he slithered toward the ramp. Four times he skidded to a stop on the car's side. He fumed.

"Lucky!" I said. "Forget it! You've already given everybody plenty of thrills."

He looked me in the eye, said nothing and slammed himself into the car. The motor roared, the car careening in a full circle of the track. This time he managed to catch the ramp straight, shoot the left wheels up in the air and flip the car completely over. As he landed flat on his four wheels, the audience screamed.

Lucky embellished his performance further and further. In the automobile broad jump, he first landed on the track where he could jolt to a halt. Not satisfied, he make it tougher on himself by landing on a ramp where, without stopping, he had to keep the wheels under control. I naturally feared he might someday fail to reach the receiving ramp.

He had a close call in Charlotte, North Carolina, when he agreed to jump his car into a lake in the middle of the racetrack. He disappeared in a huge splash. We waited an endless two minutes before Lucky finally sputtered to the surface.

When Lucky decided to retire, after a final performance in Indianapolis, I congratulated him on his good sense. The fans filled the stands, Lucky giving them a rip-roaring show. For his closing stunt, Lucky placed a regulation-size bus lengthwise between the jumping and receiving ramps. With a wave to the audience, he swept away, speeding around the track once, heading straight for the take-off ramp. He swooped into the air, flew over the bus, but landed short. With a bomb-like crash, he nose-dived into the receiving ramp. He died instantly – at the wheel of one of his cars.

In 1936, I was asked to take over another state fair – the faltering one at Trenton, New Jersey.

"I can't do it," I said. "Reviving a fair is backbreaking. I did it in North Carolina for two seasons because I needed the money. Now I don't."

Someone suggested, "Buy the whole thing – fair grounds, charter and all."

"A hundred acres almost inside Trenton," I gasped. "I don't have that much money."

In spite of myself, I rode to the property, climbed to the top of the large grandstand and surveyed barns, exhibition buildings, coliseum and racetrack – a beautiful fair plant in sub-par condition.

The terms eased as weeks passed, until I felt I could manage the deal. A few days later, pocketing the deed and charter, I drove alone to look at *my* fairgrounds. I wandered through the vast state building, the Grange Hall, planning new layouts of exhibits. I walked to the carnival area, mentally evicting petty thieves from "grifters alley." I decided to invite a dozen prominent Jerseyites to serve on my board.

Then, to the livestock building, checking for needed repairs. I wandered toward two horse barns in a far corner of the grounds. Men hammered on the second barn.

"What are you doing?" I asked.

"Starting to rip her down," a man said. "It's old and rickety – might catch fire and kill some horses."

Advising them I was the new owner and wanted to check further before proceeding with the work, I waved off the workmen.

I stood in a horse stall, kicking at the dirt. Something wouldn't let me leave, something from a long time ago. I turned from the inside darkness toward the barn door, where sunlight streamed in. At the door, I looked upon a wide expanse of grass. In the distance was a large grandstand. I turned and looked into the shadows. My breath caught. In my mind's eye, I saw Shaheen and George Simon, asleep on the hay in the stall.

This was the barn "somewhere in New Jersey," where I had slept my first night in America.

I gave orders that the barn be restored. "Imagine!" I said to myself. "People tearing down a wonderful horse barn like that!"

The old sting of Hamid's Oriental Circus never died. Mugivan's smirk penetrated through twenty intervening years, though Jerry, by this time, lay in his grave. My old circus fever prompted me to bid on benefit shows, indoor circuses sponsored by the Shriners, Police and Knights of Columbus. When I won the contract I assembled fifteen or so acts to comprise what I fancied as "Hamid's Circus."

In Buffalo, I decided to bid on a major indoor circus. My only real competition came from Bob Morton, who had an outdoor circus in Texas and didn't need this contract any more than I. We went to dinner together while awaiting a committee's decision.

"Say," Bob remarked, "you and I would make a great team, with your connections and your big assortment of acts from all over the world – and my circus know-how."

I ruffled. "What's the matter with my circus know-how? Did you know that when I was twenty-one years old I organized the first circus ever to roll on truck wheels?"

"What happened to it?" Bob wanted to know.

"Bad roads and flat tires. I even lost a golden bear."

"Wow, " responded Morton, "were you ever ahead of yor time!"

We talked on. Morton, I gathered, didn't like lugging canvas through the hot dust of Texas, even though he had the whole state to himself. "George," he asked, "how about you and me making a deal?

We can be kingpins in the circus world, if we work it right."

We conceived of a year-round tour for a circus – indoors.

We shook hands, needing no written contracts. I was to organize and produce the shows; Bob would tour them, We finished dinner and returned to hear what the Buffalo Indoor Circus' committee had decided. The committee head, who knew Bob quite well, walked to him and said, "Bob, I'm sorry. The committee decided that this year the circus will go to Mr. Hamid."

"Hooray!" Bob shouted.

"Hooray?" echoed his friend. "Didn't you understand what I said?"

"Sure, you just booked the greatest combine on the continent – the Hamid-Morton Circus."

Sam Gumpertz operated the Ringling Circus until 1936, retaining me as exclusive booker. He then retired to enjoy life in Sarasota, Florida. Not able to cope with loafing, Sam responded to my call to Atlantic City.

On his arrival, I told him, "Frank Gravatt, who owns the Steel Pier, is taking over the Million Dollar Pier with me. We want you to manage it. For three months each year, you enjoy the breezes of Atlantic City, and the rest of the time, you can bask in Florida. The best part of it, Sam, is you don't have to worry about money. We won't pay you the whole time you're here."

"What kind of deal is this, George Hamid? Don't fiddle with me. I may be getting old, but I can still beat you at your own game."

He could. I'd seen him send shivers through a hundred roustabouts with one command from his powerful voice. He had stirred men to move wagons out of hub-deep mud holes, to lift gigantic tents under impossible conditions by sheer mental and physical strength of his command.

"You can beat me at almost any game, Sam. You wouldn't take a salary, so Frank and I are going to give you a piece of the company."

"Three months a year. That's all you get, plus I don't take orders!"

"Okay, I book and pay the bills. The operation belongs to you."

We met to sign contracts with Frank Gravatt in his office on the

Steel Pier. I looked longingly out of the window. "I wish we were dealing for this one," I said to Sam, "instead of the orphan on the other end of the boardwalk."

"She won't be any orphan starting tomorrow." Sam answered.

Frank had a funny look. "I'm not sure I want that orphan, I've decided to back off."

Sam and I understood. Frank owned the sweetest amusement operation in the country. Why would he want another pier, which was little competition in the first place?

Sam and I conferred. "I sure hate to give this up," I said. "With help from you, I'll go it on my own."

"How would you operate it? You book acts for Frank. Can you compete with him, too?"

"I'll run it the way he runs his pier. Bands, vaudeville, pictures. He's proved the formula. With Frank in, we wouldn't compete. Things are different now."

"In that case," answered Sam, "count on me."

With one eye on Steel Pier, I leased Million Dollar Pier for ten years, installed a fun house, renovated the interior, built a new marquee, buying fading or blossoming names for our theater and ballroom – Paul Whiteman, Artie Shaw, the Andrew Sisters, Vaughn Monroe and Glenn Miller.

We ran Gravatt a merry chase until 1942 brought the war's oceanside brownout.

At war's end, Gravatt, with the opportunity to buy two magnificent hotels, put his Steel Pier up for sale. Frank would never sell to his opposition, me. So my attorney worked on the deal, totally avoiding mentioning my name. For two months, he maneuvered terms with no success.

On a May afternoon, 1945, my lawyer called me.

"Come to the Steel Pier right away, George."

The Million Dollar Pier was a mile up the boardwalk, so I decided to walk, passing Child's restaurant, where Shaheen's waitress had given us full-course dinners for twenty cents. I looked at the sand under the boardwalk, where Shaheen, George Simon and I slept. George Simon was dead now.

I looked ahead at the gigantic structure of the Steel Pier; with its four theaters, mammoth ballroom, and its circus stadium half a mile over the ocean. I climbed the ramp, nodded to the gate man and entered the office.

I bid my attorney hello, sitting across the desk from him. To my surprise, we were alone. "Over thirty years ago," I told him, "I sat in this very office, in a bathing suit, dead broke."

I looked around the room. "Where are the others?" I asked.

"They've gone. They left these papers for you."

"What are they?"

"They're exactly what you wanted. Sign them." I picked up the pen.

"Wait a minute, George, "he said. "Sit on this side of the desk. It's yours now."

Chapter 25
Return of the Native

The following Spring, Bess and I traveled to Lebanon – my first return after forty years. At the last moment, we included Shaheen.

Our initial stop was Marseilles, where we had first encountered Buffalo Bill. A few days later, we watched the mountains of Lebanon climb the horizon.

"There it is, Bess," I said. "The land that gave you me."

"Did I ever tell you," I asked, "about the time Shaheen and I stood on the roof and threw rocks at the school kids?"

"Ten or twelve times."

"I thought so." I grinned at Shaheen. "Bess, you'd never believe what a devil Shaheen was.".

Hundreds of people lined the Beirut dock to welcome me. Relatives of all kinds and degrees sought me. Within twenty-four hours, my Lebanese relatives exceeded my previous estimate of Lebanon's population.

The President organized a state dinner and made a speech. "George Hamid," he said. "We of Lebanon are proud of you. We delight in your accomplishments in the wonderful American world of show business. You have done your name, likewise ours, an honor. As a symbol of our esteem, we present you with the Lebanese Cross, our highest award."

He produced a lovely gold medal from a velvet box and pinned it on me. For a moment I stood speechless, because of my emotion and because I'd forgotten most of my Arabic. I thanked him as best I could. Feeling more at ease, I began to retrieve much of my Arabic, resulting in my personal advice on how to handle the political situation in the Near East.

Bess tugged at my coattails. She smiled sweetly at the President, kicked me in the shins and whispered in my ear, "Thank heavens they don't understand English. You'd talk for an hour."

We visited Transjordan, Syria and Palestine. I sank hip deep in the River Jordan, walked solemnly through Bethlehem.

"George," Shaheen philosophized, "we had to become Americans to see the Middle East."

My biggest thrill came at the young orphanage, which Bess supports. Twelve of the boys presented an acrobatic act, specially prepared for us. Tears wet Bess's cheeks as she watched the kids form pyramids, turn cartwheels and somersaults. One little tumbler caught Shaheen's eye.

He said, "He's a natural. If we trained him, he might learn tinsicas as well as you. No, I guess not. Close, maybe. But never like you."

I wondered about that kid. His bright, alert face sparkled with eagerness. Shaheen discovered, to our amazement, that the boy was Ameen's son, born in Lebanon after Uncle returned to the old country to die.

The rare and wonderful vacation ended – a vacation made possible because my son could handle my business while I was away. He and my daughter are both married, have given me four grandchildren, including of course, a third George Hamid.

On the trip home, I meditated. Buffalo Bill had died in 1917. I occasionally visited his grave on a mountainside near Denver. Annie Oakley lived a plentiful life and passed on at a comfortable age. I haven't seen Long John, Pete Cazzazza or Gloomy Gus for years. Absalom, I was told, tried to impersonate an FBI man (for what reason I can't imagine), landing in jail. Mustafa married an American girl in Chicago, became a waiter, quietly raising several children. Bess's sister, Christina, married Juan and moved to Spain, where Juan suffered a crippling stroke. The stroke, the Spanish Civil War and near starvation made hers a life of hell.

"Uncle" Alex Pantages broke up his theater empire. He lived into the early thirties. Anita Goldie married a Hawaiian orchestra leader named Johnny Pineapple.

Larry Boyd, his petite wife, Birdie, leaving him for a conventional-sized companion, grieved himself to death two years after he returned to my office.

Jerry Mugivan stayed on top, or near it, until the day he died. I wonder if he made the heaven he treasured. Forty million thieves couldn't fix that for him. He might have squeezed in at that. His wife would surely carry a store of celestial influence if anybody ever did.

I wish I could talk to him. "Mugivan, meet my partner, Bob Morton," I'd say. "He and I operate a circus. It just completed its three hundred and seventh week, Mugivan. A lot more than the four you predicted. Bob pays his performers well and doesn't try to get it back cutting craps games.

"Last week, two days after payday, he loaned a sick wire-walker a hundred and ten dollars. I bawled him out, wanting to know when in tarnation he'd get it back. He shrugged his shoulders and laughed. What's to be done with a guy like that, huh? From wherever you are, Mugivan, take a look at our kind of circus."

"I'm not concerned about bringing Uncle Ameen's son back to today's America with us. He wants to be an acrobat. Mugivan. Imagine that! He won't have the tough time I did, because he won't run into Mugivans or even Quigleys or Washburns. There aren't many of you left in circuses today.....I'm sure my little cousin will have it easier than I did. But what do you think, Turk? Will he have as much satisfaction?"

The Christian priest who ran the school in Broumana, Lebanon, along with my classmates. I am seven years old. I am on the bottom left row.

From the first moment I saw him, I worshipped Buffalo Bill. When he spoke I listened attentively – even though I couldn't understand a word.

Annie Oakley offered me and my cousins our first real smile of American friendliness. With or without a gun in her hands, she was one of the finest women I've ever known. Thanks to her, I learned to read and write.

I'm Puabla, the little top-mounter at the head of the line, just beginning my career with Uncle Ameen (second from the right). Behind me are my cousins, Shaheen and George Simon, in that order.

Travelling the circus circuit around
1916 by wagons did not work out as I
had planned

Uncle Ameen, holding eight acrobats
in the big formation in acrobatics
known as the *tukul*. I'm the boy to
the far left, having progressed
downward one level from the top
position.

Bess at age 19 in 1915.

After Buffalo Bill had me learn to ride a horse, he put me in this Arab costume. Later, he made me director of the Far East troupe in The Ride of Death.

Old Minnie looks gentle enough here, but if I had been in the pony's position beneath her, I'd never have lived to tell the tale.

My Streets of Cairo unit ended in riot one night when we were playing Washburn's Carnival, and I came close to being lynched.

A typical travelling railroad circus around 1915.

Another *tukul* formation, shown here with me in one of my early stints as understander. I'm the one on the bottom, holding up the rest of the Tuzaneen troupe. The tumbler pointing to us is one of the traditional "flourish men."

I'm in the middle, with Shaheen on my left and Uncle Ameen on my right. This was taken in the early 1900s while we were traveling the vaudeville circuits as The Sons of the Desert.

Tumbling on the beach in Atlantic City in 1914. Shaheen's waitress girlfriend looks on.

(Above) We toured the Pantages vaudeville circuit in 1917 as "The International Nine." I'm in the center with the Stars and Stripes across my chest, George Simon is on my right (he's Great Britain), Sweeney is on my left (France), and Shaheen (Switzerland) is next to him.

(Left) Bess and I look much more confident than we felt during our early married days.

(Above) Thousands gasped as Lucky Teter drove his cars and himself in and out of "impossible" feats. Lucky, the greatest daredevil of them all, died when he just missed a jump and crashed into the ramp.

(Below) A dream come true. Jerry Mugivan didn't believe me when I told him I'd own a circus – but here it is – The Hamid-Morton Circus.

— GEORGE A. HAMID —
HONORS AND AWARDS
BY HIS PEERS

- Winner of the first annual Horatio Alger Award in the company of Cardinal Spellman and Bernard Baruch.

- Founder, President, and President Emeritus of New York's National Showmen's Association.

- Inducted into the Circus Hall of Fame within 48 hours of his passing – the shortest time ever, in all three categories: performer, producer, and owner – another first.

- Inducted into the prestigious International Association of Amusement Park's Hall of Fame.

- Elected to the First Annual Atlantic City Hall of Fame.

- Billboard Amusement Business published its centennial edition, honoring the live entertainment industry. The ten "Showmen of the Century" were chosen. Along with Buffalo Bill (ironically), the five Ringling Brothers (as one), Walt Disney and six others, George Hamid was named…

SHOWMAN OF THE CENTURY

George A. Hamid

– Part Two –
Episodes and Incidents from the Perspective of George A. Hamid, Jr.

George will still be called "George" and Bess will be designated "Bess," despite my never, ever, doing so in their presence!

In prior pages you listened to George's voice. Now you will learn more about George only I will be doing the telling, in my voice, of episodes I fondly remember.

Why and how did I write George's life for him?

Why? Because it deserved to be written.

How? Because my treasured Princeton literary award (see Author's Introduction) suggested that I might be capable of doing it.

My reward? Editorial approval, particularly the closing words of John Lardner's *New York Times* review: "*The book comes close to being the best entertainment ever supplied by an acrobat.*"

Having lived within the quick-paced, sharp-eyed, loving/angry world of George Hamid, I shall now, in my own words, present a son's eye view of his dauntless personality.

George. Me call him "George?" Never. Nor did I ever call Bess, "Bess." Since, however, that is how you know them, I will invoke executive privilege, first-name them, and hope that neither will in turn invoke heavenly sanctions against their only son, the one who could never gratify George by producing a single, proper, cartwheel.

The impossibility of mastering the awesome sideways, foot-to-foot, whirling tinsica years ago affixed itself clear and permanent in my non-tumbler's brain.

Chapter 26
The Ferry Boat Ride

George had no favorite song, perhaps because of his one-note singing voice.

Launching into these few pages, I am reminded of a forties recording that might do.

"Accentuate the positive,
Eliminate the negative,
Latch onto the affirmative,
Don't mess with Mr. In-between."

The validity of which could be demonstrated in instances such as The Ferry Boat Ride.

Our 1929 motor trip through Florida, the highlight of which, for me, was a ferry boat ride to St. Petersburg, on which vessel were carried not only George, his wife, mother-in-law and two children, but the entire 1928 Championship New York Yankees baseball team.

As I, then a Yankees worshipper, stood apart trying to recognize the players, some easy, some not as easy, George urged, "Go get their autographs."

"Oh my gosh, I wouldn't dare." George opened the back door of the car. Finding my fairly new baseball, he hustled a protesting me to the nearest player.

"What's your name, son?" asked George, who at thirty-three wasn't much older than the accosted athlete.

"Earl Combs."

"Where do you play?" was the next question. I, of course, knew...

"Centerfield."

"Will you autograph my son's baseball?"

Earl looked at it. "It's a little scuffed up. I'll try."

I trembled as George selected another, huskier Yankee.

"What's your name?"

"Lou Gehrig."

George thought for a moment.. "You went to Columbia didn't you? My brother-in-law, George Raab, was captain of Rutgers. You remember him?"

Gehrig nodded, whether to appease his inquisitor, I couldn't tell.

"Beat us, I believe."

"That's what LaLa says," George responded. "Will you sign my son's baseball?"

Gehrig signed opposite Combs.

Nobody needed to identify the big fellow wearing knickers buckled to long, thin legs. George pulled me towards the man, already legend, who was talking to an associate.

"Babe," George introduced. "I'm George Hamid. Shake hands with my son, George, Jr."

The Babe paused, then took my hand. Babe Ruth! I was shaking Babe Ruth's hand!

"Here, sign my son's baseball," George smiled.

Babe looked at it. "Combs, Gehrig, ain't no clean spot left for me."

My heart stopped. I would give the entire American League for his signature.

The Babe eyed his companion. "Twink, got a fresh ball?"

"Over there, in my bag," was the answer as "Twink" moved away.

"That's "Twinkeltoes" Selkirk. He'll play right field when I quit. His name's George, too. Hey, four out of four George's. Combsey, Lou, come here," as Twinkletoes returned. "You got to sign again."

As the hand that propelled baseballs more often and farther than people believed possible gave me the signed ball, George informed, "Ruth, you are a hero to my son."

"Hero? Me, a hero? Wow." The other three joined the Babe in a hearty laugh.

As we returned to our car, Babe Ruth called out, "Next time I go four for four, I'll think of the four George's."

Chapter 27
Pin A Rose On Me

An early September Fair in Reading, Pennsylvania. was one of George's favorites. He enjoyed the half dozen Pennsylvania Dutch board members, almost all of whom called him "Chawch."

At twelve, I relished a visit to the Reading fair where I once sped around the dirt track in the mechanic's seat of a race car, spewing dust, stones and roar, where I could get passes for the ten cent rides, eat candied apples to the horror of my silver braces, then drink pop to dilute the cavity threat of the apples' red goo.

Sure enough, on a September Tuesday of my earliest teens, George herded Bess and me into the front and back seats of his Lincoln (not my younger sister, she hated rides) heading west for a meeting with his pet committee.

George wheeled his car alongside the fair office, a George Hamid prerogative on traditionally sparse Tuesdays.

He silenced the engine, Bess informing us, "I have to see a few friends on the midway about my Sunshine fund."

The early afternoon disclosed a mere scattering of fair goers, only a few riders turning, rows of games manned by indifferent operators, working to few or no players.

I said, "Dad, I need passes, the rides are starting."

George responded, "I don't have any and I don't have time to walk to the other end of the grounds to get them."

"Aw, how am I going to go on the rides?"

"Here's two bucks." He handed me a dollar and four quarters. "You can ride yourself dizzy. Be back in two hours."

"Gee, thanks."

The route to the carnival perimetered the curve of the track, winding past a long row of games – numbered wheels, dart throws and B.B. pistols – side by side.

Waiting for more ride start-ups, I drifted toward the midway.

A lean gamesman hooked a finger at me. In a loud whisper he said, "Hey, fella, do me a favor."

I stopped, impressed. He hadn't said, "Hey, kid."

"I need help," the splinter continued, "There ain't many folks around today."

I could hardly dispute that.

"C'mere." He pointed to a large wheel.

As I approached, he ran his hand across the counter, where each colored number matched its equal on the wheel.

"You know how to play this?"

"Sort of," I answered. "You put a nickel on a number and hope the wheel spins to it."

"A dime," contradicted the wheezy one. "You don't have to lose it."

"You don't?"

"No," he explained. "This wheel's my baby. If I pull it just so, I know most of the time where it will stop."

I said, "Is the wheel broken?" He ignored the question.

"What I need is a tip! Some players. You can help me."

"How?"

"Nobody will notice when I point to a number. You put your dime on the number. You win. Don't pick up your dime. I add one, you add another."

"Why?"

"Other people will see you winning and come over to play."

"Why do you want everybody to win?"

"I don't," explained the now excited splinter. "Only you, because you're doing me a favor to start my tip."

I eyed the wheel. Fortune beckoned.

My benefactor asked, "How much you got?"

"Not quite two dollars," I fibbed, understating my true worth.

"Okay, fella, I'll give you change." He handed me ten dimes for my paper dollar, pointing to nine.

I dimed the nine, the wheel spun, slowed and stopped on nine.

The splinter produced his dime, I, my second.

He shouted, "Lucky winner, this wheel's hot today!" subtly guiding his fingers to three.

I loaded three with the four dimes. The wheel rolled a couple of times, looking for three, appeared to speed ever so slightly before gasping to a halt on three.

An old lady appeared beside me and chose her number. The splinter's and my dimes moved to seven.

Seven it was, to the old lady's chagrin. After a short scold, she wagered on eight. The hand fingered two.

He whispered, "Put all your money on this spin. I got to let the old lady win the next."

I dug out everything except one quarter.

"Here we go," croaked the splinter. "Where she lands, nobody knows."

Nobody, except the splinter, and now me.

The wheel slowed dutifully toward two, then somehow picked up enough speed to reach eight.

The splinter's darting fingers swept away my unbanked fortune.

"You had a good run, kid, even if you lost. Want to try again?"

I shook my head. I lost my money, and now I lost "fella."

He beckoned, " I don't want you to leave without nuthin'. I'm pinnin' this nice rose on your shirt. Take it home to your mother."

Almost $2.00 for an artificial yellow rose bud.

My one remaining quarter and I completed the walk to the rides, with no interference from the game operators. After two good rides, plus a little one, I retraced my brooding steps to the car.

"I'm glad Dad won't find out what I did," I thought. "He always warned me about carnival games."

Bess had already returned. I slid into the back.

George appeared, smiling his way toward us. "Good meeting, Bess."

He turned to me. His head stopped, the smile disappeared, then reappeared. I expected him to jam his foot on the starter and zoom off as he usually did.

"How were the rides?"

"Okay."

"How many did you go on?"

"A bunch. They didn't open up very fast."

"How many?" I said.

Bess frowned. "Why this inquisition?"

"What's that on your shirt?"

"A rose. A guy gave it to me to give to Mom."

"What kind of guy?"

"A game guy."

"Now, son, *how many rides did you ride?*"

"Three. How do you know?"

"When you left the game, did any other game operators bother you?"

"No. Not one, see." My words sounded good to me.

"None, right?"

"Gee, Dad, I don't remember any. Why?"

Bess shifted her frown to me.

George yanked the yellow rose from my shirt.

"That's why. That rose tells every other operator that you were suckered out of your dough, not to waste their time on you."

To Bess, "You want the rose?"

I don't know why, but I heard myself say, "Keep it, Mom. Please."

She placed it in her purse, "I'm glad it's artificial."

"Why?" hissed George. "If it was real, it might be worth a few cents."

Responded Bess, "When I put it on my dresser, it will remind him of his game skills a lot longer than a real one."

I still wasn't satisfied. "When I didn't win, the old lady did," I challenged.

George clenched his words. "He's your son Bess, not mine. My son would recognize a shill, even an old one. George Jr., that innocent old lady was part of the scheme to steal your money. My money, I mean."

His foot jammed the starter, the engine caught and the gearshift shot us eastward to the Holland Tunnel, across Manhattan, with an exception.

George drove alertly, aggressively, perhaps more so on that good-meeting-dumb-son day.

Emerging from the Holland Tunnel into lower New York, George violated an intersection, not in his opinion, but in mine, Bess's and the husky cop who fiercely whistled us to the curb.

A ticket, no doubt, this time.

George always contended he was never ticketed.

"Sure you were," I would assert. "Remember when we…."

George would interrupt, never permitting a conclusion. Therefore, his contention prevailed.

The policeman, pad in hand, advanced on George's open window, his face afire, fury pouring into the car.

"Where you think you're going?"

"Well officer, my son here…"

"You ain't going nowhere, that's where. I should throw you in jail, you idiot." *He called George an idiot!*

I thought, "It's a good thing the cop has a gun or somebody's blood would decorate the sidewalk."

"I'm sorry, officer, I really am."

Were my ears inventing this?

I whispered to Bess, "What's wrong with Dad?"

The cop licked his pencil point. "This is MY intersection. I don't let people like you dynamite through it." A pause. "Look at that black mustache. You must be a *Wop*. Are you?"

George urgently needed to avoid being a *Wop*.

"Sir, I'm Syrian."

The law enforcer's eyes widened.

"Them's the people that drive camels. No wonder you can't drive a car."

George's jaw muscles tightened and loosened. I sickened with frustration, wondering when George would explode and go to jail.

"Gimme your license."

George obliged.

The angry eyes perused the license.

"Hamid. Ain't never seen that name before."

"As I told you, Sir…"

Sir? Oh, no.

"I am Syrian, even if I can't help it. No more than you can help being Irish."

"I'm only half Irish."

"I know you're doing your duty. You can see I've been telling the truth," apologized George. "Like I told you, my son is sick to his stomach."

Indeed I was.

The cop looked at me. "You sick?"

I nodded.

"Well, Hamid," handing George his license, "if you barrel through my intersection again, I'll make you wish you was back in Syria."

The ticket. Where was the ticket?

As we crept away from the Irishman's intersection I asked, "Dad, how could you take that abuse? I never saw you do that."

George said, slowly, "He didn't give me a ticket, did he?"

"He should have given you two tickets," Bess declared.

"Ketchel," George muttered after a minute. He hadn't mentioned his boxing idol in a year.

"What does Ketchel have to do with anything?" I asked.

"He taught me there's a time to punch, and now and then, a time to back off."

My mind drifted to roses. Pink ones like the lady next door grew in her garden, red ones like my grandmother grew in summer, and especially the yellow rose resting in Bess's pocketbook.

Chapter 28
The Lady Next Door

When the family moved from Jersey City to Forest Hills, Long Island, Forest Hills was spacious, pastoral. Our house, next to last on the block, was separated from the community sleigh hill by only the attractive house of Gus Van, a friendly man who vaudevillized with his partner, Joe Schenk. After Schenk died in the mid-thirties, Gus continued as a single, later playing for us in Atlantic City.

We lived on Fife Street, with Euclid Street one block east and Gown Street a block west.

The Vans never minded that the kids from Euclid, Fife, Gown and elsewhere circled their property to trudge a hundred yards to the sleigh hill. Even though the devices we "belly flopped" on were sleds, nobody ever called it the "sled hill." In fact, none of us called the various "Flexible Flyers" sleds at all – only "sleighs."

The sleigh hill was perfect, so much so that we often prayed out loud for snow. It ran more than a quarter of a mile from its crest to the edge of Flushing Meadow's frozen bull rushes, as yet undisturbed by two World's Fairs, the Expressway, and one of New York's major airports.

In the middle rose a glorious bump that rifled the sleds four feet into the air, a dozen feet down the hill unless one fell off or was yanked off by a sometime friend.

Country, indeed. It belonged to all of us.

On the other side of our house, visible from Bess and George's bedroom, was a large, green hedged-in yard within which lay a flowered section 20 feet by 30 feet. A lovely arboretum, it rested directly under the bedroom window. In the warmer seasons, it flooded itself with beautiful and varied flowers. In winter, it resembled most other places, unfoliated and bare, except when it snowed. Then it sparkled.

Within the arboretum/snow place curled a stone walkway with metal rails on each side, accessible from the antique house, which was conveniently offset from our view.

Through the arboretum, a lady walked three hours every day. In warm weather, she wore taffeta, in the cold, a cloth coat with calf-length boots.

She was neither tall nor short, plump nor thin. Her walk was steady, somewhat halted – despite that, somehow graceful.

One day, looking out the window, I said to Bess, " Mom, why does she walk so much in her yard?"

"She likes it."

"How? She can't see."

"She can smell and she can feel."

I had often noticed the lady feel the flowers. Though she would lean to smell them, I never remember her picking one.

"I guess so," I responded, shaking my head. "She can't even hear."

"She can't speak either. That's why she does all her walking on the safe stone path."

By the early thirties, all the kids on Euclid, Fife, and Gown knew the lady's name. Helen Keller. No one approached her yard. We would run through everybody else's yard, but not the Keller yard, even on Halloween. None of us entered her house either, including the local adults. Were we spooked? Were we awestruck? Were we both? Or just frightened of what we might find in the antique dwelling of a deaf, dumb and blind woman?

One night, after supper, George left the house for about an hour. Two weeks later, he left for almost two hours.

"Mom, where's Dad going? He's suppose to stay home when he isn't on the road." I was fourteen years old.

"He's next door."

"With Gus Van? I'll go over."

"No," replied Bess. "The other next door."

"Helen Keller's? He's inside Helen Keller's house?"

Bess nodded.

"Mom, what's he doing there?"

"Talking to her, I guess, and to Mrs. Sullivan." (Helen Keller's companion and tutor.)

"How can he talk to Helen Keller when she can't hear?"

"You'll have to ask your father."

I did.

"Dad," I asked when he came home, "how can you have a conversation with a lady who can't talk or hear, or even see?"

"Because I want to, because I like her."

"You mean because you're sorry for her."

"No," he said, "because I like her."

I wouldn't be stopped. "How can you get yourself to go inside that spooky house? No one else from around here does."

"Don't say spooky. It's bright and they're cheerful ladies."

I wondered how a blind, deaf-mute could be cheerful.

Two weeks later, George beckoned, "Come on, we're going out."

"Okay, where."

"Next door."

I thought Gus Van's next door, putting on my jacket. Outside, we turned right, not left.

I pointed at the Keller house.

"There?"

George nodded.

"Gosh, I forgot, I didn't finish my homework."

"Finish it later." George was not to be defied.

He knocked on the door. Without waiting, he opened it. The house was bright.

We entered the living room. First a rustle, then a squeak.

"See, son, she knows it's me."

I wasn't remotely convinced.

A middle-aged lady emerged from a nearby room and walked straight to George, stretching her hand to his moustache, that firm carefully trimmed wedge of black bristle.

She touched his mouth, uttering strange sounds, nothing more than that, sounds.

"It's me, George."

Helen Keller nodded, breaking into a smile, her fingers never leaving the moustache.

"How are you feeling?" asked George. Helen nodded, then rolled up a sleeve showing a small arm bandage.

"Where'd you get that, the rose bushes? I told you to be careful."

She looked apologetic.

As yet, she hadn't noticed me. I was merely another aroma alongside George's.

She paused, turned her head and looked toward me through blind eyes.

"That's my son," George said.

Helen seemed not to understand. Miss Sullivan, who had entered the room, offered George a pad with an unusual pencil.

Using careful strokes, he printed, "my son." Helen slowly pulled his fingers over the words, then touched George on the chest with one hand, me on the chest with the other. A mild embrace followed. Because I was "Son of George," the mind and awareness of Helen Keller instantly accepted me. Without Helen's fingers leaving Dad's mouth, he told her about me, my school, how I could run faster than almost all the other junior high school boys, how I loved the girl up the street who didn't love me.

Helen frowned. I thought she might cry. She took the pad from the table and wrote. George read the words slowly.

"Tell him there are better girls up another street."

Everybody laughed, except lovesick me.

The neighborhood kids, as neighborhood kids will, quickly discovered my visit, demanding a report.

"Is it spookier than it looks?" asked Billy Galbraith.

"Do they have green mice?" a female queried.

"Do weeds grow through cracks in the walls?"

I told them it wasn't spooky at all with the lights on, that their mice, if any, would be brown, like everybody else's. I reported how Miss Keller "heard," how she 'spoke', how she laughed. I was too embarrassed to report that Helen Keller embraced me.

Winter came. I had accompanied George next door one other time.

On a crisp, snowy afternoon, George suggested the Keller house.

"Oh, no," I complained. "We haven't had much snow. Today the hill is perfect."

He walked to the Keller house. I dashed to the sleigh hill.

Perfect, indeed. The sleds had packed the snow into an exhilarating speedway. The "bump" outdid itself.

After a half hour, Billy Galbraith pointed over my shoulder. Approaching the top of the hill was my father, with what appeared to be a heavily clad woman, wearing calf-length boots.

"My God," I thought. "It can't be."

It was.

George, with Helen Keller, stood waiting for me.

"Go get the big sleigh from the garage."

The big sleigh was a six passenger, pre-war monster, imported from Jersey City when we moved to Long Island. It had five sets of foot rungs, plus a steering bar for whomever was lucky, or unlucky enough to steer.

"What for?"

"We're taking Miss Keller for a sleigh ride. She's never been on one."

Of course she hadn't ridden a sleigh. What deaf, dumb and blind person could be expected to.

"Dad, we'll kill her. Besides, it's too heavy for one person to bring."

Billy Galbraith, seeing my discomfort, volunteered, "I'll help you."

At the top of the hill, George organized me at the steering bar, followed by Helen Keller, himself, two neighborhood kids, and finally Billy Galbraith, who earned his reward by being a "help" to me.

I steered a slow course, far wide of the bump, ending in deep snow. George, Billy and the neighborhood kids tugged the monster back up. I helped an obviously pleased Helen Keller to the top.

"Well, Dad, you made it without killing her. You and Billy take the sleigh back."

"What do you mean take it back? That ride was tame. If you put it in an amusement park, you'd go broke. Is that all this fabulous hill has to offer?"

Billy piped in, "Gosh, no, if you go to the middle, you get a terrific ride."

"And," I added, "hit a bump that will throw this Mack Truck on its side."

George ignored me, asking Helen if she would like another ride. She nodded eagerly.

In the center of the hill we huddled. George pointed the big sleigh downhill. I was now official steerer.

"Dad," I protested, "this is crazy. If we kill Helen Keller, we'll go to jail. It's premeditated."

George, "You'll never get anywhere being a pantywaist."

"That's true, Mr. Hamid," called Galbraith. "He sure won't."

Galbraith didn't fool me. He wasn't there to help. He wanted to tell every kid at the private school where he went that he rode on a sleigh with Helen Keller, or, better yet, presided over her demise.

We assumed the same running order. I looked back at Billy. "Don't you fall off. If you do, this thing will fly at the bump." And to myself, "If I get that far."

Kids were belly flopping over the bump from all directions. We sat upright. We could see better. We could also flip better. I felt the hard snow, saying to George, who ignored me, "If she lands on this, she'll get a lot more than a rosebud cut."

I noticed a lull in the random belly flopping and yelled, "Go!" Shoving with our feet, we began our plunge into whatever fate and my two steering feet had in store for us.

Faster we flew, on snow packed into near ice.

The wind blasted at our faces, mine in particular.

In front of us "loomed" the bump. To our right, I spied a belly flopper speeding toward the bump. I thought, "here we go." The sleigher looked up, eyed the six-headed monster thundering toward him, panicked and barrel rolled out of the way.

I must have over steered because the bump launched us at an unanticipated angle. For an eternity we fishtailed right, tilted left, finally landing runners down. I heard a yell. There went Galbraith.

At least he held on until we reached the ground. We skidded semi-sideways, managing to stay upright until we sank into the deep, loose snow. Over we went.

As we rolled, Helen Keller's grip released from my shoulder. I scrambled to my feet, finding her buried, motionless in the snow.

Close to tears, I said, "Dad, I told you we'd kill her."

Helen stirred, then rolled on her back. Her hands reached for some snow to rub on her face. Then she laughed. A laugh of pure joy. Climbing to her feet, she reached for George's moustache, then pulled him into the friendliest hug I had ever seen.

George said, "How was that for a ride, Helen?" She nodded again and again.

I looked into the darkening skies. "No more Dad, please."

"Why? You're an expert steerer."

"I don't want to push my luck."

My unrequited, up-the-street love, ghosted through the dusk onto the crest.

"See you later."

I overheard the parting comment, "No more rides, Helen. We just lost our lovesick steerer."

Chapter 29
Kingswood Camp

George's winner instinct manifested itself early nowhere more emphatically than during parent's weekend at Kingwood Camp.

At an age when most kids ended their camp experience, my folks initiated mine.

Our summers had always been spent in Rahway, New Jersey (actually in diminutive Clark Township, its twelve houses spread over fifty acres). Grandma (Bess's mother) owned the bungalow where many an oil lamped, hand-pumped, outhoused, July-August guest had leisurely wandered through their 62 days. George dubbed the place "Mud Hollow."

Billy Galbraith, of Helen Keller fame, was returning to Camp Kingswood, Bridgeton, Maine for the second time.

"How about you?" asked Bess. "You ought to go to camp, be a better swimmer."

I had mastered the dog paddle, only after several attempts by young, Mud Hollow residents to drown me in the Rahway River.

"I'll go, Mom, if you say so."

After a wonderful sleeper ride, cinders and all, the Boston and Maine spit its New York contingent of thirty-odd former and erstwhile campers onto the tiny Bridgeton station. Two carryalls bumped us over a country road, down a narrower drive and through a half mile of woods to the main lodge. A large, grassy clearing sloped from the lodge to a lake, named Woods Pond, bigger than any "pond" I had ever seen – it stretched a mile across.

Escorted to our cabins, shown to our bunks, we were ordered to unpack, stow, then meet our cabin master, "Cousin Bill." His wife,

"Cousin Bert," not pretty, though attractive, won me. Not only would she sew our felt awards on our shirts (campcraft, swimming, etc.), but she had the nicest legs in the whole camp, maybe in all of Maine.

Kingswood was great. I won awards, learned to boil water in three minutes from scratch. After a period of self-doubt, I conquered the width of Wood's Pond, sidestroke, not dog paddle. Another patch for Cousin Bert to sew on. Great, except for Parents' Weekend.

Kingswood, as all camps did, or do, selected a summer weekend of primp for the parents of its various occupants, scheduling an engaging assortment of events.

Kingswood's hospitality weekend coincided with the Skowhegan Fair, one where George played some of his best acts.

On Friday, as I walked out of the lodge, I noticed all the kids curled into a wide, grassy circle.

They joined in a "Yay," apparently yaying me.

Billy Galbraith, now my cabin mate, nudged me, as I asked, "Billy, what's the yay for?"

"Don't you know? I guess it's a surprise. Your father is bringing an extravaganza from the state fair to the camp."

Kids, since time began, dreaded parental involvement with their peers. I was no exception. My consolation (if any) was I might (which I did) see a certain teenage juggler unto whom I had transferred my up-street adoration.

George, with Bess, led five acts, including my juggling heartthrob, into the clearing.

We greeted, parental greeting warmer than sibling greetings.

Everybody laughed, clapped and responded to George's less-than extravagant extravaganza. He instantly gained unofficial membership in Kingswood Camp.

My juggler and I tiptoed toward the trees for five minutes of handholding.

As parents, juggler and performers departed, George reminded, "See you tomorrow."

Bess said, "Not me. I'll stay in Skowhegan."

The annual Apple Fight centerpieced Parents' Weekend. I still recall lines from a camp song:

In baseball and in Apple Fights, we play the game to win,
If we win or tie or lose, we always try to grin.
Oh, jolly Kingswood, happy go lucky and free.
We're strong for Kingswood loyal forever,
With earnest endeavor… etc.

George never heard the song. The only words that applied to him were "endeavor" and "win."

Kingswood's blue and white colors, equally divided its juvenile population. I was labeled blue. Billy Galbraith, who scorned Blues, led the Whites.

George arrived, as feared, displaying an indescribable, powder blue upper garment, connected to barely matching knee-length pants. I said, "How are you going to hide in that?", hoping that no one would see him, yet knowing that everyone would.

The camp master collected us in the main clearing to pronounce the rules.

Blues glared at Whites. Whites glared at Blues.

"The battle is engaged when I ring the camp bell. The battlefield consists of the camp woods. Whites start down from the road, Blues up from the clearing."

Old campers yawned. The rest of us pictured the conflict area. Okay, not Antietam, but suitable.

"The ammunition is crabapples. The woods are full of them. You were allowed to pick twelve yesterday. Does anyone have more than twelve?"

Nobody confessed. Everybody suspected.

George, an adopted Blue, nudged me, "How many do you have?"

"Twelve."

"Dumb kid. Us Blues are doomed. You're the only kid in camp who doesn't have two dozen."

"If you are hit by an apple," continued the camp master, "you are finished, a killed soldier. All un-killed soldiers line up here when the second bell rings. Does everybody, including fathers, understand?"

"You bet!"

"Sure!"

"Let's go!"

"Whites, up the road. Blues, here. When the bell rings," he recanted, "Kingswood starts its Annual Apple Fight."

At the bell, George and I slithered into the woods.

"Stay way from me so we don't get ambushed," I ordered.

George stowed apples in every pocket.

"Use the trees to hide you," I further ordered.

Blues tiptoed uphill. We heard shouts from the upper road, the Whites devising a soon-to-be forgotten battle plan.

Crunch! An apple hit a tree between us.

The conflict erupted. "I hit you. You're dead. Go down to the clearing you dirty White."

A Blue next to me caught an apple on the nose. He began to cry as blood trickled from his nostrils and quickly retreated to the lodge.

I watched for Galbraith. I knew he yearned for one target, my father.

I spied him just as he spotted George. Hurrying my throw, I missed. Billy aimed, fired, and splattered George, center forehead.

I didn't miss the second time, appleing Billy just below the shoulder.

I would have missed him had he been less exuberant about exterminating George.

Billy paid attention to me long enough for George to whip out a handkerchief, wiping apple juice and apple parts from his face.

"I gotcha, Mr. Hamid. You're dead," screamed Billy.

"Whaddaya mean," said George. "You missed."

I couldn't believe my ears.

"I did not." Billy noticed the handkerchief in the right hand. "How come that thing's wet?"

"I was wiping off sweat. It's hot in these darned woods."

"You're dead. All dead," insisted Billy.

They noticed me. "You're dead, too, Bill."

"What do you mean, 'too'?" threatened George. "He missed me by a foot."

"Come on you guys, get out of here. I'm still alive." I ducked somebody's errant crabapple.

Galbraith spotted an undead White. "Here, here." Either the White couldn't aim or misunderstood. An apple whistled by my eye, catching Billy on the ear.

"Serves you right," sympathized George.

In the confusion, I whacked a crabapple into the White's stomach.

From tree, to underbrush, to big rock, to tree, I crept.

After two eons, the bell rang. Yells rose as the surviving campers trudged to the clearing.

I squeezed between George and Billy, the two still feuding.

"All the Whites who were not killed, step forward, " ordered the camp master.

Of the seventy Whites, less than a third took the step.

I was suddenly glad Billy did George in. If he had jumped forward in his garish outfit, I would have headed for the woods.

Twenty-two were counted.

"Now the Blues."

As I started forward, so did George. Billy grabbed one arm, I restrained the other arm.

"Mr. Hamid, if you go up there I'll have the Whites burn you at the stake so you'll know you're dead."

Seeing we both meant business, George acquiesced.

"You're just a bum sport Billy Galbraith, and you….," pointing a finger at me, "I don't know what you are. I think your mother made you over-honest."

They counted, "Eighteen, nineteen, twenty, twenty-one. The Whites win the apple fight."

George tossed me a faceful of scorn., "If you'd done what I wanted, the Blues would have tied."

"What about being fair?" I wanted to know. "What do you mean, fair? Fathers should have two chances. What do we know about apple fights? Even if he hit me, I would only be half dead."

George strode to the car. I sulked to the lodge. I called goodbye, adding, "Twenty-one and a half still wouldn't tie."

The next day tested my capacity for embarrassment.

George appeared in the powder blue shirt, this time attached to its lower garment counterpart, powder blue, mid-thigh shorts.

His stumpy, muscle-bulged legs rippled from under the powder blues with every step.

Short pants, except on children (and campers), were rare in the thirties.

"Hey, Mr. Hamid," called one of the campers. "I don't want to mix it with you. You got muscles."

Indeed he had, for all to see. Only the mandated father/son baseball game kept me from swimming across Wood's Pond.

Again, Blues vs. Whites.

I hid George in right field where nobody ever hit the ball. I didn't worry about him getting on base, his muscular construction restricted his swing to an arc from right shoulder to left knee, his overall coordination a defiance to baseball.

I placed George last in the batting order.

My plan worked. "Powder Blue" got no balls in right, striking out his first time up.

He did not strike out the second time.

With the game tied in the bottom of the fifth, the last inning, George came to the plate.

Blue voices implored, "Come on, Mr. Hamid. Get a hit. Smoke one. Get on base."

Not my voice. A tie would be just perfect.

Though George's staccato, north/south swing never varied, the pitcher's inadvertent toss somehow found the bat. The ball bounced by the second baseman into right field, George taking off for first. Did he run? No. He cartwheeled, landing on first, to the delight of the Blues, the dismay of his son, the awe of the right fielder.

Zoom. George flip flapped feet, hands, feet, hands backwards to second and, as the right fielder took much too long to throw, on to third, Galbraith territory. A yard shy of third, George left his feet in a full back-somersault through Billy's hands, where the ball had finally arrived, onto the bag.

"You're out," called Galbraith.

"Safe!" yelled the third base umpire (a Blue).

As the argument erupted, George headed for home.

Billy whipped a bullseye to his suddenly bewildered catcher. Bewildered because of a baseball impossibility, to wit, tagging out a base runner turning tinsicas.

George pulled me and a resistant Galbraith into a huddle of joyous Blues.

"Aka lacka ching, akalaka chow,
Aka lacka ching, ching, chow chow chow.
Booma laka, booma laka
Sis boom bah
Blue team, Blue team,
Rah, rah, rah."

I must have joined in the salute to Powder Blue. Why else would I still remember the cheer?

Chapter 30
Lover Lion

During the Depression, George and Steel Pier owner Frank Gravatt became friends as they innovated, contrived and concocted public surprises.

Such as marathon dances.

Shipwreck Kelly, the Flagpole Sitter.

A twenty-minute ride from Forest Hills to Long Island City Bowl to gasp at Primo Carnera whiffing Jack Sharkey to the canvas for the heavyweight championship of the world.

A visit to Carnera's dressing room.

Next day, a limo ride to Steel Pier.

Canera measured six and a half feet tall with a 44 inch waist and wearing shoes longer than my forearm.

"The forever Champion of the World" clarioned the *New York News* (Primo lasted one more fight).

Since Carnera spoke only Italian, we could barely grunt a meager communication until our arrival at the Pier four hours later. Crowds greeted the champ, flooding inside to watch Carnera spar with a conveniently available trained kangaroo (which, in the opinion of many on-lookers, won both rounds).

More public surprises, such as importing Zachini The Human Cannonball and, after two years on the circus end of the Pier, George and Gravatt designing its successor, The Human Rocket.

Resembling what they supposed was a rocket, tracking the cannon in design and mechanism, the device was to shoot its occupant across 70 feet of ocean, into a net on the outdoor stage.

Press and performers alike, including six Hawaiian Divers, crowded to the world premier of Circusdom's newest sensation.

The wisdom of shooting over water became apparent in the Rocket's first boom.

The mechanism welshed on its job, looping the human projectile only 35 feet, plopping him in the foam.

Four Hawaiian divers plunged into the sea, grabbing the fallen rocketeer. Using a rope and a life ring, they pulled him from his watery termination.

The Human Rocket act started and ended in one jump, not for lack of merit, but for lack of would-be rocketeers.

George blamed Frank, Frank blamed George. When the publicity erupted, each smiled and forgave.

Million Dollar Pier, the toast of the Twenties, had sagged in the Thirties as its owner Captain John Young, declined in health and theatrics.

The Showplace, now ripe for the taking, beckoned the two Depression-beaters.

George proposed to a seemingly agreeable Gravatt, "You and I should buy the Million Dollar and squelch the only competition."

Frank's withdrawing and George's proceeding have been recorded earlier.

In addition to populating the Ballroom of States with aspiring Big Bands, George, supported by the indomitable Sam Gumpertz, developed a circus area at the Pier's far end with bleachers on one side and a 50 foot access way across the Pier's tip to a large stage facing the bleachers. Between bleachers and stage, dipping into 20 feet of ocean, stretched the intricacies of the gigantic fish net haul, which four, salty seamen winched deckward, twice daily, to the delight of visitors and the profit of nearby fish stores.

Patrons occupying the wooden seats looked across the nets, consecutively enjoying the circus and the reluctantly emerging sea creatures.

George prided himself in Captain Young's home – Number One Atlantic Ocean, its registered post office address.

Majestic, surprisingly sound on its many pilings and located over water halfway between the boardwalk and Pier's end, it replaced Mud

Hollow as our summer residence.

The structure displayed a stucco exterior. Inside were classic wood paneling, seashell lighting fixtures and a carved stairway. Outside, there was even a collar of salt-defiant lawn.

Young's only architectural flaw was no basement or subflooring. Dampness challenged wave noise and vice versa. Neither, or both, triumphed.

Late at night, alone, on foot, accomplishing the 1000-foot journey from Boardwalk to Number One Atlantic Ocean was a nerve-grabbing challenge to any nocturnal foot venturer.

Pier closed, lights out, the watchmanless, silent Ballroom of States brooded only darkness. Then came the hollow Hippodrome theatre, a relic from the turn of the century, surely housing a variety of vaudeville ghosts. The venturer then slid through squeaky iron gates into the nearly invisible mid-pier outdoors. Occasional moonlight grudgingly outlined the now attainable mansion.

It was no wonder I preferred my second-hand Chevy. Vehicle Boardwalk crossings, however, were restricted to a period from 2:00 a.m. to noon.

If the good cop (Jimmie Sermania) patrolled the night, I drove in and out on reasonable timetables.

If the bad cop (Ambrose) had the duty, I was commanded into the Pier parking lot to deposit the Chevy and undertake the grim trip oceanward on foot.

On a moonless Friday night in late June, I coasted toward the ramp, encountered Ambrose, stopped and rolled 90 degrees into the parking lot.

"Aw, Mr. Ambrose, we're only open Saturday and Sundays. There's nobody around a closed Pier. I'll creep the car. Please?"

"You know the rules, Junior. It ain't fifteen minutes past twelve."

I walked through the small pass gate, whose sole purpose it now seemed was to extinguish light. I snuck alongside the Ballroom, no longer bubbling with pretty girls, but frothing with echoes of bandleaders past, then measuring my way by the seemingly cobwebbed wall of the Hippodrome Theatre. Another 40 feet of cover brought me to the mansion's lawn.

"What evil lurketh in thy near and distant dark?" Coleridge? Milton? Shakespeare? For a moment, I regretted college.

Gaining the outdoor gate brought no comfort. Clouds obscured whatever illumination the moonless stars might render.

A light in the living room window calmed my panting. I entered.

"Hi, Dad."

"Well, George, Jr., you're home early," he observed, as if there weren't a spook on the entire Pier.

"Have you seen Eddie?" I breathed.

Eddie Roeker, a six-foot-two baritone, one of George's pre-season favorites, roomed with me on the third floor of our citadel of dampness and ocean chatter.

"I'm up here," called Roeker.

I climbed onto one of two benches in the second floor hall.

"Ambrose made me park in the lot. I sure don't like that walk."

"Why?" wondered Eddie. "It's more dangerous crowded with Zoot Suiters than when it's empty."

The downstairs door banged, followed by prolonged hinge squeakings, then, the unmistakable growl of Mr. Gumpertz, the powerful creature of now diminishing strength, who had sustained the Ringling Show, through mud, drought and debt.

"That fisherman you pay $5 a night to keep his eye on the end of the Pier just woke me up."

"Why?"

"A problem, George, a serious problem."

"More holes in the fish net?" prompted George.

"Worse than that."

"What?"

"One of the Baron's mangy lions looks like it died."

I suggested to Roeker that we beat it to the third floor.

"Sh-sh-sh," Eddie replied. "I want to hear this."

"Sam, did it die, or looks like it died?"

"Died," according to Gumpertz. "The fisherman knows something dead when he smells it. We got to get rid of that lion, George Hamid."

"Let the Baron drag him off to someplace in his pickup."

"The Baron ain't here," roared Gumpertz. "Where is the someplace you drag a dead lion to?"

"It's the middle of the night, Sam. We'll think of something."

"We should. If we're caught with a mangy, dead lion tomorrow morning, the paper will kill us. Remember the lady's letter?"

"What letter?"

"The lady who wrote that when the wind comes off the ocean, she can't stand the animal smell."

"Oh my gosh, yes."

"The paper," growled Gumpertz, "will say the lion died of stink. There goes our season."

"Sit down, Sam. Let's reason this out."

"Eddie," I implored, "upstairs, quick, before he remembers we're here."

Too late. "George Junior, come down here. I want to talk to you. Have you seen the Baron?" asked and ordered George.

Lion trainers, other than Clyde Beatty, George's protegé, were always "Captain" or even "Colonel." George conferred Baronhood on one Ludwig Heinrich Schultz.

"Not since 10:30 when he was beering at McGettigan's. He blasphemed the Irish."

"Where is he?"

"Looked like he was making speed toward Philly."

The scene. George under the seashell chandelier. Sam pacing north and south. Roeker and George Junior seeking escape.

"I've got it," George exclaimed.

"Thank God," graveled Gumpertz, "this is awful late."

"Where's the wagon?" asked George, remembering my second-hand Chevy napping in the asphalt lot.

"Ambrose made me park it."

"Get it out here. We'll load the lion into the back. You and Roeker ride to Egg Harbor, dig a ditch and bury him."

I gasped. This out-scared skirting the Ballroom.

Eddie Roeker evaluated, "It's midnight. If Ambrose, who hardly worships your son, even lets him bring the wagon out here, it'll be dawn by the time we start 20 miles up the road."

"Guess what, Dad," I added, "Eddie and I will be caught in broad daylight burying a lion, in, of all places, Egg Harbor. That's if we could even lift 400 pounds of lion into and out of the wagon."

"Well, let's get out there and look," commanded George. "Keep thinking."

"I can think better right here, Dad. Besides, I report early tomorrow." Another thousand feet seaward, through the darkest night I'd ever seen? Not if I could help it.

George's eyes told me I couldn't help it.

Roeker started up the stairs.

"Where you going?"

"To bed. Need to rest my voice."

"Roeker, you're the strongest person here," pronounced George, casting a brown-eyed dig at his not as strong son. "We're all going."

"What's the matter," grumbled Gumpertz, "you afraid of the dark?"

"Not me," I lied.

"Me either," from Eddie, compounding the lie.

Outdoors, Sam gimped to the front. In daylight, his aging eyes could barely distinguish faces. George pushed me ahead.

"Sam, stay right behind George Junior."

"I'm only the assistant manager," I complained. "I shouldn't lead."

"Not me," snapped Eddie. "I'm just a singer."

I led.

The heretofore unnoticed unevenness of the deck planks unsettled my feet. I half tripped, slowing to a shuffle.

"Get a move on. We don't have all night," George called.

Since our residence faced the boardwalk we executed a long half-circle toward Portugal, skirting the dormant Funhouse. I tried to think of my skill at the air button, blowing up girls' dresses. Only for a moment. Due to a long ago hip crushing by a runaway Ringling circus wagon, Mr. Gumpertz's walk barely equalled his vision.

An over-eager deck plank seized his heel, toppling him onto my back. His grunt and handclasp on my shoulder, coupled with his weight, almost brought the two of us to the dismal deck.

"What on earth are you doing to Sam?" George asked, since he couldn't observe the near collapse a yard in front of him.

The pounding in my throat forbade an answer.

Three hundred feet short of the bleachers, the roof quit. We found ourselves in the open, the already uneven deck now turning wet.

As we groped past the bleachers, a yellow beam appeared in my face.

If Gumpertz could see better, the fisherman's dim flashlight would have choked even him.

"What are you trying to do, kill us?" I asked the five dollar fisherman.

The old salt had no answer, then, "How could I kill you with a flashlight?"

"At least take us over the access to the stage."

"Where's the light switch?" asked Roeker.

"Good God," exclaimed George. "Don't turn on the lights. Ambrose will come running."

A big, steel arena, made up of 24-foot by 10-foot interlocking sections, stood invisible in the center of the stage. Behind it, a line of lion cages. The front of the arena contained a three-foot door for the Baron's entry and departure.

The thin, yellow shaft revealed an open door.

"That ain't ever supposed to be open," exploded Gumpertz. "Where's the groom? He didn't go to Philly too?"

The fisherman howled the groom's name, "Fingers!"

The groom, crawling out of sleep, found his sightless way to the front of the arena.

"What's the door doing open?" raged Mr. Gumpertz.

The fisherman rescued Fingers. "I opened it when I saw the lion was dead."

George stepped forward. "How did you know he wasn't sleeping?"

"I poked him enough times with the strongest rod we got. Didn't budge."

"Fingers," asked George, "What was that lion doing in the arena, instead of in his cage?"

"That's Kingpin. Ain't been looking good lately. Always muzzling Queendolly in her cage. I thought it would do them both good to leave him out in the arena overnight."

"Kingpin? Queendolly?" whispered Eddie.

"Leaving him out didn't do Kingpin much good," I observed.

The thin, yellow beam found the motionless lion, five feet inside the arena door, lying on his back, legs out, feet stiffened in the night nothingness.

As the breeze shifted, animal stench filled our nostrils.

"Has anybody thought of anything?" asked George.

"I thought of throwing up," replied Roeker.

"Why don't we dump Kingpin in the ocean?" I snarled.

"Don't be a smart alec," George snarled back.

"Hold it a minute," Sam thought aloud. "What could happen if we did do that?"

I answered, "He'd wash up on the beach or he'd float out to sea."

"Either way," commented Eddie, "he'd smell better."

I pondered, "If he washes out to sea, no problem."

A trace of excitement gripped George's voice, "If he washes up on the beach, I can tell the papers he jumped overboard. A brilliant idea, son."

"How do we get him to jump overboard?" squelched Roeker. "That's 400 pounds of dead lion. There are twenty poisonous paw nails, plus God knows how many dirty fangs."

Fingers offered his opinion, "He'll roll, sure as shooting, likely catch somebody in this black…"

George interrupted, "He's seven feet from the edge of the stage. There are six of us. How many heavy rods by the net haul?"

"Four," answered the fisherman.

"We'll manhandle him to the edge of the stage, then into the drink. Find a couple of two-by-fours."

"We couldn't get him through the door if we could see," I objected. "And we can't!"

"Sam Gumpertz, why did I saddle you with such an ignorant assistant manager? He might get to be a Pier man, never a circus man." To me, "We'll make an eight-foot opening by taking out two sections of arena. Even in pitch black we can do that. Fingers, get some rags. Tie them around his paws."

The fisherman, Roeker and I pushed, pulled and lifted two sections from the arena, laying them on the stage, our invisible movements directed by George.

Fingers completed his bandaging.

Four rods, with two two-by-fours, urged Kingpin toward the edge. Sweat and profanity shared equal billing.

"Watch out for the net ties," yelled the fisherman, as I tripped on one. But for Eddie Roeker, I would have preceded the lion into the Atlantic.

We budged the feline corpse to the edge of the stage, George stopping us. "Off with the bandages. We'd never explain them if he's discovered on the beach," he said.

Fingers whined, "That's all that kept us from being blood poisoned."

"We can see a little now. Be extra careful. One big shove and he's overboard."

Five big shoves later, Kingpin rolled past the edge into the ocean.

Or so we thought.

The fisherman turned his light toward the surface.

"Mr. Hamid," said the fisherman, "that lion ain't going out to sea. He ain't headin' for the beach either."

"What?"

"He caught himself cockeyed on a rope. The lion's in the fishnet."

George's weary voice sought the fisherman. "Get him out. We can't leave him in the net all summer."

The fisherman acquired a name, Louie. I glimpsed Louie through the first scant light of dawn.

"We can winch up the net and grapple him out. We grappled a three hundred pound dolphin once," Louie offered.

"Great," I grumbled. "We'll be right back where we started."

"How soon?" George wanted to know.

"About ten when Moe comes in. He's the grappler."

"Eddie," George's voice brightened, "get some sleep. Son, find Ambrose and tell him we lost a lion."

"Ambrose?" I yelled. "We nearly killed ourselves in the pitch black to hide from Ambrose."

"Do as I said. Make him think the lion is most likely on the Pier."

"Sam," barked George, "get Fingers to clean this place up. Louie, here's an extra five. Help Fingers."

Bossing a circus guy, even one as lowly as Fingers, was Sam Gumpertz's specialty.

"Disinfectant! You must have plenty, since you ain't never used it. Mop that stuff everywhere. Wake up the animals, put them in the arena, hose every one. Flush out their cages, disinfect, then get the pickup and take your four crap cans to the dump. Here's ten bucks. Buy new cans, more disinfectant."

I walked Eddie to Number One, then alone to the deserted Boardwalk, finding Ambrose in the lobby of the nearby Warner Theatre.

"You smell bad," was his only greeting.

"Can I drive the car over the Boardwalk?"

"I ain't stopping you. It's six o'clock."

"By the way, Mr. Ambrose, did you see a lion leave the Pier?"

"What?"

"A lion. We lost one. Couldn't find him in the dark. That's why I'm still up."

Ambrose shook his head. "I seen lots of things on this boardwalk, no lions."

He made a note in a little book.

"Got to go on my report. 'Lion lost on Hamid's Pier.' I'm warning you now, if I do see him, he'll get shot. You don't want a dead lion on your hands, do you Hamid?"

"Absolutely not, Mr. Ambrose, no way."

"Then be careful with your damn lions."

As I drove to the house, I wondered, "What did I do wrong? He's reporting us."

George, undressing for a short nap, heard my tale.

"Just fine," he approved.

"You're not mad?"

"Nope, you did just fine."

George left instructions for our carpenter to rush a crude six-foot box into being. "Load it onto the pickup when it returns from the dump and have Fingers park in near the stage," it said.

My new duty was to intercept any reporter coming on the Pier and instead escort him slowly to the end.

"Give me time to get out there," stated George. "Don't mention a word about the lion, you hear me?"

At nine thirty, per instructions, I stationed myself alongside the watchman's door. Some one rapped.

Sure enough, a newspaper reporter, not a stringer, a familiar veteran in his mid-twenties. I excused myself to the phone.

"Dad, he's here. Donovan. The guy who wrote the lady's stink story."

"Take it slow. I'll be sitting in the bleachers."

Turning to the reporter, I asked, "What can I do for you, Sy? Sit down."

Donovan stood. "I see on the police blotter you lost a lion. How do you lose a lion?"

"You'll have to ask Dad."

"Is your father here?" I nodded. "Where?"

"Out in the circus area, I guess," was my answer.

"Then you did lose a lion. Otherwise, why would he be out there?"

"Fish," I responded. "The best thing about Million Dollar, to my father, is fresh fish from the net haul every morning."

"At twelve, not ten. I know your schedule." Donovan started toward the end.

"What's your hurry, Sy? I'll walk with you. Dad will be here all day."

I paced our trip as slowly as Donovan would permit.

Five hundred feet from the bleacher, I spotted George. At the same time, I heard footsteps.

The Baron, cloaked in animal/beer aroma, stepped past us, hastening toward George.

I quickened our pace, sensing an unknown catastrophe.

I steered Donovan to the outer rails, trying to shut him off from, and enable me to hear, the ensuing conversation.

"Vot's going on here?"

George responded, "Shut up!"

Baron Von Schultz looked into the net. "Mein Gott, dots Kingpin. Vhy's he in with the fishes?"

"I'll tell you later, maybe. Now, you get in your dressing room. Don't speak to anybody, *Anybody*. You understand?"

"But…"

"Look, I made you a Baron. In two seconds I can turn you into a serf. Don't think I'm not thinking about it."

The Baron ran into his dressing room, preferring the company of hungry lions to the ferocity of George Hamid.

I returned my attention to Donovan.

"Isn't that your father's voice?" he asked.

"Sure, let's go around to the seats."

I introduced Donovan, "Dad, this is Sy Donovan, the reporter from the paper, the fellow who wrote the article on the animal smell."

George frowned, "What animal smell? I don't smell any animal smell. Do you, Mr. Donovan?"

Sy shook his head, "All I smell is disinfectant. Whew! Atlantic City Hospital never smelled like this."

"That dame was a crank. We use disinfectant every day."

In the future, not in the past.

"Look, Mr. Hamid, I didn't come here to smell your Pier. What about the lost lion?"

"You may not believe what I'm going to tell you, but every word is gospel." I crossed my fingers for forgiveness.

"First I knew of it was about midnight, from the fisherman. Louie," George beckoned, "come over here."

Louie stood only a dozen feet away. "Tell him what happened."

"Well, we shoved, and…"

"No, not that," interrupted George. "The arena door. Yeah."

I opened that arena door. It was black dark. I know no lion would ever be in the arena at night…

The winching of the rising net distracted Donovan and released Louie. "What in God's name is that?" he asked, pointing at the tan stranger in the net. "That's not a fish."

"Nope," agreed George. "That's our Kingpin. As you can see, he may be dead, but he isn't lost. I wouldn't want the public to think we had an uncaged lion prowling around Hamid's Million Dollar Pier."

"This is ridiculous. What happened? How did he get dead?" asked a shocked Donovan.

"Look Donovan, you're the only one in town who's got this story, or will get it. Your scoop!"

"Fingers," George shouted. "Come here."

Fingers, stationed nearby and better rehearsed than Louie, approached the reporter.

"Go ahead," prodded George.

"Well, you see, we always leave up the gates between cages so the lions can move around. Soon's we did it, Kingpin would mosey into Queendolly's cage and nuzzle her all to hell."

"Who, pray tell, is Queendolly?"

By arrangement, Queendolly strolled about the arena.

"That's her. Anyway, it got so bad that Kingpin was going to mate Queendolly, whether she wanted to or not.

"You couldn't call it rape," defined George. "You also couldn't call her a willing partner."

"So," continued Fingers, "last night I shoved Kingpin into the arena for everybody's good."

Trusting Fingers memory no longer, George assumed command.

"When Louie opened the gate, the frustrated, love-sick Kingpin jumped, or fell, overboard. I don't think he expected to wind up in the net haul."

"I'm suppose to write this?" asked Donovan.

"You don't think those simple guys could make this up, do you?" asked George.

"Try George Junior. He followed me out."

Sy looked at me. "Is that how it happened?"

I paused and reflected, "You know, Sy, everything you heard is the truth." Except who followed who, and certain things left unsaid.

"What are you going to do with him now?" Donovan asked as the grappled Kingpin swayed slowly into the box on the pickup.

"I'll pack him in ice, send him to a pet cemetery near my

fairgrounds in Trenton and bury Kingpin there." A possibility, except I wouldn't bet on the Baron buying ten dog graves to bury one lion.

"To finish my story, George....mind if I call you George?"

"Okay with me."

"George, tell me, in your opinion what was the cause of death?"

"Suicide. No doubt about it."

George misunderstood Donovan's roaring laughter.

"Do we get a retraction on the smell story?"

Sy shook his head, "Nope. That story is as dead as Kingpin."

Father and son in 1945.

Steel Pier on the Boardwalk in Atlantic City – all 2400 feet of it – jutting a half mile into the Atlantic Ocean with its three theatres, 10,000 square-foot ballroom, and circus stadium – "all for one low admission."

Steel Pier's famous High Diving Horse, still talked about to this day.

George with Franklin's marvelous First Lady, promoting war support in 1943 for Army and Navy relief in outdoor show business. Eleanor Roosevelt assigned this job to George and he never let her down.

Both of us with our all time favorite bandleader Glenn Miller in 1942. George presented Glenn with a five-foot horseshoe floral piece in appreciation of Glenn's breaking an all-time attendance record on Million Dollar Pier in Atlantic City. Glenn then turned the floral piece over to me, an ensign in the Navy, telling me that I will need a little luck if the horseshoe is a symbol. I returned from the war. Glenn never did.

Our home, Captain Young's mansion on the Million Dollar Pier in Atlantic City – Number One Atlantic Ocean, its registered post office address.

George and Frankie Boy (Sinatra) backstage at Steel Pier in Atlantic City in 1950 doing what they did best – entertaining guys who needed it.

Here are Kingpin and the Baron in happier, (at least healthier) times. We wonder why Ambrose is ticketing Kingpin.

George and Ed Sullivan on the Steel Pier in Atlantic City in 1964 planning the Beatles concert at Atlantic City Convention Hall.

George (standing behind the Fab Four) at the Beatles' press conference before their 1964 show in Atlantic City.

"The Acrobat" and "Showman of the Century" George A. Hamid, at the New Jersey State Fairgrounds, where he spent his first night in America and later owned in the 1960s.

The Hamid showman tradition continues today at the office of Hamid Enterprises outside of Atlantic City, NJ. (L-R) Jim Hamid, George A. Hamid, Jr., and Jim Hamid, Jr.

Chapter 31
Big Band Man

Big Bands were George's and my specialty. By 1941 none were bigger than Glenn Miller. Glenn drew more than Tommy Dorsey and Benny Goodman combined.

We did not yet own Steel Pier. Frank Gravatt did. Ours was Million Dollar Pier. Through an oft-broken truce, Steel Pier booked the MCA agency bands, Goodman, Dorsey, Lombardo, Harry James.

Million Dollar Pier played General Artist bands, newcomers like Jimmy Dorsey, Artie Shaw, Woodie Herman, Johnnie Long. In 1938 an unknown band, headed by bespectacled Glenn Miller, joined The General Artist (GAC) team, and thus played Million Dollar Pier.

In two years Miller's musicianship and melodic touch lifted his band to the pinnacle of popularity. Glenn was a "Hamid" band and in 1940 gave our pier the biggest weekend in its history.

Even though one might figure Shaw, who cared only for Shaw, might defect to the world-renowned glamorous Steel Pier, (which he did), we knew that Miller never would.

Until spring of 1941.

Mike Nidorff, GAC's head booker, brought the 1941 contracts to George. J. Dorsey, W. Herman, Johnnie Long, Charlie Spivak.

George rifled through them and began signing. He stopped.

"Mike, there's something missing."

Nidorff averted George's eyes. "Miller?"

"Yes, Glenn is almost a part of my family. He wouldn't play any place else."

Mike finally looked at George. Then, "How much is Gravatt paying him?"

"$4000 a day."

"I paid him $2500 last summer. Gravatt's gone crazy."

"Maybe so," responded Nidorff. "It's signed. Nothing can be done, even if you pay $4000."

"So much for loyalty. I expected this from Shaw. Never from Miller."

George waved Mike Nidorff from his office.

On a Friday in late August, 1941, close to my departure for the Navy, George and I sat on the porch of Number One Atlantic Ocean, discussing Labor Day logistics without the Miller Band.

George had gotten to know Sally Rand (of strip-tease fame) at the Chicago World's Fair. In July, George booked her for Labor Day weekend over the pious objections of Gumpertz, Bess, and even me.

"Don't worry," George countered, "the heck with the do-gooders. I'm booking Sally for Labor Day weekend."

At the time I shook my head.

George continued, "It's so dark in that creepy old Hippodrome Theater, they won't know if it's skin or muslin under those fans."

Now, a day before opening, we planned.

As we talked, a black limousine pulled in front of the mansion.

A tall, eye-glassed man strode from the limo to our porch.

"Glenn Miller." I gasped.

Glenn extended his hand to George, who reluctantly took it.

"I'm exhausted. Can I sit down?"

George nodded.

"Twelve hours from Youngstown here. They should do something about those roads."

George asked, "What are you doing?"

Glenn answered. "Relaxing, this is my home in Atlantic City, isn't it?"

"Not anymore, it isn't."

Miller opened his eyes, looking narrowly at George.

"What do you mean by that?"

George answered. "It's on every billboard from Philadelphia to Atlantic City. You saying you didn't see it?"

"Slept all the way."

"Well," concluded George, "You're playing Steel Pier. Don't kid me, Glenn. I saw your signature on a contract in May."

"Must have been stuck in the middle of a batch. You know I sign contracts a dozen at a time. Did Nidorff show it to you?"

George nodded.

"So that's it! Wait till I see him." Pause. "Do you want my band next year?"

I jumped up. "Do you really mean it?"

Glenn grabbed George's hand. "Not one weekend, but two."

"Young man," ordered George. "Get Glenn Miller some iced tea."

Sunday was the second day of the two-day weekend, a surprisingly good (and harmless) one for Hamid's Million Dollar Pier, a sensational one for Steel Pier.

Mike Nidorff tiptoed into our office. George looked up and saw him. "What do you want?"

"You win," said Nidorff, "I have two contracts for you to sign."

George frowned. "Miller? Next summer? What's the price?"

"Four thousand a day. Do you want them?"

"It's a lot of money."

"It'll be more if you wait till May."

Because of those two weekends, despite the war, despite a Boardwalk brownout, 1942 became the biggest season in Million Dollar Pier's history.

After the last set on closing night I walked to the bandstand.

"Next year?" I asked.

Glenn Miller shook his head. "I'm taking the band on military tour till this war is over."

As I said goodbye, Miller smiled, "Stay afloat sailor."

Chapter 32
The Physics Professor

On an autumn Friday in 1939, the beginning of my senior year in college, George sent word that he would meet me to watch the game.

Circus and fairs, put to bed for the year, this mid-fall respite allowed him to visit campus, warm up his 16 mm movie camera, sit in the small stands and watch the one-fifties (light-weight football team) perform.

Leaving the field house after a training table lunch, I headed toward my nearby eating club.

George, on time for a change, greeted me.

"Where you been?"

"Having lunch."

"What did they feed you?"

"Dad, you know, a slice of beef and a baked potato."

"How come you're playing on Friday?"

"You know that, too. When the fat boys are in town, we play on Friday."

"The fat boys?"

"The Varsity. That's what we call them."

"I like that sweater, especially the orange 'P'. Are you going to get another one?"

"We won the title last year, that's why we got a major letter. If we win it again, all we get is the orange 'P', no second sweater."

"That's okay. I'll get Bess to buy me a black sweater. Give me the 'P' for Christmas."

I shook my head. "After today, there's Yale, Penn and Rutgers. We haven't lost, but they're tough."

As we walked along Prospect Street toward campus, George said, "Who are you playing this afternoon?"

"Lafayette."

"How come you invite me to the Lafayette game?"

"I didn't invite you, Father, you invited yourself. Penn is next week, in Philadelphia. Then Yale, you're invited."

"Too bad," George consoled. "Conventions."

We climbed stairs through a red brick arch.

"What is this?"

"Seventy-Nine Arch," I answered.

"Be serious. That's one of your football plays."

"Sorry, Dad, this dorm was built by the class of 1879. Just came back to their sixtieth reunion."

"How many of them?"

"Very few. They graduated almost 300. Maybe a dozen."

From Seventy-Nine Arch, a flagstone path curved graciously in a wide arc, past the iron-fenced gardens of the president's home, where fall flowers were winning (for the moment) their golden war against winter, then, another thousand feet through campus.

George and I directed ourselves onto the path, the shortest route to my other-end-of-the-campus dorm room.

"Who's that?" asked George, looking toward a strolling figure 30 feet in front of us.

"One of our physics professors."

"You took physics, didn't you?"

"All I could digest."

"Are you taking it now?"

"Nope," I answered. "Switched to English Lit."

"All the money I'm paying for your education and you switch from something important to English Lit."

I thought out loud, "Readin' and ritin' are as important as 'rithmatic."

"If I went to college," mused George, "I would have taken physics."

"I did. Anyway, the Tumble Bug is paying for this. Seven hundred dollars tuition, 400 for room and twenty a week to the club."

"Add in the books and your dates," George responded. "Anyway, White City Park's Tumble Bug wasn't your idea. Your mother made me give it to you."

The summer receipts from the amusement park ride went directly into my account at the Boulevard Bank, Gown Street, Forest Hills, ostensibly, and as it turned out, actually, to purchase my college education.

We strolled only slightly faster than the professor.

"Were you in his class?"

"Not me."

"Did he ever teach you anything? He looks shaggy enough to be a good professor."

"Nothing much. Well, he has a theory I heard about." I recited it to him.

George's curiosity continued, "What does it mean? Capital letters or small?"

"Small."

"Three little letters and a tiny two, and you don't know what it means?"

"I don't. Only the professors and three other people in the world really understand it."

George accelerated through the now 20 feet to the professor, ringed his arms and chatted alongside.

The professor seemed to return the conversation. He looked back at me, then at George, shaking his head.

"Uh-oh," I thought. "I'm in trouble."

Passing our turnoff, I called, "Come here, we go left."

George patted the professor on his back, shook hands and returned.

I said, "So?"

"Well, so, I told him you quit physics for English Lit. He said 'A lot of them do.' I offered to show him how to make his shaggy mustache trim like mine. He said, 'It cannot be as comfortable.' I asked him if he could recognize you as one of his students. He looked back, shook his head and said that he couldn't."

"Dad, thank heavens. I thought I was in some kind of trouble."

"You are."

"I am?"

"Yes, you are. I asked him about E=mc2."

"What did he say?"

"The professor told me, 'It is simply the relationship of time, motion and matter'."

"Simply?" I observed.

"Any dummy should be able to figure that out. No reason to run off to English Lit."

"What was it you handed him?"

"My business card."

"You haven't had one for years."

"I have three left," explained George, "from when I started out in the booking business." He paused. "By the way, what is the physics professor's name?"

"Albert Einstein."

George repeated the name. "I've read about him. Jewish, isn't he?"

I nodded.

After a few steps, George mumbled, more to himself than to me, "Back in the old country, I would bring him to my side of the well."

At Christmas, George's present from me failed to arrive. All I could produce was an envelope.

Gathering near the morning Christmas tree, my sister and Bess savored their treats, I mine.

Late-sleeping George entered as we finished. After George exulted over his usual pajamas, shirts and handkerchiefs, Bess handed him an envelope.

"What's that?"

"I don't know," she answered. "It came from the office."

"Well, open it."

Bess fumbled it open. A small card fell to the floor. Picking it up, she read, "Wirth and Blumenfeld. This card must be fifteen years old."

Turning the card over, she shook her head, "I can't read the back. It's in Arabic."

Bess handed the card to me.

"I don't think so, more like Hebrew."

"You can't read that, " said George.

"A logical Jew," I answered, "would reason that a fellow named Blumenfeld could. I bet I know what it says."

"You're not Blumenfeld," observed George.

"Don't have to be. I'll bet you my Tumble Bug it says 'Happy Hannukah.' Look at the signature."

George read it. "A. Einstein."

He opened my envelope.

Out tumbled a felt, orange 'P.'

"Bess, where's my black sweater?"

"What black sweater?" She paused. "You'd think *you* went to Princeton, not George Jr."

"Doesn't matter. All we need is a little snow and this will be a perfect Christmas," George concluded, casting his gaze at the yellow sun in the bright blue sky.

Chapter 33
Frankie Boy

In the years that followed, George and Bess spent partial summers in Number One Atlantic Ocean. During these years, I graduated from college, accompanied the U.S. Navy in and about the South Pacific, returned from the service to work on the Steel Pier (now ours), and married an Irish girl named Patricia.

"Partial summers" because in mid-June Bess traditionally departed for Maine, leaving our domestic destinies in the hands of first Grandma and, after her departure to eternity, in the large hands of large, black, pleasant Ethel. Partial summers because George spent at least half of each summer on the road, working with his beloved fairs.

With the children gone, for whatever reason, they searched Atlantic City and surrounding communities for a large, land-borne home.

They found it, bought it, and the rest of us quickly christened it the Big House. Big it was.

Built by Luden (cough drop Luden) before World War I and occupying most of an entire beach block, it qualified as a true mansion. Need one or not, that's what George and Bess bought. Its 27 over-sized rooms included a beach porch, sun porch, five regular bedrooms and two master bedrooms – one masterer than the next. Its 13 bathrooms, seven with tub, all vintage, all large, were fortunately rarely used, otherwise the scrubbing would exceed the bed making.

In mid-May, Bess hired a decorator, selected carpets and curtains and proceeded to hang enough drapery to enclose a Turkish Oda. Before the bills came, she waved herself off to Maine.

I toured wife Patty through the porches, dining room, kitchen and upstairs to the master bedrooms, into the "smaller" one.

"Is this the master bedroom?" she asked. "It's huge."

"Not really, the other one's huger."

"Don't I see Dad's things here?"

"Mother's stuff is in her master bedroom."

"Hmm, it figures."

We entered Bess's room.

"I can't believe it," marveled Patty. "You could fit our entire first floor in here."

Caring for this concrete enterprise was Ethel Jacobs, late of Number One Atlantic Ocean, Million Dollar Pier. Ethel's forte was not style, taste or planning, merely occasional light work and upon demand, a touch of heavy work. On the Million Dollar Pier, Ethel wore her own clothes; at the Big House, it was starched white kitchen dresses, thankfully provided by Bess before her defection to Maine.

In early June, George had advised Bess that Frank Sinatra was booked on the Pier four weeks later. He wanted Frank over for dinner and to please stay until July.

"Take him to your favorite, Captain Starn's," Bess said.

"Look," answered George. "We bought this fortress, you're spending a mint to decorate it. I want to invite important people here."

Deadlock. It resolved itself as their deadlocks usually did. Bess traveled north, George proceeded with his invitation.

I met Sinatra briefly before the war, at Tommy Dorsey's lavish estate in Bernardsville, New Jersey. The Dorsey home was open to friends, even when Tommy played away, which he mostly did.

To the best of my recollection, Frank pursued Tommy Dorsey's singer, Edythe Wright (not too successfully, I was told). Thereafter, I visited the band on location where we struck up a minor friendship.

Toward the end of the war, Frank pioneered the vocalist break from the big bands, becoming the first band singer to reach stardom. Delighting in his success, I now anticipated his performing as a single on Steel Pier.

Friday night before opening, George did, indeed, invite Frank to the Big House for dinner – that edifice's first name guest.

Patty and I were, of course, included.

We chatted on the beachfront porch for awhile, tea-totaller George even permitting us one drink.

I whispered, "Dad, who's preparing the dinner?"

"Ethel."

I blinked. "Ethel? She never prepared a dinner in her life."

"George, don't worry, she'll do fine."

"She's got to cook, dish and serve. You'll be lucky if Sinatra doesn't sue you."

I moved next to Patty. "You're the hostess." Patty, for some reason, incorrectly judged that Bess would return for the occasion.

"Okay, I guess, what are we having?"

"I don't know, Ethel's concocting it."

"Take me home."

"I can't, not now. Besides, there's just the four of us."

We retreated to the dining room, seated ourselves, each at one side of a modest (compared to everything else) table. George, of course, reigned at the head.

"You know, George," said Frank, "these are some digs. I haven't seen anything like it since Tommy's place."

In strode a starched, smiling Ethel balancing four glass plates, each bearing a salad, which were deposited approximately in front of us. George tasted his.

"Ethel, where's the dressing?"

Her strong voice bounced wall to wall from the kitchen, "Madam ain't bought none."

Fortunately, Madam had purchased rolls and butter, which next appeared on the table as the salad dishes found their way to the kitchen.

In five minutes, the alabaster Ethel triumphed into the room bearing remarkably familiar glass dishes, each now adorned with a piece of toast and five stalks of asparagus covered by an unidentifiable sauce.

No favoritism, five each.

Patty squirmed.

I commented, "Can't be the same dishes. She didn't have time to wash them."

Ethel heard me. "We got plenty of them glass dishes. No need to worry."

There was need to worry.

Nothing from the kitchen, not even noise.

George and Frank talked about big bands, of past experiences and what tomorrow's opening Saturday would bring.

Patty nudged, "Go help Ethel with the main course."

I excused myself to the kitchen.

Table talk continued. A few laughs could be heard. None from Patty.

I checked the kitchen, finding only three wilted asparagus spears in a pan.

"Ethel, where's the main course?"

"You et it Mr. Junior. Good, wasn't it?"

"You are kidding. No meat, no fish?"

A slow head shake.

"Do you have any dessert?"

"Madam didn't call for none."

"Madam is in Maine, couldn't you think of a main course or even dessert?"

"We got some yellow jello."

"Any whipped cream?"

She shook her head again.

"Okay," I said. "Jello it is. Give us decent portions."

Ethel shook her head. "Can't make 'em too decent. Ain't got much."

I returned to the table, whispering the news to hostess Patty. She tried to crumble under the table.

"Dad will be so embarrassed," she mourned, "I could cry. How can he apologize?"

Apologize? George? If ever, this was it.

Ethel consumed the doorway, four plates of wiggling jello defying her fingers. She managed to bring the plates to a landing on the table.

After the quick yellow jello was finished, I pushed back my chair and stood up thinking, "Here goes."

"Dad," I said. "Bad news, no meat course, no chicken course. The asparagus was it."

George looked at me, frowned, then turned to Sinatra, placing his hand on Frank's arm. "Son," he announced, eyes again on me. "Do you think for one minute that I would serve a good Catholic boy like Frankie meat on Friday?"

Frank's eyes twinkled. "Geawge," as only Frank can say it, "If I keep eating with you, I'll die of malnutrition."

The engagement drew record crowds for a pre-season, nice weather weekend. George extracted a Sinatra promise that he would play Labor Day Saturday and Sunday next year. If he could, Frank would fly east for George's National Showmen's Commodore Hotel Fundraiser in November.

Annually, on Thanksgiving Eve, George, perennial President of the National Showmen's Association, commandeered the grand ballroom of the Commodore Hotel and lured outdoor show people from fairs, parks and carnivals for a fun-filled, celebrity-dotted banquet. Theatrical agencies persuaded important artists in the New York area into complimentary performances for their brother and sister show people, some of whom, less fortunate, needed financial help. The N.S.A. via Bess's Sunshine Fund, supported a children's summer camp. Newcomers relished the appearance. Giants like Como, Dinah Shore and Sinatra were virtually impossible to snare.

George never doubted Sinatra would show, despite my reminder that the man was on the Coast, eight plane hours away from New York.

Sure enough, on Tuesday we got a call that Frank might be there.

Wednesday night, the throng buzzed in anticipation. Could George Hamid really produce "Frankie Boy"?

My station, when not at Patty's table near the stage, was to rehearse performers in the impossible-to-predict order of arrival.

Forty-five minutes before show time, true to his word, Sinatra arrived. In forty-five seconds, "He's here!" sped through the giant ballroom. Surrounding backstage with four tough carnies, I greeted Frank.

"This is wonderful, even though you cost me five bucks."

"How did I cost you five bucks, Geawge?"

"I bet Dad five you wouldn't show, to get you off the hook in case you didn't."

"Do you want cash, or should I apply it to my plane fare?"

"How about, Frank, if we donate it to the Bess Hamid Sunshine Fund."

We rehearsed. "Will you have dinner at our table after the show?" I asked.

"Is it past the asparagus season?"

"I'm glad you think that's funny. Patty doesn't."

Frank paused, "Are you going to be out front when I go on?"

I nodded, "I wouldn't be much use backstage."

By now, George was taking plaudits from the N.S.A. big wigs, plus the few little wigs who could get near him.

The emcee lavished an introduction on Sinatra through thunderous applause.

The crowd hushed.

"Before I begin," said Frank, almost chuckling, eyeing me, then George, "I want to tell you that last summer, the fine things you folks do was explained to me. I, because of a certain man, a very fine man, made this trip." All eyes turned to George. "That man is George Hamid...Junior."

Gasps, downbeat, first song. Frank grinned at Patty, then me. I glanced at the other George, waved, stood up, responding to the most muted applause of the evening.

We did away with Sinatra the following September.

In the early fifties, it must be remembered, there were no concerts, no arena shows. Only Steel Pier, and an emerging Las Vegas, maintained a big name policy. A few major fairs were testing the big name waters. That was it.

Admission prices didn't venture above a dollar fifty for a movie. Steel Pier, with its one charge for three theaters, huge ballroom, circus and diving horse could be had for a dollar seventy-five.

We relied on numbers, big numbers. Our acts expected to do four shows a day, five on Saturday and Sunday. Music Hall Theatre, for decades, "Home of the Stars", only accommodated twenty-five hundred people.

Since some of our visitors bypassed the Music Hall, we could optimistically handle fourteen thousand patrons.

Two factors affected Sinatra's playdate. Labor Day Sunday, with no assistance from the weather, exceeded all of our other seventy days.

A morning drizzle inflated any day to double its norm.

How would we handle Labor Day Saturday and Sunday?

Saturday, I conducted Frank to his now familiar dressing room. On the door, I had affixed the words, 'The Frank Sinatra Room'.

"Do me a favor, Geawge," intoned Frank (to this day, I believe Sinatra's intonation or non-intonation of the letter "r" partially created his uniqueness). "Will ya?"

"Whatever you say, Frank, maybe."

"Name this dinky dressing room after Como."

"Okay, if you will walk to the Ballroom after the show."

"Why, I played there for pennies with Harry and Tommy."

"Meager as this is," I continued, "I'll show you where you dressed in the hallway."

"Don't remind me."

"It's Mr. Sinatra," said the switchboard.

"How is it going?" I asked.

"Get me a phone. Your switchboard is destroying my love life."

"How?"

"Every time I call Ava, I either get cut off or a busy signal."

"That's better than you did with Edythe Wright," I remembered.

Our sixty-year-old switchboard lady trembled. She could barely handle routine Pier inquires, let alone three calls an hour to Palm Springs.

"We never supplied a dressing room phone before. For you, there'll be one in an hour," I conceded.

"I'll even pay for it."

"Forget it, Frank. It's yours."

George heard my call to the vice president of the phone company.

"Who's paying for that phone?"

"You, me or Frank. If not Hilda." (switchboard) "She'd give up a month's pay to avoid those calls to and from Ava Gardner."

A sunny Saturday spent itself through four packed houses.

Not Sunday.

Drizzle wet the boardwalk and was predicted to continue all day.

I always arrived at the office before George.

On the phone George said, "George Junior, we'll kill them today."

"I know. I sent out the cashiers half an hour early. People are massed at the Music Hall."

"Tell Frank he'll have to do more than five shows."

"Already did. First show is one o'clock instead of two. I told him to cut. I'm dropping the movie between shows."

Backstage, I cautioned, "Frank, no more than four songs a show."

The man out-stamina'd everybody. After the eleventh show, he collapsed in a chair in the dressing room. My doctor, Jim Gleason, had attended Frank's throat since six.

At midnight, "Mr. Sinatra, sir," I offered, "you open at the Michigan State Fair tomorrow. Can I take you to the airport?"

"No need, I called them," Frank croaked. "Tomorrow, I'm a no-show."

George walked into the cramped "Perry Como Dressing Room". "Frank, my boy, you outdid yourself."

To me, "Why'd you change it? I told you to name it the Frank Sinatra Room."

"I did. At 8:00 Frank, in his infinite generosity, donated it to Como."

"What days do you want next year?"

He shook his head. The famous voice only whispered.

"Two times were tough. The third might be fatal."

Sinatra walked wearily to George's car. I watched as they drove off to his hotel room.

Sinatra was known to bestow a gift of gold on some friends and associates. A month after his departure from the Music Hall torture chamber, George and I each received a package.

George's was a beautiful, shining pocket watch, etched, "George, Sr. from Frank Sinatra."

Mine, a beautiful pair of gold cuff links: the top of one in the perfectly etched face of the muse of comedy; the other, the dramatic face of tragedy. On the square face of the cuff inserts was scripted, "To George, Jr." on one, "From Frank Sinatra" in his tiny, exact signature, on the other.

Having no cuffed shirts, I promptly bought some, upgrading my wrist visibility on special occasions. These, plus a watch, a wedding ring, and a few childhood items, constituted my entire jewelry collection.

For only eight years did Comedy prevail. In the late fifties, the muse of Tragedy took over as our house was entered by thieves. The intruder must have been frightened away because all that disappeared were Patty's pearls and, somehow, my innocuous jewelry box.

I could only sigh at the thought of those classic irreplaceables melted into some unknowing sufferer's dental work.

Chapter 34
Ricky

Although the Ricky story will be part of another telling, a piece of it belongs in George's book.

George and I shared a large office on Steel Pier, his desk on one wall....mine on the opposite.

Part of my job was to contract next season's name attractions. George paid an overviewer's attention to my accomplishments (or non-accomplishments) when he was not traveling with our circus. The circus season, January to June, coincided with the act-booking season. Thus, I did contracting with minimum interference from the overviewer.

Our summer show policy required a dozen weekly features, plus shorter presentations on the two holiday weekends – a total of fourteen headliners.

I prowled the act agencies for "sleepers" – acts visible in February, with the look of a blockbuster in July. At February prices, of course.

Because the agencies needed to showcase their prospects on the Pier, I made some surprising steals.

Jane Russell, Como and Danny Kaye in the late forties; Esther Williams, Johnnie Ray, Pat Boone, The Maguire Sisters and Tony Bennett in the fifties.

I didn't win them all.

In February of 1957, the phone brought the voice of my friend, Sol Shapiro of the William Morris office.

My side of the conversation went as follows: "Hi, Sol."

"You know I do. I always look for bargains in February."

"Tell me about him."

"If this guy's going to be so hot in August, how come I never heard of him?"

"What did you say his name is?"

"I can't believe it."

"He's open Labor Day weekend for three days and playing only a couple of other spots, maybe one? What else?"

"Get to the basics, Sol, the price."

"Twelve thousand dollars! We never paid Frank that much! I don't know anybody in the business who gets twelve grand for three days!"

"You're sorry you can't do anything about it? I'm sorry, too. I have to take it or leave it?"

"I know you would if you could, Sol. We're passing. It's not just the money. The American people will idolize a Frank, a Perry, a Pat. Never will thy go for a guy with the weird first name of *Elvis.*"

Colonel Parker appeared in the office the following July. I knew he was one of George's earliest Buffalo Bill cronies. I also knew he managed one act, one certain act.

I tried to disappear, because Presley could now command twelve thousand a performance, maybe more.

After twenty minutes of Wild West and circus talk, Tom, as George called him, leaned over the desk, "Tell me, George, how come you didn't buy my boy?"

George looked at me, "How come we didn't buy the Colonel's boy?"

I used the only approach that might save me. "I thought twelve thousand for three days was too much of a risk."

George shrugged, "You and I suffered through some tough times, Tom. Maybe some of it rubbed off on my son."

Soon after, Colonel Parker left.

"George Junior, who is Colonel Parker's boy?"

I gulped, "Elvis Presley."

George, though innocent of rock and roll, must know Presley.

"That's the nice-looking kid who shakes when he sings?"

"Yes."

"I'll call Colonel Tom and set him for next year."

I shook my head, "I didn't buy him this year, we'll never get to play him. I doubt that many others ever will, either."

Late in the following winter, I received a call from Normie Weiss, my buddy at M.C.A.

"George, I've got something for you."

"What?"

"A singer that's going to be hotter than Presley next summer."

"You're talking to the guy who fanned on the original."

"Come on, George. Don't fan twice."

"Who is it, Norm?"

"Ricky Nelson. Ozzie and Harriet's son. On their television show. You watch it, don't you?"

"Not much."

"You ought to. You're in the business."

I answered, "I let you guys watch TV for me. If I watched it, I'd get smart and make too many mistakes."

"Well, what about it?"

"What about what? Come on, Norm."

"Well," said Weiss, "the kid's filming all summer, with two days off over Labor Day. His folks played for your dad with their band. They want him to make his first personal for the Hamids."

"How do you know he can sing?"

"It doesn't matter," enthused Normie. "When that good-looking kid came down the stairs on the show, with a guitar, shaking his legs, the studio phones lit up like Las Vegas."

"A good analogy. You want your friend George, here, to take a hefty gamble on somebody who never did a performance in his life. How hefty?"

"Ten grand."

"What's this world coming to? Five grand a day for this kid? I turned down four a day for Elvis."

"Think about it, George."

"Wait a minute, Normie. I'm thinking. Give me five minutes"

I called a familiar number in Philadelphia. Dick Clark.

"Dick, this is George calling from Steel Pier."

"In March?"

"I need help."

"If your pipes are frozen," advised that mellow voice, "I can't help you."

"Ever hear of Ricky Nelson?"

"Sure. Never played for me or for that matter, for anybody."

"They're offering him to the Pier for two days. Ten grand. As much as we pay you for 10 people."

"All I can tell you is he did a walk-on at the Minnesota State Fair last September. The boppers went wild."

"Should I book him?"

A pause, then Dick's unhurried voice... "George, you're well known in these parts for turning down Elvis. Don't be twice famous."

I thanked Dick and dialed Weiss in New York

"Normie, can you do any better than the ten? My father will assassinate me."

"No chance. They've got to fly 10 people, round-trip, from the coast. They won't net anything at ten grand."

"Okay, Norman Weiss, you've got a deal. Get the contract to me fast. I want it signed and sealed before I change my mind, or have it changed for me."

Quick? No, it was early May when the signed contracts nestled into our files.

Now the problem, how to tell George.

I decided to bundle several executed contracts, shuffle them onto a desk and hope he might breeze through them, which of course, he rarely did.

He relished the postman's daily bounty.

George burst into the outer office. (George did more bursting than most people.) He entered our sanctum in the company of A. Earl O'Brien, an important circus client from Harrisburg's Zembo Shrine Temple, a genial, slightly corpulent, Pennsylvania Dutch Irishman, nicknamed O'Bie, as all amiable, male O'Briens are.

"Gee, O'Bie," I said, "It's good to see you." I meant it, also hoping he might distract the overviewer.

O'Brien and George chatted. "Do you mind if I look at my mail?" George asked O'Bie, as if he needed permission.

"No. Look at it faster than you usually do. I'm ready for lunch."

"Maybe," from George, as he picked apart the recently cluttered desk.

Four contracts crept into his hands.

"What's those?" asked O'Bie, as I winced.

"Act contracts. My son, over there, buys the Steel Pier acts."

He thumbed the contracts.

"Paul Anka, one week, thirty-five hundred dollars," looking at me.

"Thirty-five hundred dollars? I discovered the kid in the Ottawa Fair and let him sing on my show. His father and uncle are my friends. Is there no gratitude?"

"Yes," I said, "there is. He's getting five grand everyplace else, without doing 28 shows a week."

George perused the next contract. "Frankie Avalon, four thousand, one week. Didn't he used to play for nothing in our Children's Theatre?"

"He's not a child anymore. He's becoming a big star."

George shrugged, "Lennon Sisters, ten thousand dollars, 28 shows, one week."

To O'Bie, "Big television act, I think. Cute girls, but omygosh, ten thousand a week."

George paused, "Not bad. In fact, okay for a son who doesn't know the value of money."

O'Bie, "From you, George, that sounds like a compliment."

I shuddered as he examined the fourth contract.

"Ricky Nelson, who's he?"

"The son of your good friend, Ozzie Nelson."

"They have a television show, don't they?"

I took a chance, "Hotter than the Lennon Sisters."

George's jaw muscles tightened. "Young man, come over here."

O'Bie, "He's forty years old. He may be younger than us, but not young."

O'Bie gave me a wink that did not improve matters.

George said, "Sometimes I regret I learned to read English. Is this ten thousands dollars for two days? If O'Bie wasn't here, I would break your neck."

O'Bie smiled, "Don't let me interfere. Want me to apply the blindfold?"

O'Bie continued, "He did three good ones, one bad one. Not a bad average."

"The good ones," George groaned, "aren't as good as the bad one is bad."

"Calm down, George. O'Bie here will take you to lunch."

"O'Bie, you know I only eat breakfast and dinner."

(Which was true.)

"Okay," said O'Bie. "We'll go to the Children's Show and look for another Frankie Avalon."

Off they went. I said to my secretary, "File these contracts and lock the drawers."

The engagement surpassed even MCA's wildest expectations. Forty-four thousand two hundred and eleven people through the turnstiles on Labor Day Sunday, an all time, indoor, one-day record.

O'Bie visited George the day after Labor Day. We manned our respective desks.

They talked until O'Bie asked, "How was breakfast?"

George answered. "I missed it."

"By the way, George, how did that Ricky Nelson turn out?"

"Great! Ozzie and Harriet headed my list, even when they worked here with their band."

O'Bie, "How did you know Ricky would be such a sensation?"

George, "Couldn't miss with parents like that."

O'Bie, "Hmm, I thought George Junior, over there, made the booking."

"He did, and I'm proud of him."

O'Bie, "Remember, I was here in May."

George remembered. "That's right, you were."

"So, the kid hit four out of four," concluded O'Bie.

"Well, O'Bie, we must admit, as they get older they learn a thing or two, don't they?"

Arm in arm, they strolled from the office. For the first time in ages, George ate lunch.

Chapter 35
The Boys From Liverpool

In 1964, the Democrats held their Convention in Atlantic City to do what everyone knew they were going to do, nominate Lyndon Johnson to the Presidency.

In March of that year, I received a call from Normie Weiss.

"Watch the Ed Sullivan show?"

"Sure did."

"What did you think of the Beatles?"

"Your kidding? Bigger than Ricky and Elvis put together," I replied.

"Want 'em?"

"Who'll pay to rebuild the Pier when it falls in the ocean with a hundred thousand people on it?"

"George, I'm serious, we have Sunday, August 30th open and two days after for R & R. Sullivan thinks you and Atlantic City are the right combination. You gotta get Convention Hall, not Steel Pier, and at least 15,000 seats."

"Normie, it would take your salary and mine to convert Convention Hall into a 15,000-seat theater."

"George, there must be a way – Ed says your father can do anything – at least in Atlantic City. By the way, are you a Democrat?"

"Here? You must be out of your mind. This little town is the Republican stronghold of the universe."

"But you're housing the Democratic Convention there that week aren't you?"

I paused. "George, are you there?"

"I'm thinking."

"That's all I wanted to hear," concluded Weiss. "Call me by next Wednesday."

I called my father. "Get Hap (Hap Farley, the absolute Republican Monarch of Southern New Jersey) and rent Convention Hall the day after the Democratic Convention, as is. They won't be taking it apart on Sunday. It's overtime."

"What for?"

"Ed Sullivan will tell you, Dad."

In a half hour, George called. "It's yours for $2,500, all they'll do is clean it up."

"Fine."

"Now what's this all about?"

"The Beatles are touring six cities in late August. Ed is giving them to us on August 30th."

"Sullivan doesn't *give* anybody anything."

I told him that the fee was $25,000 and if we don't take the deal, Philadelphia gets them.

"Well," George philosophized. "In late August, we should have enough money to pay for your Convention Hall shenanigans."

Thus began the most harrowing sixty hours of my show business life, the details of which will be documented elsewhere.

August came. The boys were to finish their Shea Stadium gig at 10:30 Saturday night. A helicopter waited at second base to fly them to Atlantic City. Three hundred New York City policemen and 40 firemen with hoses were at the ready to deflect the Gotham fans and accomplish the take-off.

Once they were airborne, Norm Weiss called me. "Thank God they're out of my jurisdiction," he said. "Good luck!"

I had promised Weiss a hundred cops at the airport in Atlantic City. I had none.

Sufficient to say no one knew what two limousines were doing at my rural home at 10 p.m., August 23 when they were silently wheeling themselves to Atlantic City's quiet airport and not a single

Atlantic City policeman in sight.

I called George at Steel Pier. "Want to meet the Beatles?"

"You crazy? It's Saturday night at Steel Pier. Dick Clark and his group are here. You're not even around."

"Just thought I'd ask."

Since nobody knew but me, we arrived alone at the airport, two limos, my four kids – two in each waiting limo.

The helicopter arrived at midnight.

First George Harrison, then Paul, Ringo and finally John Lennon, poked their heads through the helicopter door.

No police, no screaming fans, only two black limousines and four little kids.

Knowing they had lived two weeks of life threatening existence, I could not determine if they were pleased or disappointed to observe the silent scene.

Not for long. In 10 minutes we were at the Lafayette Hotel.

Within minutes, thousands of passionate, adoring fans filled the street and surrounded the hotel. Caeser would have sacked Athens with that mob.

My kids were hustled home in the limos, 60 cops secured the five hotel entrances and secured them well, despite a handful who sneaked up the stairwell to the Beatles seventh floor, only to be quickly expelled.

On Sunday, I accompanied Brian Epstein, the manager of the quartet, through the Miss America entrance of Convention Hall.

"The press conference will be here on the main floor. When the boys arrive they go right upstairs to the Miss America dressing room. After they get settled we'll bring them back down for the press conference."

"Nobody, the Governor, the President, nobody goes upstairs."

Despite my patented secrecy, it took 30 cops to manhandle the four boys from the curb eight feet into the Miss America door, then quickly upstairs, with a police sergeant blocking the stairs.

I herded the press and a few invited guests to one side of the table, four chairs to the other side.

I felt a pinch at my shirt.

"Do you want this show to go on?" the voice of Brian Epstein.

"Brian, I can't think of anything I want more."

"Come upstairs with me, there's an oddish fellow with three or four young ones upstairs."

I stepped quickly to the cop at the stairs.

"Did you let somebody up the stairs."

"Not somebody," answered the officers. "Your father."

"How could you?"

"How couldn't I," he said. "He says he's the boss and I know he's the boss."

Up we dashed.

The scene was memorable. John Lennon asleep on a settee and the other three engaged in a conversation with George.

"Downstairs, all of you" I commanded to my intruding family.

"Hold a minute," interrupted Ringo. "He's a Brit."

"My father? A Brit?"

"He's telling us about London in the thirties when he came to England to buy circus acts. Carl Wallenda, my word."

"He hasn't even gotten to Liverpool yet," said Harrison.

"Downstairs, kids. Downstairs, Dad. You've got all day tomorrow to tell them about Liverpool." Then I whispered, "You've never been to Liverpool."

That produced a crunching blow to my ribs.

The press conference followed. It went as well as could be expected.

One radio guy who I didn't want there in the first place upset Brian by asking, "How is your sex life here in the United States?"

Ringo was up to it. "Our famous English poet described it best in *Rhyme of the Ancient Mariner: "Water, water, all around and not a drop to drink."*

A columnist from the *Philadelphia Inquirer* shouted above the hubbub, "I have a question for George."

George Harrison leaned toward the voice.

"Not you. My question is for George Hamid."

George, all five feet four of him jumped into the limelight of the table.

Beatle George looked up at Showman George and mouthed "I am sorry."

George patted Harrison on the head, rested his hand on the boy's shoulder and asked the columnist. "What's the question?"

"Well, with Philadelphia, Atlanta and Dallas begging for the Beatles, how did you pull this off in little Atlantic City?"

"First of all, Atlantic City is not little, not in the summertime anyway. Second, Ed Sullivan has been my friend for years. When he put this tour together naturally he thought of me."

"Mr. Hamid how much are you paying?"

"Thirty five thousand."

I gulped.

The columnist said, "Everyone here knows their fee is a flat twenty five thousand."

Despite the snickering, George didn't flinch. "Plus $2,500 for the hall, the 7th and 8th floor of the Lafayette Hotel for three nights, 96 off-duty cops and…"

John Lennon raised his hand, "Plus four pairs of specially made eye-glasses your son is having custom made for me. Today, on Sunday."

George concluded, "I should have said, *forty-five thousand.*"

Good natured laughter ended the press conference.

As we made our way from backstage into the already packed Convention Hall, I beckoned to George. "I have one more job for you."

"You haven't given me any yet."

"This is important Dad. The crowd almost dismembered them on the way in. I am announcing the show. See this backstage elevator? I am going to make the audience sing *God Save the Queen* at the end. That will give you time to bring the boys to this elevator and downstairs to the police paddy wagon. Get them in the truck and over to the Lafayette. Don't even wait for a cop and don't forget to press *down.*"

"What do you think I am, a dummy?"

The show was a total success. At the end I stepped forward "And now in honor of our British friends, let's all stand and sing 'God Save the Queen'."

Out of the corner of my eye I saw the retreating Beatles following George, in whom they now had great faith.

By the time the anthem ended, I hurried backstage.

"Got 'em on their way?" I asked the sergeant.

He nodded, "Smooth as a Swiss watch."

George returned in twenty minutes (via the paddy wagon) and elevatored himself upstairs.

"How did it go, Dad?"

"Okay." Then George said something slowly, a bit strange.

"You know what I said to myself when I got in the paddy wagon with these four boys?"

"What?"

"Buffalo Bill would never believe this. I must have said it out loud because the drummer Beatle said, "I don't fancy I would enjoy buffalo meat."

"What did you talk about on your way through the back streets of Atlantic City?"

"Well, the sleepy one tried to sleep. The cheerful one, named after me, the boyish one, Paul, and the grown up one, the drummer, listened to my every word."

"What did you talk about?"

"Liverpool."

Chapter 36
FINALE

It doesn't seem right that a journey like this should end. But it did, as all journeys must.

His was tough, as so many things in his life were.

Sickness tugged his strength, his body, even his wit.

George last saw his circus in Wilkes-Barre, Pennsylvania. Withered with weight loss he still insisted on the three-hour trip.

Performers and Shriners fussed over him, bringing a grin to the thinning lips under the recently-turned-white moustache.

As the show started, we sat in the front row of an end bleacher. After two acts, I felt a squeeze on my arm.

"Good opening. I can see it's a nice show. Take me back to the motel," he whispered.

At the motel, George undressed, looking into the mirror, brushing his teeth. Finishing, he shook his head.

"I can't understand St. Joseph letting me down like this."

"St. Joseph can't handle everything."

George ignored his son. "He broke his arm in California; I sent two hundred and fifty to fix it."

"You aren't hallucinating, Dad, are you? How could St. Joseph break his arm in California?"

"Sometimes I still wonder about you, George Junior. The earthquake; his statue fell and broke his arm. I sent the money in January. Here it is April."

"Pardon me for not knowing."

"I'll pardon you, but I won't pardon St. Joseph."

I chuckled. George didn't. He was serious.

"Help me open this pill bottle."

I turned away, afraid I might weep at the thought of those powerful wrists, which tumbled two and a half times around Madison Square Garden, now unable to open a pill bottle.

"You're going back to the shore tomorrow. Some rest and some Syrian food will do you good."

George shook his head, "You can't leave now. I'll be okay."

"I'm not leaving, you are. Get into bed and finish your quarrel with St. Joseph."

Since 1957, when Bob Morton died, George had kept Shaheen on the circus, painting props, working lights, guarding dressing rooms, providing him with ample (not extravagant) pay.

They had not seen each other in a year.

Shaheen knocked on the door at nine the next morning. He paled. "George, you don't look like you."

"On the outside," I agreed. "On the inside, he's still George. Guess who he's fighting with now?"

Not moving his gaze from George's withered jaws, Shaheen mumbled, "I dunno. Who?"

"St. Joseph, that's who."

George's eyes brightened. "He doesn't know St. Joseph from St. Jude. Nice of you to come see me, Shaheen."

"Get dressed. He's driving you to the shore." I said.

"Him! Even in my condition, I can drive better than him."

"Faster," contradicted Shaheen, "not better."

Within an hour, the two cousins were seated in my car, Shaheen steering it away from Wilkes-Barre, leaving behind George's circus of forty years.

By the time they were twenty minutes out of town, the irony became a realization. Shaheen, who had accompanied him to his first circus, was taking George from his last.

Shaheen returned the next day, coming to my room to hand me the car keys.

"How was the trip?"

Shaheen shook his head. "He made me take him by the fairgrounds in Trenton."

"Why?" I asked, "that's forty minutes out of the way."

Shaheen seemed to be thinking, "He talked funny."

"How?"

"He said, 'Someday, when I die, this might be a good place to bury me. We buried one of my elephants here."

"That's true," I responded, "Plus, I'd be willing to bet, a lion."

"Then your father said something like, "If only my gold bear was…"

"George Junior, your father just don't talk like that."

A tear rolled down his cheek. I put my arms around Shaheen as tears ran down mine.

"Uncle Shaheen," I said, "I think you and I are going to have a good cry."

Chapter 37
FINAL REFLECTION

George left his world of circuses, Steel Pier, big name pals, fairs, amusement parks and special family in June of 1971. Bess left deep in the night, six days later as she quietly slept.

Hard on me? Indeed.

I was with George to the end. When it came, I left Atlantic City Hospital, slowly walked the Boardwalk to Steel Pier and alone to its Ocean Stadium where I sat down.

The horizon etched the meeting of earth and sky with rare definition, making it appear possible to climb from one to the other. I thought, "Are heaven and nature conspiring to help George on his celestial journey?"

Would his first encounter be Buffalo Bill, Annie, his grandmother? Sooner or later, Ameen? Whatever else, Uncle was pivotal in George's life. Then a visit to animal kingdom to find a little white mule, a little white pony to ask how they made out with the auctioneer…a stop by elephant corner to see Minnie, Gyp, and Ginger…well at least Ginger.

Certainly Golden Jim, his precious golden bear.

Perhaps a sleigh ride down a white cloud with Helen Keller.

Or will he respond to a command performance before the celestial throne and execute the ultimate tinsica?

A song seemed to float out of the ocean. In reality, our stage manager was testing the sound system by piping in music from the radio station on the Pier.

Using a nearby phone, I called the station.

"What was that song?"

"My Way."
"Who's singing it?"
"Sinatra."
"I thought so," I said, then, "Who wrote it?"
"Paul Anka."
"Will you copy it for me?"
"Sure thing," he answered.

Three days later at the church, there were a lot of people, but no hymns, only a meaningful song composed by George's protégé and delivered by the sensitive voice of George's buddy.